Early praise for *Node.js 8 the Right Way*

Node.js 8 the Right Way is an excellent guide for building robust Node.js applications and making use of the extensive Node.js ecosystem. Using realistic applications from several different domains, it gives a highly useful and thorough description of the process of building, testing, and deploying real-world Node.js programs.

➤ **Dan Scales**
Principal Engineer, Google Inc.

Without the original *Node.js the Right Way*, I wouldn't be where I am today. This book leapfrogged me from being a casual Node.js developer to loving the event loop and knowing how to build effective distributed systems in Node.js. It led me to writing clean, idiomatic, and highly understandable JavaScript—both in Node.js and in the browser. This update will do the same for readers.

➤ **Kyle Kelley**
Senior Software Engineer, Netflix

Jim's update to his engaging, wide-ranging deep dive into how to solve actual problems using Node.js taught even this old dog some new tricks. Hats off to Jim for clearly demonstrating how to get the most out of Node.js.

➤ **Mark Trostler**
Software Engineer, Google Inc.

Jim Wilson shows the correct way, the way that will definitely make you a better Node.js developer, giving you many techniques, insights, and—most of all—some really cool stuff. *Node.js 8 the Right Way* provides loads of good practices and reveals some of the lower-level interactions of Node with the system. In a Node.js shop, this book is a must for seniors' reference *and* a must for new hires.

➤ **Peter Perlepes**
Software Engineer, Growth

Node.js 8 the Right Way

Practical, Server-Side JavaScript That Scales

Jim R. Wilson

The Pragmatic Bookshelf

Raleigh, North Carolina

Many of the designations used by manufacturers and sellers to distinguish their products are claimed as trademarks. Where those designations appear in this book, and The Pragmatic Programmers, LLC was aware of a trademark claim, the designations have been printed in initial capital letters or in all capitals. The Pragmatic Starter Kit, The Pragmatic Programmer, Pragmatic Programming, Pragmatic Bookshelf, PragProg and the linking *g* device are trademarks of The Pragmatic Programmers, LLC.

Every precaution was taken in the preparation of this book. However, the publisher assumes no responsibility for errors or omissions, or for damages that may result from the use of information (including program listings) contained herein.

Our Pragmatic books, screencasts, and audio books can help you and your team create better software and have more fun. Visit us at *https://pragprog.com*.

The team that produced this book includes:

Publisher: Andy Hunt
VP of Operations: Janet Furlow
Managing Editor: Brian MacDonald
Supervising Editor: Jacquelyn Carter
Indexing: Potomac Indexing, LLC
Copy Editor: Candace Cunningham
Layout: Gilson Graphics

For sales, volume licensing, and support, please contact *support@pragprog.com*.

For international rights, please contact *rights@pragprog.com*.

Printed in the United States of America.
ISBN-13: 978-1-68050-195-7
Printed on acid-free paper.
Book version: P1.0—January 2018

Contents

Part II — Working with Data

Part III — Creating an Application from the Ground Up

Acknowledgments

I'm so grateful to have had the opportunity to write this book. And I'm especially thankful for my editor, Jackie Carter—your thoughtful feedback made this book what it is today.

Thank you, dear reader, and readers of the Beta releases. Your errata reports made the book better than it would have otherwise been.

I'd also sincerely like to thank the whole team at The Pragmatic Bookshelf. Thanks for your kind patience, and all of your hard work to polish this book and find all of my mistakes.

I'd like to thank all of my reviewers. Your keen observations have helped make this book even more technically correct (the best kind of correct). In no particular order:

Dan Scales	Mark Ethan Trostler	Gary Chamberlain
Rick Waldron	Nick Capito	Peter Hampton
Luca Mezzalira	Peter Perlepes	Dominic Schulz
	Maricris S. Nonato	

And I want to thank my amazing family, too. Dear Ruthy, you are my inspiration; never stop fighting! Emma and Jimmy, even though you're both growing up too fast, I can't wait to see all the great things you'll do.

For anyone I missed, I hope you'll accept my apologies. Any omissions were certainly not intentional, and I have nothing but gratitude for you in my heart.

Preface

In recent years, two big shifts have happened in the practice of writing software—and Node.js has been at the forefront of both.

First, software is becoming increasingly *asynchronous*. Whether you're waiting on a Big Data job, interacting with end users, steering a quadcopter, or simply responding to an API call, chances are you'll need asynchronous programming techniques.

Second, JavaScript has quietly become the world's standard code-execution environment. It's everywhere: in web browsers, modern NoSQL databases, DIY robots, and now on the server as well.

Node.js is an integral part of these trends, and it has taken off in a big way.

Why Node.js the Right Way?

Way back in March of 2010, I gave a lightning talk titled "Full-Stack JavaScript" at the NoSQL Boston conference. Back then, and even more so now, I knew that using JavaScript for every layer of the application stack was not only possible, but was a great way to reduce software complexity.

When each layer of your stack speaks JavaScript, you sidestep impedance mismatches and facilitate code reuse. Node.js is an important piece of the puzzle, filling the middle space between your front-end user-facing code and your data-storage layer.

The *Right Way* in this book's title refers to both the process of learning Node.js and the practice of writing Node.js code.

Learning Node.js

As with any growing technology, there are plenty of resources available for learning Node.js. Unfortunately, many of those resources are narrowly focused on serving up web resources.

The web is great, but it's not enough, and it's not the whole story of Node.js. Node.js is about more than just serving web apps, and this book treats it that way.

Node.js 8 the Right Way teaches you the concepts you'll need to be an effective Node.js programmer, no matter what kinds of programs you need to write.

Writing Node.js

One thing I love about JavaScript is that there are seven ways to do anything. There's breathing room, where developers can explore and experiment and find better approaches to everything.

The community of Node.js developers, the conventions in Node.js development, and even the semantics of the JavaScript language itself are all rapidly evolving. With eyes to the near future, the code examples and recommendations in this book reflect current best practices and standards.

What's in This Book

This book is for intermediate to advanced developers who want to learn how to write asynchronous JavaScript for the server using Node.js. Some prior JavaScript experience will definitely help, but you don't have to be an expert.

The book proceeds in three parts, outlined here briefly.

Part I: Getting Up To Speed on Node.js 8

Part I is about getting you up to speed on Node.js 8. You'll write Node.js programs that use core modules—and a few external modules as well—to do things like interact with the filesystem, spin up a cluster of worker processes, and manage network connections.

Getting Started

Chapter 1, *Getting Started*, on page 3, introduces the Node.js event loop, explaining how it empowers Node.js to be highly parallel and single-threaded at the same time. This chapter also outlines the five aspects of Node.js development that frame each subsequent chapter and has some brief instructions on getting Node.js installed on your machine.

Wrangling the File System

In Chapter 2, *Wrangling the File System*, on page 11, you'll start writing Node.js programs. If you've done any server-side programming in the past, chances are you've had to access a filesystem along the way. We'll start in this familiar domain, using Node.js's filesystem tools to create asynchronous, nonblocking file utilities. You'll use Node.js's ubiquitous EventEmitter and Stream classes to pipe data, and you'll spawn and interact with child processes.

Networking with Sockets

We'll expand on those concepts while exploring Node.js's network I/O capabilities in Chapter 3, *Networking with Sockets*, on page 27. You'll create TCP servers and client programs to access them. You'll also develop a simple JSON-based protocol and a custom class for working with these messages. To develop unit tests for the code, you'll use Mocha, a popular Node.js test harness.

Connecting Robust Microservices

Then, in Chapter 4, *Connecting Robust Microservices*, on page 53, we'll branch away from the Node.js core and into the realm of third-party libraries. You'll use npm to import ØMQ (pronounced "Zero-M-Q")—a high-efficiency, low-latency library for developing networked applications. With ØMQ, you'll develop programs that communicate using several important patterns, such as publish/subscribe and request/reply. You'll create suites of programs that work together in concert, and you'll learn the clustering tools to manage them.

Part II: Working with Data

In Part II, you'll work with real data and lay the groundwork for an end-to-end application. This starts with processing data files in a testable way. You'll also learn to compose rich command-line utilities using Node.js and interact with HTTP services.

Transforming Data and Testing Continuously

Chapter 5, *Transforming Data*, on page 81, kicks off an ongoing project that spans Part II and Part III. You'll download the catalog from Project Gutenberg, an online resource for ebooks in the public domain. Using a module called Cheerio, you'll write Node.js code to parse the data files and extract the important fields. You'll use npm, Mocha, and an assertion library called Chai to set up continuous testing, and you'll learn to use Chrome DevTools for interactive debugging.

Commanding Databases

In Chapter 6, *Commanding Databases*, on page 111, you'll insert the extracted Project Gutenberg catalog into an Elasticsearch index. To get this done, you'll write a command-line utility program called esclu using a Node.js module called Commander. Since Elasticsearch is a RESTful, JSON-based datastore, you'll use the Request module to interact with it. You'll also learn to use a handy and powerful command-line tool called jq for manipulating JSON.

Part III: Implementing an Application

Part III is where everything comes together. You'll develop web services that mediate between your API users and your back-end data services. End users don't interact directly with APIs, though, so for that you'll implement a beautiful UI. At the end, you'll tie it all together with session management and authentication.

Developing RESTful Web Services

Node.js has fantastic support for writing HTTP servers, and in Chapter 7, *Developing RESTful Web Services*, on page 147, you'll do exactly that. You'll use Express, a popular Node.js web framework for routing requests. We'll dive deeper into REST semantics, and you'll use Promises and async functions for managing code flows. In addition, you'll learn to configure your services using the nconf module, and keep them running with nodemon.

Creating a Beautiful User Experience

With the web services in place, in Chapter 8, *Creating a Beautiful User Experience*, on page 185, you'll craft a front end for them. You'll learn how to assemble a front-end project using a Node.js-based build tool called webpack, along with a host of peer-dependency plugins for it. You'll transpile your code for consumption by the browser using TypeScript, a language and transpiler from Microsoft that features inferred type checking. To make your UI look modern and fabulous, you'll bring in Twitter's Bootstrap styling framework, and implement templating with Handlebars.

Fortifying Your Application

Chapter 9, *Fortifying Your Application*, on page 219, is where everything comes together. You'll combine the user experience with the web services from the previous two chapters for an end-to-end solution. Using Express middleware, you'll create authenticated APIs and implement stateful sessions. You'll also learn how to use npm's shrinkwrap option to insulate yourself from upstream module changes.

Developing Flows with Node-RED

After Part III concludes, there's a special bonus chapter on Node-RED. Chapter 10, *BONUS: Developing Flows with Node-RED*, on page 259, walks you through this clever visual editor for designing event-based code flows. It ships directly with Raspbian, the default operating system of Raspberry Pi.

Using Node-RED, you can quickly stub out exploratory HTTP APIs. I'll show you how!

Appendices on Angular and React

In case you're interested in using the front-end frameworks Angular and React, Appendix 1, *Setting Up Angular*, on page 285, and Appendix 2, *Setting Up React*, on page 291, show you how to integrate them with webpack and Express. The appendixes will help you put the pieces in place to start experimenting, but they don't take the place of a good tutorial on how to fully develop with them.

What This Book Is Not

Before you commit to reading this book, you should know what it *doesn't* cover.

Everything About Everything

At the time of this writing, npm houses more than 528,000 modules, with a growth rate of more than 500 new modules per day.[1] Since the ecosystem and community around Node.js is so large and still growing so rapidly, this book does not attempt to cover everything. Instead, this short book teaches you the essentials you need to get out there and start coding.

In addition to the wealth of Node.js modules available, there's the added complexity of working with non-Node.js services and platforms. Your Node.js code will invariably act as an intermediary between various systems and users both up and down the stack. To tell a cohesive story, we'll naturally only be able to dive deep on a few of these, but always with an eye to the bigger picture.

MEAN

If you're looking for an opinionated book that focuses only on a particular stack like MEAN (Mongo, Express, Angular, and Node.js), this is not it! Rather than prescribe a particular stack, I'll teach you the skills to put together the Node.js code, no matter which back end you connect to or front end you choose to put on top.

Instead of MongoDB, I've selected Elasticsearch to back the projects in this book because it's increasingly popular among experienced Node.js developers,

---

1. http://www.modulecounts.com/

as evidenced by a 2016 survey by RisingStack.[2] Moreover, with its REST/JSON API, Elasticsearch offers a way to ease into HTTP services as a consumer before jumping into writing your own.

This book also shies away from front-end JavaScript frameworks. The two most popular front-end frameworks at the time of this writing are React, by Facebook,[3] and Angular, by Google.[4] This book covers neither of them in detail, by design. They both deserve more coverage than fits in these pages.

I want you to be the best Node.js coder you can be, whether you use any particular database or front-end framework.

JavaScript Beginner's Guide

The JavaScript language is probably the most misunderstood language today. Although this book does discuss language syntax from time to time (especially where it's brand-new), this is not a beginner's guide to JavaScript. As a quick quiz, you should be able to easily read and understand this code:

```
const list = [];
for (let i = 1; i <= 100; i++) {
  if (!(i % 15)) {
    list.push('FizzBuzz');
  } else if (!(i % 5)) {
    list.push('Buzz');
  } else if (!(i % 3)) {
    list.push('Fizz');
  } else {
    list.push(i);
  }
}
```

You may recognize this as a solution to the classic programming puzzle called FizzBuzz, made famous by Jeff Atwood in 2007.[5] Here's another solution—one that makes gratuitous (and unnecessary) use of some of the newer JavaScript features.

```
'use strict';
const list = [...Array(100).keys()]
  .map(n => n + 1)
  .map(n => n % 15 ? n : 'FizzBuzz')
  .map(n => isNaN(n) || n % 5 ? n : 'Buzz')
  .map(n => isNaN(n) || n % 3 ? n : 'Fizz');
```

---

2. https://blog.risingstack.com/node-js-developer-survey-results-2016/

3. https://facebook.github.io/react/

4. https://angularjs.org/

5. https://blog.codinghorror.com/why-cant-programmers-program/

If you don't recognize the techniques used in this code, that's expected! You'll learn to use several of them, and many others, in this book.

A Note to Windows Users

The examples in this book assume you're using a Unix-like operating system. We'll make use of standard input and output streams, and pipe data between processes. The shell session examples have been tested with Bash, but other shells may work as well.

If you run Windows, I recommend setting up Cygwin.[6] This will give you the best shot at running the example code successfully, or you could run a Linux virtual machine.

Code Examples and Conventions

The code examples in this book contain JavaScript, shell sessions, and a few HTML/XML excerpts. For the most part, code listings are provided in full—ready to be run at your leisure.

Samples and snippets are syntax-highlighted according to the rules of the language. Shell commands are prefixed by $.

When you write Node.js code, you should always handle errors and exceptions, even if you just rethrow them. You'll learn how to do this throughout the book. However, some of the code examples lack error handling. This is to aid readability and save space, and sometimes to provide opportunities for reader tasks at the end of the chapter. In your code, you should always handle your errors.

Online Resources

The Pragmatic Bookshelf's page for this book is a great resource.[7] You'll find downloads for all the source code presented in this book, and feedback tools, including a community forum and an errata-submission form.

Thanks for choosing this book to show you Node.js *the right way*.

Jim R. Wilson
December 2017

---

6. http://cygwin.com/
7. http://pragprog.com/book/jwnode2/node-js-8-the-right-way

Part I

Getting Up to Speed on Node.js 8

Node.js is a powerful platform for developing server-side JavaScript.

In this first part, you'll write Node.js code, beginning with the familiar domain of the command line and then expanding into the realm of microservices. Along the way, you'll learn to structure your code into modules, use third-party modules from npm, and take advantage of the latest ECMAScript language features.

Getting Started

An old programming adage says that while functionality is an asset, code is a liability.[1]

Throughout this book, as you learn to harness Node.js, keep in mind that the best line of code is the one you never had to write. If you can get something for free, take it!

However, the nature of a technical book is to teach you how to do something, even if somebody has already done it for you. By understanding how things work, you'll be better able to build on top of them.

So we'll be progressing in stages. In the beginning, you'll be working at the lowest levels of Node.js—getting to know the environment, the language, and the fundamental APIs. As you master those, you'll learn how to use other peoples' modules, libraries, and services to replace some of that code and go to the next level.

By the end, you'll see where it's possible to make great gains using existing libraries, and where it makes sense to implement the functionality yourself. At the end of the day, this wisdom is the power that will distinguish you from a novice developer.

Thinking Beyond the web

A lot of the buzz around Node.js is focused on the web. In truth, Node.js serves a bigger purpose that people often miss. Let's use a map to see where Node.js fits in the broader scheme of things.

Imagine the set of all possible programs as the inhabitants of a vast sea. Programs that have similar purposes are near each other, and programs that

---

1.　http://c2.com/cgi/wiki?SoftwareAsLiability

differ are further apart. With that picture in mind, take a look at this map. It shows a close-up of one particular outcrop in this sea, the Island of I/O-Bound Programs.

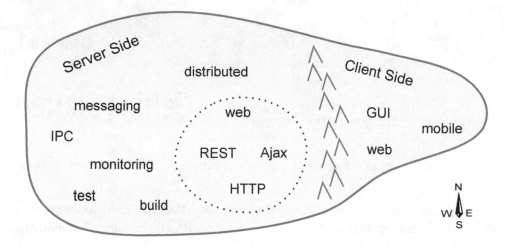

I/O-bound programs are constrained by data access. These are programs where adding more processing power or RAM often makes little difference.

East of the mountain range, we find the *client-side* programs. These include GUI tools of all stripes, consumer applications, mobile apps, and web apps. Client-side programs interact directly with human beings, often by waiting patiently for their input.

West of the mountains are the *server-side* programs. This vast expanse is Node.js territory.

Deep within the server-side region lies the web—that old guard of HTTP, Ajax, and REST, communicating with JSON. The websites, apps, and APIs that consume so much of our collective mental energy live here.

Because we spend so much time thinking about the web, we often overemphasize Node.js's use in developing web applications. People ask, "How is Node.js better for making web apps?" or "How can I make a REST service with Node.js?"

These are good questions, but they miss the point. Node.js is great for a wider range of things, and this book explores that larger area.

Node.js's Niche

Since JavaScript first appeared in 1995, it has been solving problems all along the front-end/back-end spectrum. The following figure shows this spectrum and where Node.js fits within it.

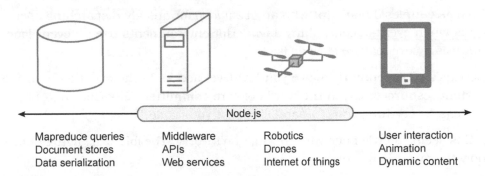

Mapreduce queries	Middleware	Robotics	User interaction
Document stores	APIs	Drones	Animation
Data serialization	Web services	Internet of things	Dynamic content

In the web browser on the right, much of the scripting involves waiting for user interaction: click here, drag that, choose a file, etc. JavaScript has been extraordinarily successful in this space.

On the left, back-end databases are investing heavily in JavaScript. Document-oriented databases like MongoDB and CouchDB use JavaScript extensively—from modifying records to ad-hoc queries and mapreduce jobs. Other NoSQL datastores, like Elasticsearch and Neo4j, present data in JavaScript Object Notation (JSON). These days, you can even write SQL functions for Postgres in JavaScript with the right plugin.

Many middleware tasks are I/O-bound, just like client-side scripting and databases. These server-side programs often have to wait for things like a database result, feedback from a third-party web service, or incoming connection requests. Node.js is designed for exactly these kinds of applications.

Node.js has also made inroads into the field of autonomous systems. Platforms for protyping the Internet of Things, such as the Raspberry Pi OS Raspbian,[2] come with Node.js, and Tessel is built on Node.js from the ground up.[3] Johnny-Five and CylonJS are two robotics-development platforms that help you develop Node.js applications for a variety of hardware components.[4] [5]

---

2. https://www.raspberrypi.org/downloads/raspbian/
3. https://tessel.io/
4. http://johnny-five.io/
5. https://cylonjs.com/

Since robotics and Internet of Things applications tend to be very hardware-specific, developing them is not covered in this book. However, the skill of developing Node.js would transfer if you decide to go that route in the future.

How Node.js Applications Work

Node.js couples JavaScript with an *event loop* for quickly dispatching operations when events occur. Many JavaScript environments use an event loop, but it is a core feature of Node.js.

Node.js's philosophy is to give you low-level access to the event loop and to system resources. Or, in the words of core committer Felix Geisendörfer, in Node.js "everything runs in parallel except your code."[6]

If this seems a little backward to you, don't worry. The following figure shows how the event loop works.

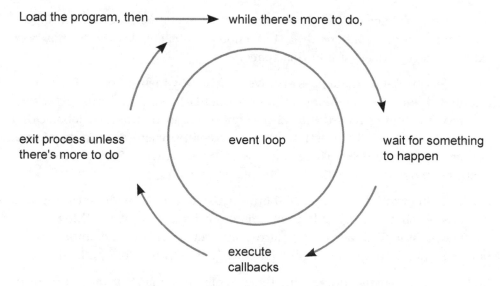

As long as there's something left to do, Node.js's event loop will keep spinning. Whenever an *event* occurs, Node.js invokes any *callbacks* (event handlers) that are listening for that event.

As a Node.js developer, your job is to create the callback functions that get executed in response to events. Any number of callbacks can respond to any event, but only one callback function will ever be executing at any time.

---

6.   http://www.debuggable.com/posts/understanding-node-js:4bd98440-45e4-4a9a-8ef7-0f7ecbdd56cb

Everything else your program might do—like waiting for data from a file or an incoming HTTP request—is handled by Node.js, in parallel, behind the scenes. Your application code will never be executed at the same time as anything else. It will always have the full attention of Node.js's JavaScript engine while it's running.

Single-Threaded and Highly Parallel

Other systems try to gain parallelism by running lots of code at the same time, typically by spawning many threads. But not Node.js. As far as your JavaScript code is concerned, Node.js is a single-threaded environment. At most, only one line of your code will ever be executing at any time.

Node.js gets away with this by doing most I/O tasks using *nonblocking* techniques. Rather than waiting line-by-line for an operation to finish, you create a callback function that will be invoked when the operation eventually succeeds or fails.

Your code should do what it needs to do, then quickly hand control back over to the event loop so Node.js can work on something else. We'll develop practical examples of this throughout the book, starting in Chapter 2, *Wrangling the File System*, on page 11.

If it seems strange to you that Node.js achieves parallelism by running only one piece of code at a time, that's because it is. It's an example of something I call a backwardism.

Backwardisms in Node.js

A *backwardism* is a concept that's so bizarre that at first it seems completely backward. You've probably experienced many backwardisms while learning to program, whether you noticed them or not.

Take the concept of a *variable*. In algebra it's common to see equations like $7x + 3 = 24$. Here, x is called a variable; it has exactly one value, and your job is to solve the equation to figure out what that value is.

Then when you start learning how to program, you quickly run into statements like x = x + 7. Now x is still called a variable, but it can have any value that you assign to it. It can even have different values at different times!

From algebra's perspective, this is a backwardism. The equation x = x + 7 makes no sense at all. The notion of a variable in programming is not just a little different than in algebra—it's 100 percent backward. But once you understand the concept of *assignment*, the programming variable makes perfect sense.

So it is with Node.js's single-threaded event loop. From a multithreaded perspective, running just one piece of code at a time seems silly. But once you understand event-driven programming—with nonblocking APIs—it becomes clear.

Programming is chock-full of backwardisms like these, and Node.js is no exception. Starting out, you'll frequently run into code that looks like it should work one way, but it actually does something quite different.

That's OK! With this book, you'll learn Node.js by making compact programs that interact in useful ways. As we run into more of Node.js's backwardisms, we'll dive in and explore them.

Aspects of Node.js Development

Node.js is a surprisingly big subject, so let's break it down into different *aspects*. We might talk about many aspects of Node.js development, ranging from basic JavaScript syntax to revision control. This book focuses on five in particular:

- Practical programming
- Node.js core
- Patterns
- JavaScriptisms
- Supporting code

Let's explore each of these briefly.

Practical Programming

Practical programming is all about producing real code that does something useful. Interacting with a filesystem, establishing socket connections, and serving web applications are all examples of practical programming.

Each remaining chapter of this book focuses on one particular practical domain. Through code examples specific to each domain, you'll learn Node.js's architecture, patterns, JavaScriptisms, and supporting code.

Node.js Core

Understanding Node.js's core modules and behavior will help you to harness its features while avoiding pitfalls. For example, Node.js uses an event loop written in C for scheduling work. But it executes application code in a

JavaScript environment. How information is shuttled between these layers is the kind of impactful architectural detail you'll learn.

Patterns

Like any successful codebase with a healthy ecosystem, Node.js has a number of repeating patterns. Some of these patterns are baked into the core while others mostly appear in third-party libraries. Examples include the use of callbacks, error-handling techniques, and classes like EventEmitter and Stream, which are used liberally for event dispatching.

As we progress through different practical programming domains, we'll naturally encounter these and other patterns. When we do, you'll discover why they're useful and how to use them effectively.

JavaScriptisms

JavaScript is the language of Node.js programs, so you'll be seeing quite a lot of it. The code examples in this book make use of the latest available JavaScript features that Node.js supports. Some of these features may be unfamiliar to you, even if you've done JavaScript development before.

Modern JavaScriptisms discussed in this book include things like arrow functions, spread parameters, and destructuring assignment.

Supporting Code

Code does not live in isolation; it takes a village to support any individual program. Supporting code covers lots of things, from unit testing to deployment scripts. We'll use supporting code throughout the book to make our programs more robust, more scalable, and more manageable.

With these five aspects, you'll be able to develop applications that make the most use of the platform while employing idiomatic Node.js style. The example applications you'll develop in this book are functional and small, and aim to clearly demonstrate these concepts. But to use them, you'll need to get Node.js installed first.

Installing Node.js

To install Node.js, you have several choices based on your operating system and your comfort with building from source code.

This book assumes you are using the latest stable version of Node.js 8. If you install a different version—for example, by building from the latest source code—the code examples in this book may not work. From the command line you can run node --version to see what version you have installed if you are not sure:

```
$ node --version
v8.0.0
```

One of the easiest ways to get Node.js is to download an installer from nodejs.org.[7]

Another popular option (the one that I use personally) is Node.js Version Manager (nvm).[8] If you're using a Unix-like OS (such as Mac OS X or Linux), you can install nvm like so:

```
$ curl https://raw.github.com/creationix/nvm/master/install.sh | sh
```

Then install a specific version:

```
$ nvm install v8.0.0
```

If you have trouble, you can get help on the Node.js mailing lists and IRC channel, both linked from the Node.js community page.[9]

We've got a lot of ground to cover, and we don't have many pages to do it. So if you're ready, let's begin in the oh-so-familiar domain of filesystem access.

---

7. http://nodejs.org/download/
8. https://github.com/creationix/nvm
9. http://nodejs.org/community/

CHAPTER 2

Wrangling the File System

As a programmer, chances are you've had to access a filesystem at some point: reading, writing, renaming, and deleting files. We'll start our Node.js journey in this familiar area, creating useful, asynchronous file utilities. Along the way we'll explore the following aspects of Node.js development:

Node.js Core
> On the architecture front, you'll see how the event loop shapes a program's flow. We'll use Buffers for transporting data between Node.js's JavaScript engine and its native core, and we'll use Node.js's module system to bring in core libraries.

Patterns
> Inside our programs, we'll use common Node.js patterns like callbacks for handling asynchronous events. We'll harness Node.js's EventEmitter and Stream classes to pipe data around.

JavaScriptisms
> We'll take a look at some JavaScript features and best practices such as block scoping and arrow-function expressions.

Supporting Code
> You'll learn how to spawn and interact with child processes, capture their output, and detect state changes.

We'll begin by creating a tool that watches a file for changes. This'll give you a peek into how the event loop works while introducing Node.js's filesystem APIs.

Programming for the Node.js Event Loop

Let's get started by developing a couple of simple programs that watch files for changes and read arguments from the command line. Even though they're short, these applications offer insights into Node.js's event-based architecture.

Watching a File for Changes

Watching files for changes is a convenient problem to start with because it demands asynchronous coding while demonstrating important Node.js concepts. Taking action whenever a file changes is just plain useful in a number of cases, ranging from automated deployments to running unit tests.

Open a terminal to begin. Create a new directory called filesystem and navigate down into it.

```
$ mkdir filesystem
$ cd filesystem
```

You'll use this directory for all of the code examples in this chapter. Once there, use the touch command to create a file called target.txt.

```
$ touch target.txt
```

If you're in an environment that doesn't have the touch command (like Windows), you can alternatively echo something to write the file.

```
$ echo, > target.txt
```

This file will be the target for our watcher program. Now open your favorite text editor and enter the following:

```
filesystem/watcher.js
'use strict';
const fs = require('fs');
fs.watch('target.txt', () => console.log('File changed!'));
console.log('Now watching target.txt for changes...');
```

Save this file as watcher.js in the filesystem directory alongside the target.txt file. Although this is a short program, it deserves scrutiny since it takes advantage of a number of JavaScript and Node.js features. Let's step through it.

The program begins with the string 'use strict' at the top. This causes the program to be executed in strict mode, a feature introduced in ECMAScript version 5. Strict mode disables certain problematic JavaScript language features and makes others throw exceptions. It's always a good idea to use strict mode, and we'll use it throughout the book.

Next, notice the const keyword; this sets up fs to be a local variable with a constant value. A variable declared with const must be assigned a value when declared, and can never have anything assigned to it again (which would cause a runtime error).

It might surprise you, but it turns out that most of the time, in most code, variables don't need to be reassigned, making const a good default choice for declaring variables. The alternative to const is let, which we'll discuss shortly.

The require() function pulls in a Node.js *module* and returns it. In our case, we're calling require('fs') to incorporate Node.js's built-in filesystem module.[1]

In Node.js, a module is a self-contained bit of JavaScript that provides functionality to be used elsewhere. The output of require() is usually a plain old JavaScript object, but may also be a function. Modules can depend on other modules, much like libraries in other programming environments, which import or #include other libraries.

Next we call the fs module's watch() method, which takes a path to a file and a callback function to invoke whenever the file changes. In JavaScript, functions are first-class citizens. This means they can be assigned to variables and passed as parameters to other functions. Take a close look at our callback function:

```
() => console.log('File changed!')
```

This is an *arrow-function expression*, sometimes called a fat arrow function or just an arrow function. The empty pair of parentheses () at the beginning means this function expects no arguments. Then the body of the function uses console.log() to echo a message to standard output.

Arrow functions are new in ECMAScript 2015 and you'll be writing many such functions throughout this book. Prior to the introduction of arrow functions, you'd have supplied a callback using the more verbose function(){} construction:

```
function() {
  console.log('File changed!');
}
```

Aside from having a terser syntax than older function expressions, arrow functions have another big advantage over their ancestral counterparts: they do not create a new scope for this. Dealing with this has been a thorn in the side of many JavaScript developers over the years, but thanks to arrow functions, it's no longer a major source of consternation. Just like const should be your go-to means of declaring variables, arrow functions should be your first choice in declaring function expressions (such as callbacks).

---

1. http://nodejs.org/api/fs.html

The last line of the program just informs you that everything is ready. Let's try it out! Return to the command line and launch the watcher program using node, like so:

```
$ node watcher.js
Now watching target.txt for changes...
```

After the program starts, Node.js will patiently wait until the target file is changed. To trigger a change, open another terminal to the same directory and touch the file again. The terminal running watcher.js will output the string *File changed!*, and then the program will go back to waiting.

If you see duplicate messages, particularly on Mac OS X or Windows, this is not a bug in your code! There are a number of known issues around this, and many have to do with how the operating system surfaces changes.

Since you'll be touching the target file a lot this chapter to trigger changes, you might want to use the watch command to do this automatically:

```
$ watch -n 1 touch target.txt
```

This command will touch the target file once every second until you stop it. If you're on a system that doesn't have the watch command, don't worry. Any means of writing to target.txt is fine.

Visualizing the Event Loop

The program we wrote in the last section is a good example of the Node.js event loop at work. Recall the event-loop figure from *How Node.js Applications Work*, on page 6. Our simple file-watcher program causes Node.js to go through each of these steps, one by one.

To run the program, Node.js does the following:

- It loads the script, running all the way through to the last line, which produces the *Now watching* message in the console.

- It sees that there's more to do because of the call to fs.watch().

- It waits for something to happen—namely, for the fs module to observe a change to the file.

- It executes our callback function when the change is detected.

- It determines that the program still has not finished, and resumes waiting.

In Node.js the event loop spins until there's nothing left to do, there's nothing left to wait for, or the program exits by some other means. For example, if an exception is thrown and not caught, the process will exit. We'll look at how this works next.

Reading Command-Line Arguments

Now let's make our program more useful by taking in the file to watch as a command-line argument. This will introduce the process global object and how Node.js deals with exceptions.

Open your editor and enter this:

```
filesystem/watcher-argv.js
const fs = require('fs');
const filename = process.argv[2];
if (!filename) {
  throw Error('A file to watch must be specified!');
}
fs.watch(filename, () => console.log(`File ${filename} changed!`));
console.log(`Now watching ${filename} for changes...`);
```

Save the file as watcher-argv.js and run it like so:

```
$ node watcher-argv.js target.txt
Now watching target.txt for changes...
```

You should see output and behavior that's nearly identical to that of the first watcher.js program. After outputting *Now watching target.txt for changes...* the script will diligently wait for changes to the target file.

This program uses process.argv to access the incoming command-line arguments. argv stands for *argument vector*; it's an array containing node and the full path to the watcher-argv.js as its first two elements. The third element (that is, at index 2) is target.txt, the name of our target file.

Note the use of backtick characters (`) to mark the strings logged in this program:

```
`File ${filename} changed!`
```

These are called *template strings*. They can span multiple lines and they support expression interpolation, meaning you can place an expression inside of ${} and it will insert the stringified result.

If a target filename is not provided to watcher-argv.js, the program will throw an exception. You see try that by simply omitting the target.txt parameter:

```
$ node watcher-argv.js
/full/path/to/script/watcher-argv.js:4
  throw Error('A file to watch must be specified!');
  ^

Error: A file to watch must be specified!
```

Any unhandled exception thrown in Node.js will halt the process. The exception output shows the offending file and the line number and position of the exception.

Processes are important in Node. It's pretty common in Node.js development to spawn separate processes as a way of breaking up work, rather than putting everything into one big Node.js program. In the next section, you'll learn how to spawn a process in Node.

Spawning a Child Process

Let's enhance our file-watching example program even further by having it spawn a child process in response to a change. To do this, we'll bring in Node.js's child-process module and dive into some Node.js patterns and classes. You'll also learn how to use streams to pipe data around.

To keep things simple, we'll make our script invoke the ls command with the -l and -h options. This will give us some information about the target file whenever it changes. You can use the same technique to spawn other kinds of processes, as well.

Open your editor and enter this:

filesystem/watcher-spawn.js
```
'use strict';
const fs = require('fs');
const spawn = require('child_process').spawn;
const filename = process.argv[2];

if (!filename) {
  throw Error('A file to watch must be specified!');
}

fs.watch(filename, () => {
  const ls = spawn('ls', ['-l', '-h', filename]);
  ls.stdout.pipe(process.stdout);
});
console.log(`Now watching ${filename} for changes...`);
```

Save the file as watcher-spawn.js and run it with node as before:

```
$ node watcher-spawn.js target.txt
Now watching target.txt for changes...
```

If you go to a different console and touch the target file, your Node.js program will produce something like this:

```
-rw-rw-r-- 1 jimbo jimbo 6 Dec  8 05:19 target.txt
```

The username, group, and other properties of the file will be different, but the format should be the same.

Notice that we added a new require() at the beginning of the program. Calling require('child_process') returns the child process module.[2] We're interested only in the spawn() method, so we save that to a constant with the same name and ignore the rest of the module.

```
spawn = require('child_process').spawn,
```

Remember, functions are first-class citizens in JavaScript, so we're free to assign them directly to variables like we did here.

Next, take a look at the callback function we passed to fs.watch():

```
() => {
  const ls = spawn('ls', ['-l', '-h', filename]);
  ls.stdout.pipe(process.stdout);
}
```

Unlike the previous arrow-function expression, this one has a multiline body; hence the opening and closing curly braces ({}).

The first parameter to spawn() is the name of the program we wish to execute; in our case it's ls. The second parameter is an array of command-line arguments. It contains the flags and the target filename.

The object returned by spawn() is a ChildProcess. Its stdin, stdout, and stderr properties are Streams that can be used to read or write data. We want to send the standard output from the child process directly to our own standard output stream. This is what the pipe() method does.

Sometimes you'll want to capture data from a stream, rather than just piping it forward. Let's see how to do that.

Capturing Data from an EventEmitter

EventEmitter is a very important class in Node.js. It provides a channel for events to be dispatched and listeners to be notified. Many objects you'll encounter in Node.js inherit from EventEmitter, like the Streams we saw in the last section.

Now let's modify our previous program to capture the child process's output by listening for events on the stream. Open an editor to the watcher-spawn.js file from the previous section, then find the call to fs.watch(). Replace it with this:

---

2. https://nodejs.org/api/child_process.html

```
filesystem/watcher-spawn-parse.js
fs.watch(filename, () => {
  const ls = spawn('ls', ['-l', '-h', filename]);
  let output = '';

  ls.stdout.on('data', chunk => output += chunk);

  ls.on('close', () => {
    const parts = output.split(/\s+/);
    console.log([parts[0], parts[4], parts[8]]);
  });
});
```

Save this updated file as watcher-spawn-parse.js. Run it as usual, then touch the target file in a separate terminal. You should see output something like this:

```
$ node watcher-spawn-parse.js target.txt
Now watching target.txt for changes...
[ '-rw-rw-r--', '0', 'target.txt' ]
```

The new callback starts out the same as before, creating a child process and assigning it to a variable called ls. It also creates an output variable, which will buffer the output coming from the child process.

Notice the output variable declared with the keyword let. Like const, let declares a variable, but one that could be assigned a value more than once. Generally speaking, you should use const to declare your variables unless you know that the value should be able to change at runtime.

What about var?

Prior to the introduction of const and let, the keyword var was used for declaring variables in JavaScript. var is like let, except that it's scoped to the nearest function or module, not to the nearest block.

You should always prefer const or let over var. Here's an example to make it clear why:

```
if (true) {
  var myVar = "hello";
  let myLet = "world";
}

console.log(myVar); // Logs "hello".
console.log(myLet); // throws ReferenceError.
```

It is unintuitive, but the variable myVar is available outside of the if() block. This JavaScript language quirk is called *hoisting*. Using var hoists the variable up from its declared block to the nearest function or module scope.

When you really want a variable to be scoped to the module or function, use const or let to declare the variable there.

Next we add *event listeners*. An event listener is a callback function that is invoked when an event of a specified type is dispatched. Since the Stream class inherits from EventEmitter, we can listen for events from the child process's standard output stream:

```
ls.stdout.on('data', chunk => output += chunk);
```

A lot is going on in this single line of code, so let's break it down.

Notice that the arrow function takes a parameter called chunk. When an arrow function takes exactly one parameter, like this one, you can omit the parentheses around the param.

The on() method adds a listener for the specified event type. We listen for data events because we're interested in data coming out of the stream.

Events can send along extra information, which arrives in the form of parameters to the callbacks. data events in particular pass along a Buffer object. Each time we get a chunk of data, we append it to our output.

A *Buffer* is Node.js's way of representing binary data.[3] It points to a blob of memory allocated by Node.js's native core, outside of the JavaScript engine. Buffers can't be resized and they require encoding and decoding to convert to and from JavaScript strings.

Any time you add a non-string to a string in JavaScript (like we're doing here with chunk), the runtime will implicitly call the object's toString() method. For a Buffer, this means copying the content into Node.js's heap using the default encoding (UTF-8).

Shuttling data in this way can be a slow operation, relatively speaking. If you can, it's often better to work with Buffers directly, but strings are more convenient. For this tiny amount of data the impact of conversion is small, but it's something to keep in mind as you work more with Buffers.

Like Stream, the ChildProcess class extends EventEmitter, so we can add listeners to it, as well.

```
ls.on('close', () => {
  const parts = output.split(/\s+/);
  console.log([parts[0], parts[4], parts[8]]);
});
```

After a child process has exited and all its streams have been flushed, it emits a close event. When the callback printed here is invoked, we parse the output

---

3.   https://nodejs.org/api/buffer.html

data by splitting on sequences of one or more whitespace characters (using the regular expression /\s+/). Finally, we use console.log() to report on the first, fifth, and ninth fields (indexes 0, 4, and 8), which correspond to the permissions, size, and filename, respectively.

We've seen a lot of Node.js's features in this small problem space of file-watching. You now know how to use key Node.js classes, including EventEmitter, Stream, ChildProcess, and Buffer. You also have firsthand experience writing asynchronous callback functions and coding for the event loop.

Let's expand on these concepts in the next phase of our filesystem journey: reading and writing files.

Reading and Writing Files Asynchronously

Earlier in this chapter, we wrote a series of Node.js programs that could watch files for changes. Now let's explore Node.js's methods for reading and writing files. Along the way we'll see two common error-handling patterns in Node.js: error events on EventEmitters and err callback arguments.

There are a few approaches to reading and writing files in Node. The simplest is to read in or write out the entire file at once. This technique works well for small files. Other approaches read and write by creating Streams or staging content in a Buffer. Here's an example of the whole-file-at-once approach:

filesystem/read-simple.js
```
'use strict';
const fs = require('fs');
fs.readFile('target.txt', (err, data) => {
  if (err) {
    throw err;
  }
  console.log(data.toString());
});
```

Save this file as read-simple.js and run it with node:

```
$ node read-simple.js
```

You'll see the contents of target.txt echoed to the command line. If the file is empty, all you'll see is a blank line.

Notice how the first parameter to the readFile() callback handler is err. If readFile() is successful, then err will be null. Otherwise the err parameter will contain an Error object. This is a common error-reporting pattern in Node.js, especially for built-in modules. In our example's case, we throw the error if there was one. Recall that an uncaught exception in Node.js will halt the program by escaping the event loop.

The second parameter to our callback, data, is a Buffer—the same kind that was passed to our various callbacks in previous sections.

Writing a file using the whole-file approach is similar. Here's an example:

filesystem/write-simple.js

```
'use strict';
const fs = require('fs');
fs.writeFile('target.txt', 'hello world', (err) => {
  if (err) {
    throw err;
  }
  console.log('File saved!');
});
```

This program writes *hello world* to target.txt (creating it if it doesn't exist, or overwriting it if it does). If for any reason the file can't be written, then the err parameter will contain an Error object.

Creating Read and Write Streams

You create a read stream or a write stream by using fs.createReadStream() and fs.createWriteStream(), respectively. For example, here's a very short program called cat.js. It uses a file stream to pipe a file's data to standard output:

filesystem/cat.js

```
#!/usr/bin/env node
'use strict';
require('fs').createReadStream(process.argv[2]).pipe(process.stdout);
```

Because the first line starts with #!, you can execute this program directly in Unix-like systems. You don't need to pass it into the node program (although you still can).

Use chmod to make it executable:

```
$ chmod +x cat.js
```

Then, to run it, send the name of the chosen file as an additional argument:

```
$ ./cat.js target.txt
hello world
```

The code in cat.js does not bother assigning the fs module to a variable. The require() function returns a module object, so we can call methods on it directly.

You can also listen for data events from the file stream instead of calling pipe(). The following program called read-stream.js does this:

filesystem/read-stream.js

```
'use strict';
require('fs').createReadStream(process.argv[2])
  .on('data', chunk => process.stdout.write(chunk))
  .on('error', err => process.stderr.write(`ERROR: ${err.message}\n`));
```

Here we use process.stdout.write() to echo data, rather than console.log(). The incoming data chunks already contain any newline characters from the input file. We don't need the extra newline that console.log() would add.

Conveniently, the return value of on() is the same emitter object. We take advantage of this fact to *chain* our handlers, setting up one right after the other.

When working with an EventEmitter, the way to handle errors is to listen for error events. Let's trigger an error to see what happens. Run the program, but specify a file that doesn't exist:

```
$ node read-stream.js no-such-file
ERROR: ENOENT: no such file or directory, open 'no-such-file'
```

Since we're listening for error events, Node.js invokes our handler (and then proceeds to exit normally). If you don't listen for error events, but one happens anyway, Node.js will throw an exception. And as we saw before, an uncaught exception will cause the process to terminate.

Blocking the Event Loop with Synchronous File Access

The file-access methods we've discussed in this chapter so far are *asynchronous*. They perform their I/O duties—waiting as necessary—completely in the background, only to invoke callbacks later. This is by far the preferred way to do I/O in Node.

Even so, many of the methods in the fs module have synchronous versions, as well. These end in *Sync, like readFileSync, for example. Doing synchronous file access might look familiar to you if you haven't done a lot of async development in the past. However, it comes at a substantial cost.

When you use the *Sync methods, the Node.js process will *block* until the I/O finishes. This means Node.js won't execute any other code, won't trigger any callbacks, won't process any events, won't accept any connections—nothing. It'll just sit there indefinitely waiting for the operation to complete.

However, synchronous methods are simpler to use since they lack the callback step. They either return successfully or throw an exception, without the need for a callback function. There actually are cases where this style of access is OK; we'll discuss them in the next section.

Here's an example of how to read a file using the readFileSync() method:

```
const fs = require('fs');
const data = fs.readFileSync('target.txt');
process.stdout.write(data.toString());
```

The return value of readFileSync() is a Buffer—the same as the parameter passed to callbacks of the asynchronous readFile() method we saw before.

Performing Other File-System Operations

Node.js's fs module has many other methods that map nicely onto POSIX conventions. (POSIX is a family of standards for interoperability between operating systems—including filesystem utilities.)[4] To name a few examples, you can copy() files and unlink() (delete) them. You can use chmod() to change permissions and mkdir() to create directories.

These functions rely on the same kinds of callback parameters we've used in this chapter. They're all asynchronous by default, but many come with equivalent *Sync versions.

The Two Phases of a Node.js Program

Given the cost that blocking has on the Node.js event loop, you might think it's always bad to use synchronous file-access methods. To understand when it's OK, you can think of Node.js programs as having two phases.

In the initialization phase, the program is getting set up, bringing in libraries, reading configuration parameters, and doing other mission-critical tasks. If something goes wrong at this early stage, not much can be done, and it's best to fail fast. The only time you should consider synchronous file access is during the initialization phase of your program.

The second phase is the operation phase, when the program churns through the event loop. Since many Node.js programs are networked, this means accepting connections, making requests, and waiting on other kinds of I/O. You should never use synchronous file-access methods during this phase.

---

4.   http://pubs.opengroup.org/onlinepubs/9699919799/utilities/contents.html

The require() function is an example of this principle in action—it synchronously evaluates the target module's code and returns the module object. Either the module will successfully load or the program will fail right away.

As a rule of thumb, if your program couldn't possibly succeed without the file, then it's OK to use synchronous file access. If your program could conceivably continue about its business, then it's better to take the safe route and stick to asynchronous I/O.

Wrapping Up

In this chapter we've used Node.js to perform file operations in Node.js's evented, asynchronous, callback-oriented way. You learned how to watch files for changes and to read and write files. You also learned how to spawn child processes and access command-line arguments.

Along the way, we covered the EventEmitter class. We used the on() method to listen for events and handle them in our callback functions. And we used Streams—which are a special kind of EventEmitter—to process data in buffered chunks or pipe it directly to other streams.

Oh, and let's not forget about errors. You learned Node.js's convention of passing an err argument to callbacks, and how error events can be captured from an EventEmitter.

Keep these patterns in mind as you continue through the book. Third-party libraries sometimes have different styles, but the concepts you've learned here reappear throughout the Node.js ecosystem.

In the next chapter we'll dig into the other form of server-side I/O: network connections. We'll explore the domain of networked services, building on the concepts and practices developed here.

The following are some bonus questions for you to try out your newly gained Node.js knowledge.

Fortifying Code

The various example programs we developed in this chapter lack many safety checks. Consider the following questions, and how you'd change the code to address them:

- In the file-watching examples, what happens if the target file doesn't exist?
- What happens if a file being watched gets deleted?

Expanding Functionality

In an early example of our file-watcher program, we pulled the filename to watch from process.argv. Consider these questions:

- Instead, how would you take the *process to spawn* from process.argv?
- How would you pass an arbitrary number of additional parameters from process.argv to the spawned process (e.g., node watcher-spawn-cmd.js target.txt ls -l -h)?

CHAPTER 3

Networking with Sockets

Node.js was designed from the ground up to do networked programming. In this chapter, we'll explore Node.js's built-in support for low-level socket connections. TCP sockets form the backbone of modern networked applications, and understanding them will serve you well as we do more complex networking through the rest of the book.

As you develop socket-based servers and clients, you'll learn about the following Node.js aspects.

Node.js Core

    The asynchronous programming techniques we explored in the last chapter will be even more important here. You'll learn how to extend Node.js classes such as EventEmitter. You'll create custom modules to house reusable code.

Patterns

    A network connection has two endpoints. A common pattern is for one endpoint to act as the server while the other is the client. We'll develop both kinds of endpoints in this chapter, as well as a JSON-based protocol for client/server communication.

JavaScriptisms

    The JavaScript language has an interesting inheritance model. You'll learn about Node.js's utilities for creating class hierarchies.

Supporting Code

    Testing is important to ensure that our programs behave the way we expect them to. In this chapter, we'll develop a unit test with a framework called Mocha, which we'll install with npm.

To begin, we'll develop a simple and complete TCP server program. Then we'll iteratively improve the code as we address concerns such as robustness, modularity, and testability.

Listening for Socket Connections

Networked services exist to do two things: connect endpoints and transmit information between them. No matter what kind of information is transmitted, a connection must first be made.

In this section, you'll learn how to create socket-based services using Node.js. We'll develop an example application that sends data to connected clients, then we'll connect to this service using standard command-line tools. By the end, you'll have a good idea of how Node.js does the client/server pattern.

Binding a Server to a TCP Port

TCP socket connections consist of two *endpoints*. One endpoint *binds* to a numbered port while the other endpoint *connects* to a port.

This is a lot like a telephone system. One phone binds a given phone number for a long time. A second phone places a call—it connects to the bound number. Once the call is answered, information (sound) can travel both ways.

In Node.js, the bind and connect operations are provided by the net module. Binding a TCP port to listen for connections looks like this:

```
'use strict';
const
  net = require('net'),
  server = net.createServer(connection => {
    // Use the connection object for data transfer.
  });
server.listen(60300);
```

The net.createServer() method takes a callback function and returns a Server object. Node.js will invoke the callback function whenever another endpoint connects. The connection parameter is a Socket object that you can use to send or receive data.

The callback function defined here is an arrow-function expression, the same kind we used extensively in Chapter 2, *Wrangling the File System*, on page 11.

Calling server.listen() binds the specified port. In this case, we're binding TCP port number 60300. To get an idea of the setup, take a look at the figure on page 29.

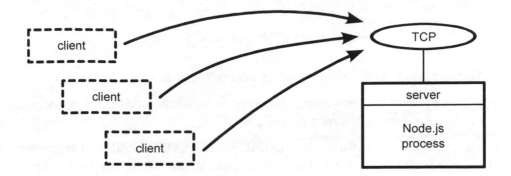

The figure shows our one Node.js process whose server binds a TCP port. Any number of clients—which may or may not be Node.js processes—can connect to that bound port.

Our server program doesn't do anything with the connection yet. Let's fix that by using it to send some useful information to the client.

Writing Data to a Socket

In Chapter 2, *Wrangling the File System*, on page 11, we developed some simple file utilities that would take action whenever a target file changed. Let's reuse the file changes as a source of information for our example networked service. This will give us something to code against as we dig into aspects of Node.js development.

To begin, create a directory named networking to hold the code you'll be writing. Then open your favorite text editor and enter this:

```
networking/net-watcher.js
'use strict';
const fs = require('fs');
const net = require('net');
const filename = process.argv[2];

if (!filename) {
  throw Error('Error: No filename specified.');
}

net.createServer(connection => {
  // Reporting.
  console.log('Subscriber connected.');
  connection.write(`Now watching "${filename}" for changes...\n`);

  // Watcher setup.
  const watcher =
    fs.watch(filename, () => connection.write(`File changed: ${new Date()}\n`));
```

```
  // Cleanup.
  connection.on('close', () => {
    console.log('Subscriber disconnected.');
    watcher.close();
  });
}).listen(60300, () => console.log('Listening for subscribers...'));
```

Save this file in your networking directory as net-watcher.js. At the top, we pull in the Node.js core modules fs and net.

The name of the file to watch, if supplied, will be the third (index 2) argument in process.argv. If the user didn't supply a target file to watch, then we throw a custom Error. Uncaught errors like this will cause the Node.js process to halt after sending a stacktrace to standard error.

Now let's take a look inside the callback function given to createServer(). This callback function does three things:

- It reports that the connection has been established (both to the client with connection.write and to the console).

- It begins listening for changes to the target file, saving the returned watcher object. This callback sends change information to the client using connection.write.

- It listens for the connection's close event so it can report that the subscriber has disconnected and stop watching the file, with watcher.close().

Finally, notice the callback passed into server.listen() at the end. Node.js invokes this function after it has successfully bound port 60300 and is ready to start receiving connections.

Connecting to a TCP Socket Server with Netcat

Now let's run the net-watcher program and confirm that it behaves the way we expect. This will require a little terminal juggling.

To run and test the net-watcher program, you'll need three terminal sessions: one for the service itself, one for the client, and one to trigger changes to the watched file.

In your first terminal, use the watch command to touch the target file at one-second intervals:

```
$ watch -n 1 touch target.txt
```

With that running, in a second terminal, run the net-watcher program:

```
$ node net-watcher.js target.txt
Listening for subscribers...
```

This program creates a service listening on TCP port 60300. To connect to it, we'll use netcat, a socket utility program. Open a third terminal and use the nc command like so:

```
$ nc localhost 60300
Now watching "target.txt" for changes...
File changed: Wed Dec 16 2015 05:56:14 GMT-0500 (EST)
File changed: Wed Dec 16 2015 05:56:19 GMT-0500 (EST)
```

If you're on a system that doesn't have nc, you can use telnet:

```
$ telnet localhost 60300
Trying 127.0.0.1...
Connected to localhost.
Escape character is '^]'.
Now watching "target.txt" for changes...
File changed: Wed Dec 16 2015 05:56:14 GMT-0500 (EST)
File changed: Wed Dec 16 2015 05:56:19 GMT-0500 (EST)
^]
telnet> quit
Connection closed.
```

Back in the net-watcher terminal, you should see this:

```
Subscriber connected.
```

You can kill the nc session by typing Ctrl-C. If you're using telnet, you'll need to disconnect with Ctrl-] and then type *quit* Enter. When you do, you'll see the following line appear in the net-watcher terminal:

```
Subscriber disconnected.
```

To terminate the net-watcher service or the watch command, type Ctrl-C from their terminals.

The following figure outlines the setup we just created. The net-watcher process (box) binds a TCP port and watches a file—both resources are shown as ovals.

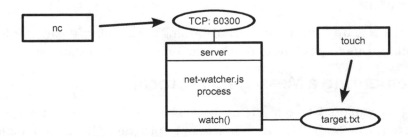

Multiple subscribers can connect and receive updates simultaneously. If you open additional terminals and connect to port 60300 with nc, they'll all receive updates when the target file changes.

TCP sockets are useful for communicating between networked computers. But if you need processes on the same computer to communicate, Unix sockets offer a more efficient alternative. The net module can create this kind of socket as well, which we'll look at next.

Listening on Unix Sockets

To see how the net module uses Unix sockets, let's modify the net-watcher program to use this kind of communication channel. Keep in mind that Unix sockets work only on Unix-like environments.

Open the net-watcher.js program and change the .listen() call at the end to this:

```
.listen('/tmp/watcher.sock', () => console.log('Listening for subscribers...'));
```

Save the file as net-watcher-unix.js, then run the program as before:

```
$ node net-watcher-unix.js target.txt
Listening for subscribers...
```

Note that if you get an error containing EADDRINUSE, you may have to delete the watcher.sock before running the program again.

To connect a client, we can use nc as before, but this time specifying the -U flag to use the socket file.

```
$ nc -U /tmp/watcher.sock
Now watching target.txt for changes...
```

Unix sockets can be faster than TCP sockets because they don't require invoking network hardware. However, by nature they're confined to the machine.

That concludes the basics of creating network socket servers in Node. We discovered how to create socket servers and connect to them using the common client utility program nc. This framework will supply the backdrop for the rest of the examples in the chapter.

Next, we'll beef up our service by transforming the data into a parsable format. This will put us in position to develop custom client applications.

Implementing a Messaging Protocol

We've just explored how to create socket servers that listen for incoming connections in Node. So far, our example programs have sent plain-text messages that are meant to be read by a human. In this section we'll design and implement a better protocol.

A *protocol* is a set of rules that defines how endpoints in a system communicate. Any time you develop a networked application in Node.js, you're working with one or more protocols. Here we'll create a protocol based on passing JSON messages over TCP.

JSON is incredibly prevalent in Node.js. We'll use it extensively for data serialization and configuration throughout the book. It is significantly easier to program clients against than plain text, and it's still human-readable.

We'll implement client and server endpoints that use our new JSON-based protocol. This will give us opportunities to develop test cases and refactor our code into reusable modules.

Serializing Messages with JSON

Let's develop the message-passing protocol that uses JSON to serialize messages. Each message is a JSON-serialized object, which is a hash of key-value pairs. Here's an example JSON object with two key-value pairs:

```
{"key":"value","anotherKey":"anotherValue"}
```

The net-watcher service we've been developing in this chapter sends two kinds of messages that we need to convert to JSON:

- When the connection is first established, the client receives the string *Now watching "target.txt" for changes....*

- Whenever the target file changes, the client receives a string like this: *File changed: Fri Dec 18 2015 05:44:00 GMT-0500 (EST)*.

We'll encode the first kind of message this way:

```
{"type":"watching","file":"target.txt"}
```

The type field indicates that this is a watching message—the specified file is now being watched.

The second type of message is encoded this way:

```
{"type":"changed","timestamp":1358175733785}
```

Here the type field announces that the target file has changed. The timestamp field contains an integer value representing the number of milliseconds since midnight, January 1, 1970. This happens to be an easy time format to work with in JavaScript. For example, you can get the current time in this format with Date.now().

Notice that there are no line breaks in our JSON messages. Although JSON is whitespace agnostic—it ignores whitespace outside of string values—our protocol will use newlines only to separate messages. We'll refer to this protocol as line-delimited JSON (LDJ).

Switching to JSON Messages

Now that we've defined an improved, computer-accessible protocol, let's modify the net-watcher service to use it. Then we'll create client programs that receive and interpret these messages.

Our task is to use JSON.stringify() to encode message objects and send them out through connection.write(). JSON.stringify() takes a JavaScript object, and returns a string containing a serialized representation of that object in JSON form.

Open your editor to the net-watcher.js program. Find the following line:

```
connection.write(`Now watching "${filename}" for changes...\n`);
```

And replace it with this:

```
connection.write(JSON.stringify({type: 'watching', file: filename}) + '\n');
```

Next, find the call to connection.write() inside the watcher:

```
const watcher =
  fs.watch(filename, () => connection.write(`File changed: ${new Date()}\n`));
```

And replace it with this:

```
const watcher = fs.watch(filename, () => connection.write(
    JSON.stringify({type: 'changed', timestamp: Date.now()}) + '\n'));
```

Save this updated file as net-watcher-json-service.js. Run the new program as always, remembering to specify a target file:

```
$ node net-watcher-json-service.js target.txt
Listening for subscribers...
```

Then connect using netcat from a second terminal:

```
$ nc localhost 60300
{"type":"watching","file":"target.txt"}
```

When you touch the target.txt file, you'll see output like this from your client:

```
{"type":"changed","timestamp":1450437616760}
```

Now we're ready to write a client program that processes these messages.

Creating Socket Client Connections

So far in this chapter, we've explored the server side of Node.js sockets. Here we'll write a client program in Node.js to receive JSON messages from our net-watcher-json-service program. We'll start with a naive implementation, and then improve upon it through the rest of the chapter.

Open an editor and insert this:

networking/net-watcher-json-client.js
```javascript
'use strict';
const net = require('net');
const client = net.connect({port: 60300});
client.on('data', data => {
  const message = JSON.parse(data);
  if (message.type === 'watching') {
    console.log(`Now watching: ${message.file}`);
  } else if (message.type === 'changed') {
    const date = new Date(message.timestamp);
    console.log(`File changed: ${date}`);
  } else {
    console.log(`Unrecognized message type: ${message.type}`);
  }
});
```

Save this program as net-watcher-json-client.js.

This short program uses net.connect() to create a client connection to localhost port 60300, then waits for data. The client object is a Socket, just like the incoming connection we saw on the server side.

Whenever a data event happens, our callback function takes the incoming buffer object, parses the JSON message, and then logs an appropriate message to the console.

To run the program, first make sure the net-watcher-json-service is running. Then, in another terminal, run the client:

```
$ node net-watcher-json-client.js
Now watching: target.txt
```

If you touch the target file, you'll see output like this:

```
File changed: Mon Dec 21 2015 05:34:19 GMT-0500 (EST)
```

Success! This program works, but it's far from perfect. Consider what happens when the connection ends or if it fails to connect in the first place. This program listens for only data events, not end events or error events. We could listen for these events and take appropriate action when they happen.

But there's actually a deeper problem lurking in our code—caused by assumptions we've made about message boundaries. In the next section we'll develop a test that exposes this bug so we can fix it.

Testing Network Application Functionality

Functional tests assure us that our code does what we expect it to do. In this section, we'll develop a test for our networked file-watching server and client programs. We'll create a mock server that conforms to our LDJ protocol while exposing flaws in the client.

After we write the test, we'll fix the client code so that it passes. This will bring up many Node.js concepts, including extending core classes, creating and using custom modules, and developing on top of EventEmitters. But first we need to understand a problem lurking in our client/server programs as currently written.

Understanding the Message-Boundary Problem

When you develop networked programs in Node.js, they'll often communicate by passing messages. In the best case, a message will arrive all at once. But sometimes messages will arrive in pieces, split into distinct data events. To develop networked applications, you'll need to deal with these splits when they happen.

The LDJ protocol we developed earlier separates messages with newline characters. Each newline character is the *boundary* between two messages. Here's an example of a series of messages, with newline characters specifically called out:

```
{"type":"watching","file":"target.txt"}\n
{"type":"changed","timestamp":1450694370094}\n
{"type":"changed","timestamp":1450694375099}\n
```

Recall the service we've been developing so far in this chapter. Whenever a change happens, it encodes and sends a message to the connection, including the trailing newline. Each line of output corresponds to a single data event in the connected client. Or, to put it another way, the data event boundaries exactly match up with the message boundaries.

Our client program currently relies on this behavior. It parses each message by sending the contents of the data buffer directly into JSON.parse():

```
client.on('data', data => {
  const message = JSON.parse(data);
```

But consider what would happen if a message were split down the middle, and arrived as two separate data events. Such a split could happen in the wild, especially for large messages. The following figure shows an example of a split message.

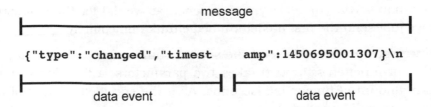

Let's create a test service that sends a split message like this one and find out how the client responds.

Implementing a Test Service

Writing robust Node.js applications means gracefully handling network problems like split inputs, broken connections, and bad data. Here we'll implement a test service that purposefully splits a message into multiple chunks.

Open your editor and enter this:

networking/test-json-service.js
```
'use strict';
const server = require('net').createServer(connection => {
  console.log('Subscriber connected.');

  // Two message chunks that together make a whole message.
  const firstChunk = '{"type":"changed","timesta';
  const secondChunk = 'mp":1450694370094}\n';

  // Send the first chunk immediately.
  connection.write(firstChunk);

  // After a short delay, send the other chunk.
  const timer = setTimeout(() => {
    connection.write(secondChunk);
    connection.end();
  }, 100);

  // Clear timer when the connection ends.
  connection.on('end', () => {
    clearTimeout(timer);
    console.log('Subscriber disconnected.');
  });
});

server.listen(60300, function() {
  console.log('Test server listening for subscribers...');
});
```

Save this file as test-json-service.js and run it:

```
$ node test-json-service.js
Test server listening for subscribers...
```

This test service differs from our previous net-watcher-json-service.js in a few ways. Rather than setting up a filesystem watcher, as we did for the real service, here we just send the first predetermined chunk immediately.

Then we set up a timer to send the second chunk after a short delay. The JavaScript function setTimeout() takes two parameters: a function to invoke and an amount of time in milliseconds. After the specified amount of time, the function will be called.

Finally, whenever the connection ends, we use clearTimeout() to unschedule the callback. Unscheduling the callback is necessary because once a connection is closed, any calls to connection.write() will trigger error events.

At last, let's find out what happens when we connect with the client program:

```
$ node net-watcher-json-client.js
undefined:1
{"type":"changed","timesta
                  ^

SyntaxError: Unexpected token t
    at Object.parse (native)
    at Socket.<anonymous> (./net-watcher-json-client.js:6:22)
    at emitOne (events.js:77:13)
    at Socket.emit (events.js:169:7)
    at readableAddChunk (_stream_readable.js:146:16)
    at Socket.Readable.push (_stream_readable.js:110:10)
    at TCP.onread (net.js:523:20)
```

The error *Unexpected token t* tells us that the message was not complete and valid JSON. Our client attempted to send half a message to JSON.parse(), which expects only whole, properly formatted JSON strings as input.

At this point, we've successfully simulated the case of a split message coming from the server. Now let's fix the client to work with it.

Extending Core Classes in Custom Modules

The Node.js program we made in the last section exposed a flaw in our client code; namely, that it doesn't buffer its inputs. Any message that arrives as multiple data events will crash it.

So really the client program has two jobs to do. One is to buffer incoming data into messages. The other is to handle each message when it arrives.

Rather than cramming both of these jobs into one Node.js program, the right thing to do is to turn at least one of them into a Node.js *module*. We'll create a module that handles the input-buffering piece so that the main program can reliably get full messages. Along the way, we'll need to talk about custom modules and extending core classes in Node.

Extending EventEmitter

To relieve the client program from the danger of split JSON messages, we'll implement an LDJ buffering client module. Then we'll incorporate it into the network-watcher client.

Inheritance in Node

First let's have a look at how Node.js does inheritance. The following code sets up LDJClient to inherit from EventEmitter.

```
networking/lib/ldj-client.js
const EventEmitter = require('events').EventEmitter;
class LDJClient extends EventEmitter {
  constructor(stream) {
    super();
  }
}
```

LDJClient is a *class*, which means other code should call new LDJClient(stream) to get an instance. The stream parameter is an object that emits data events, such as a Socket connection.

Inside the constructor function, we first call super() to invoke EventEmitter's own constructor function. Whenever you're implementing a class that extends another class, you should start with calling super(), with the appropriate constructor arguments for it.

You might be interested to know that under the hood, JavaScript uses *prototypal inheritance* to establish the relationship between LDJClient and EventEmitter. Prototypal inheritance is powerful, and can be used for more than just classes, but this usage is increasingly rare. Code to use 'LDJClient' might look like this:

```
const client = new LDJClient(networkStream);
client.on('message', message => {
  // Take action for this message.
});
```

The class hierarchy is now in place, but we haven't implemented anything to emit message events. Let's look at this next, and talk about buffering data events in Node.

Buffering Data Events

It's time to use the stream parameter in the LDJClient to retrieve and buffer input. The goal is to take the incoming raw data from the stream and convert it into message events containing the parsed message objects.

Take a look at the following updated constructor. It appends incoming data chunks to a running buffer string and scans for line endings (which should be JSON message boundaries).

```
networking/lib/ldj-client.js
constructor(stream) {
  super();
  let buffer = '';
  stream.on('data', data => {
    buffer += data;
    let boundary = buffer.indexOf('\n');
    while (boundary !== -1) {
      const input = buffer.substring(0, boundary);
      buffer = buffer.substring(boundary + 1);
      this.emit('message', JSON.parse(input));
      boundary = buffer.indexOf('\n');
    }
  });
}
```

We start out by calling super, just like before, and then set up a string variable called buffer to capture incoming data. Next, we use stream.on() to handle data events.

The code inside the data event handler is dense, but it's not fancy. We append raw data to the end of the buffer and then look for completed messages from the front. Each message string is sent through JSON.parse() and finally emitted by the LDJClient as a message event via this.emit().

At this point, the problem we started with (handling split messages) is effectively solved. Whether ten messages come in on a single data event or only half of one does, they'll all precipitate message events on the LDJClient instance.

Next we need to put this class into a Node.js module so our upstream client can use it.

Exporting Functionality in a Module

Let's pull together the previous code samples and expose LDJClient as a module. Start by creating a directory called lib. You could name it something else, but there is a strong convention in the Node.js community to put supporting code in the lib directory.

Prototypal Inheritance

Consider the LDJClient class we just made. Prior to the availability of the class, constructor, and super keywords, we would have written that code as follows:

```
const EventEmitter = require('events').EventEmitter;
const util = require('util');

function LDJClient(stream) {
  EventEmitter.call(this);
}

util.inherits(LDJClient, EventEmitter);
```

LDJClient is a *constructor function*. It's the same as if you'd used the class and constructor keywords. Instead of super(), we invoke the EventEmitter constructor function on this.

Finally, we use util.inherits() to make LDJClient's *prototypal parent* object the EventEmitter *prototype*. If this sounds cryptic to you, don't worry. It means that if you look for a property on an LDJClient and it's not there, the EventEmitter is the next place to look.

Consider when we make an LDJClient instance called client and call client.on(). Even though the client object itself and the LDJClient prototype both lack an on method, the JavasScript engine will find and use the on method of EventEmitter.

In the same fashion, if we call client.toString(), the JavaScript engine will find and use the native implementation on the EventEmitter's prototypal parent, Object.

In general, you shouldn't have to deal with this level of abstraction. Library authors sometimes take advantage of these features to do clever things, but by far the most common use of prototypal inheritance is to set up class hierarchies.

Next, open your text editor and insert the following:

networking/lib/ldj-client.js

```
'use strict';
const EventEmitter = require('events').EventEmitter;
class LDJClient extends EventEmitter {
  constructor(stream) {
    super();
    let buffer = '';
    stream.on('data', data => {
      buffer += data;
      let boundary = buffer.indexOf('\n');
      while (boundary !== -1) {
        const input = buffer.substring(0, boundary);
        buffer = buffer.substring(boundary + 1);
        this.emit('message', JSON.parse(input));
        boundary = buffer.indexOf('\n');
      }
    });
  }
```

```
  static connect(stream) {
    return new LDJClient(stream);
  }
}
module.exports = LDJClient;
```

Save the file as lib/ldj-client.js. The code for this module is the combination of previous examples plus a static method—the new module.exports section at the end.

Inside the class definition, after the constructor, we're adding a *static* method called connect(). A static method is attached to the LDJClient class itself rather than applied to individual instances. The connect() method is merely a convenience for consumers of the library so that they don't have to use the new operator to create an instance of LDJClient.

In a Node.js module, the module.exports object is the bridge between the module code and the outside world. Any properties you set on exports will be available to upstream code that pulls in the module. In our case, we're exporting the LDJClient class itself.

Code to use the LDJ module will look something like this:

```
const LDJClient = require('./lib/ldj-client.js');
const client = new LDJClient(networkStream);
```

Or, using the connect() method, it could look like this:

```
const client = require('./lib/ldj-client.js').connect(networkStream);
```

Notice that in both cases, the require() function takes an actual path here, rather than the shorthand module names we've seen previously, like fs, net, and util. When a path is provided to require(), Node.js will attempt to resolve the path relative to the current file.

Our module is done! Now let's augment the network-watching client to use the module, to bring it all together.

Importing a Custom Node.js Module

It's time to make use of our custom module. Let's modify the client to use it rather than reading directly from the TCP stream.

Open a text editor and enter the following:

```
networking/net-watcher-ldj-client.js
'use strict';
const netClient = require('net').connect({port: 60300});
const ldjClient = require('./lib/ldj-client.js').connect(netClient);

ldjClient.on('message', message => {
  if (message.type === 'watching') {
    console.log(`Now watching: ${message.file}`);
  } else if (message.type === 'changed') {
    console.log(`File changed: ${new Date(message.timestamp)}`);
  } else {
    throw Error(`Unrecognized message type: ${message.type}`);
  }
});
```

Save this file as net-watcher-ldj-client.js. It's similar to our net-watcher-json-client from *Creating Socket Client Connections*, on page 35. The major difference is that instead of sending data buffers directly to JSON.parse(), this program relies on the ldj-client module to produce message events.

To make sure it solves the split-message problem, let's run the test service:

```
$ node test-json-service.js
Test server listening for subscribers...
```

Then, in a different terminal, use the new client to connect to it:

```
$ node net-watcher-ldj-client.js
File changed: Tue Jan 26 2016 05:54:59 GMT-0500 (EST)
```

Success! You now have a server and client that use a custom message format to reliably communicate. To round out this chapter, we'll bring in a popular testing framework called Mocha and use it to orchestrate our unit tests.

Developing Unit Tests with Mocha

Mocha is a popular, multiparadigm testing framework for Node.js. It features several different styles for describing your tests. We'll be using the behavior-driven development (BDD) style.

To use Mocha, first we'll install it with npm, Node.js's built-in package manager. Next we'll develop a unit test for the LDJClient class. And finally we'll use npm to run the test suite.

Installing Mocha with npm

Installing Node.js packages with npm can be quite easy, which partly explains the abundance of modules available to you. Even so, it's important to understand what's going on so you can manage your dependencies.

npm relies on a configuration file called package.json, so let's create one now. Open a terminal to your networking project and run this:

```
$ npm init -y
```

Calling npm init will create a default package.json file. We'll go through this important file in future chapters; for now let's move on to installing Mocha by running npm install.

```
$ npm install --save-dev --save-exact mocha@3.4.2
npm notice created a lockfile as package-lock.json. You should commit this file.
npm WARN networking@1.0.0 No description
npm WARN networking@1.0.0 No repository field.

+ mocha@3.4.2
added 34 packages in 2.348s
```

You can safely ignore the warnings in the output for now. npm is just suggesting that you add some descriptive fields to your package.json.

When the command finishes, it will have made a few changes. You'll now have a directory called node_modules in your project, which contains Mocha and its dependencies. And if you open your package.json file, you should find a devDependencies section that looks like this:

```
"devDependencies": {
  "mocha": "3.4.2"
}
```

In Node.js, there are a few different kinds of dependencies. Regular dependencies are used at runtime by your code when you use require() to bring in modules. Dev dependencies are programs that your project needs during development. Mocha is the latter kind, and the --save-dev flag (-D for short) told npm to add it to the devDependencies list.

Note that both dev dependencies and regular runtime dependencies are installed when you run npm install with no additional arguments. If you specifically want only the regular runtime dependencies and not the dev dependencies, you can run npm install with the --production flag, or by setting the NODE_ENV environment variable to *production*.

npm also created a file called package-lock.json. This file contains the exact version of every module that Mocha depends on, transitively. We'll talk more about this file in a bit, but first it helps to understand semantic versioning and how npm resolves package versions.

Semantic Versioning of Packages

The --save-exact (or -E) flag tells npm that we really want the version specified, in this case 3.4.2. By default, npm will use *semantic versioning* (or SemVer) to try to find the best available, compatible version of a package.[1]

Semantic versioning is a strong convention in the Node.js community, which you should definitely follow when setting version numbers on your packages. A version number consists of three parts joined by dots: the major version, the minor version, and the patch.

To abide by the semantic versioning convention, when you make a change to your code you have to increment the correct part of the version number:

- If your code change does not introduce or remove any functionality (like a bug fix), then just increment the patch version.

- If your code introduces functionality but doesn't remove or alter existing functionality, then increment the minor version and reset the patch.

- If your code in any way breaks existing functionality, then increment the major version and reset the minor and patch versions.

You can omit the --save-exact flag if you want npm to pull in the nearest matching version. You can even omit the version number entirely when running npm install, in which case npm will pull down the latest released version.

For the purposes of this book, all version numbers will be rigorously specified. This makes the code examples more future-proof and guards against potential violations of semantic versioning in packages we use.

If you leave off the --save-exact flag when installing a module through npm, it will append the version number with a caret (^) in the package.json. For example, "^3.4.2" instead of just "3.4.2". The caret means that npm will use the latest minor version greater than or equal to the one you specified.

For example, if your dependency version is set to ^1.5.7, and the module authors release a new minor version at 1.6.0, then anyone installing your module will get 1.6.0 of your dependency. They would not, however, pick up version 2.0, since major versions are assumed not to be backward compatible.

As long as everyone abides by the semantic versioning convention, everything should be fine, since minor versions can only add new functionality without

---

1. http://semver.org/

breaking existing functionality. In practice, things don't always work out that way.

If you want to have some leeway but still be a little more strict, you can use the tilde (~) prefix character instead. To continue the previous example, if your dependency is set to ~1.5.7 and the authors release 1.5.8, your users will get 1.5.8 but would not automatically be upgraded to 1.6.0. Prefixing with ~ is somewhat safer than prefixing with ^ because people are somewhat less likely to introduce breaking changes in patch releases, but you never know.

Although semantic versioning has been widely adopted by the community, authors sometimes make breaking changes in minor and patch releases prior to major version 1. For example, a project might start at version 0.0.1 and make breaking changes in each of 0.0.2, 0.0.3, and so on. Likewise for projects that go from 0.1.0 to 0.2.0 to 0.3.0, etc. npm accounts for this by ignoring leading zeros when trying to figure out which version to use for caret- and tilde-prefixed version numbers.

My advice: always use --save-exact when installing packages. The downside is that you'll have to explicitly update the version numbers of packages you depend on to pick up newer versions. But at least you get to tackle this on your own terms instead of having a surprise breakage introduced by an upstream dependency you don't control.

I have one more parting tip on version numbers before we move on. Even if you meticulously manage your direct dependencies with --save-exact, those dependencies may not be as strict in their own dependencies. This is why the package-lock.json is so important. It cements the versions of the entire dependency tree, including checksums.

If you're serious about having identical files on disk from one install to the next, you should commit your package-lock.json to your version-control system. When you're ready to perform updates, use npm outdated to get a report showing which of the modules you depend on have updated versions. Then when you install the latest version of a module, your package-lock.json will have the newly updated tree.

By committing the package-lock.json as you develop your project, you create an audit trail that allows you to run the exact same code stack from any point in the past. This can be an invaluable resource when trying to track down bugs, whether they're in your own code or your dependencies.

That's enough for now about semantic versioning, package.json, and package-lock.json. Let's move on to writing unit tests with Mocha.

Writing Mocha Unit Tests

With Mocha installed, now we'll develop a unit test that uses it.

Create a subdirectory named test to hold your test-related code. This is the convention for Node.js projects generally, and by default Mocha will look for your tests there.

Next, create a file in your test directory called ldj-client-test.js and add the following code to it.

```
networking/test/ldj-client-test.js
'use strict';
const assert = require('assert');
const EventEmitter = require('events').EventEmitter;
const LDJClient = require('../lib/ldj-client.js');

describe('LDJClient', () => {
  let stream = null;
  let client = null;

  beforeEach(() => {
    stream = new EventEmitter();
    client = new LDJClient(stream);
  });

  it('should emit a message event from a single data event', done => {
    client.on('message', message => {
      assert.deepEqual(message, {foo: 'bar'});
      done();
    });
    stream.emit('data', '{"foo":"bar"}\n');
  });
});
```

Let's step through this code. First we pull in the modules we'll need, including Node.js's built-in assert module. This contains useful functions for comparing values.

Next we use Mocha's describe() method to create a named context for our tests involving LDJClient. The second argument to describe() is a function that contains the test content.

Inside the test, first we declare two variables with let—one for the LDJClient instance, client, and one for the underlying EventEmitter, stream. Then in beforeEach(), we assign fresh instances to both of those variables.

Finally we call it() to test a specific behavior of the class. Since our class is asynchronous by nature, we invoke the done callback that Mocha provides to signal when the test has finished.

In the body of the test, we set up a message event handler on the client. This handler uses the deepEqual() method to assert that the payload we received matches our expectations. At last we tell our synthetic stream to emit a data event. This will cause our message handler to be invoked in a few turns of the event loop.

Now that we have a test written, it's time to run it!

Running Mocha Tests from npm

To run Mocha tests using npm, we have to add an entry to the package.json file. Open your package.json and update the scripts section so that it looks like this:

```
"scripts": {
  "test": "mocha"
},
```

Entries in scripts are commands you can invoke from the command line using npm run. For example, if you do npm run test, it'll run mocha as a command-line tool.

And for test in particular (and a few other scripts), npm has an alias so you can omit the run and just do npm test.

Let's run it now. Open a terminal and run npm test:

```
$ npm test

> @ test ./code/networking
> mocha


  LDJClient
    ✓ should emit a message event from single data event

  1 passing (9ms)
```

Great! Our test passed on the first try. Next, let's convert the chunked test from test-json-service.js into a true Mocha test.

Adding More Asynchronous Tests

With this infrastructure in place, we can also easily upgrade the test-json-service.js to be a Mocha test. Open your test/ldj-client-test.js file and add the following inside the describe() block:

```
networking/test/ldj-client-test.js
it('should emit a message event from split data events', done => {
  client.on('message', message => {
    assert.deepEqual(message, {foo: 'bar'});
    done();
  });
```

```
  stream.emit('data', '{"foo":');
  process.nextTick(() => stream.emit('data', '"bar"}\n'));
});
```

This test breaks up the message into two parts to be emitted by the stream one after the other. Notice the use of process.nextTick() on the second chunk. This Node.js built-in method allows you to schedule code as a callback to be executed as soon as the current code finishes.

If you've done front-end JavaScript programming, you may be familiar with using setTimeout() with a delay of 0 for this purpose. The difference between setTimeout(callback, 0) and process.nextTick(callback) is that the latter will execute before the next spin of the event loop. By contrast, setTimeout() will wait for the event loop to spin at least once, allowing for other queued callbacks to be executed.

This test will pass irrespective of which of these methods you use to delay the second chunk, as long as the delay is less than Mocha's test timeout. By default, this timeout is 2 seconds (2000 ms), but you can change it for the whole suite or on a test-by-test basis.

To set the Mocha timeout for the whole run, use the --timeout flag to specify the timeout in milliseconds. Set the timeout to 0 to disable it entirely.

If you want to set a specific timeout for a particular test, you can call the timeout() method on the object returned by Mocha's it() method. Here's an example:

```
it('should finish within 5 seconds', done => {
  setTimeout(done, 4500);  // Call done after 4.5 seconds.
}).timeout(5000);
```

You can also call timeout() on the describe() returned object to set a default timeout for a set of tests.

OK, let's review what we've covered before moving on to even bigger things.

Wrapping Up

This chapter explored how to write socket-based networked applications in Node. We developed both ends of a server/client interaction and created a JSON-based protocol for them to communicate.

When our assumptions about the protocol began to fail us, we developed a test case to expose the problem. You wrote a custom Node.js module that extended EventEmitter, a core Node.js class. You also learned one technique for buffering streamed data and incrementally scanning it for messages.

Using npm, you installed Mocha, a popular test framework, and used it to develop a unit test.

Writing simple networked applications in Node.js, like those in this chapter, doesn't take very much code. After only a few lines, you have a functioning server or client application.

However, writing robust applications is harder when you consider the many ways in which a networked application might fail. In the next chapter, we'll use high-performance messaging libraries and infrastructure to take our Node.js applications to the next level.

The following tasks ask you to improve the code from this chapter, making it more testable and more robust.

Testability

In this chapter, we developed a unit test to run with Mocha. Currently it only tests one behavior of the LDJClient class, namely that it emits a message event for a message that came in as a single data event.

The following questions ask you to think about and implement additional tests.

- Add a unit test for a single message that is split over two (or more) data events from the stream.

- Add a unit test that passes in null to the LDJClient constructor and asserts that an error is thrown. Then make the test pass by modifying the constructor.

Robustness

The LDJClient developed in this chapter is somewhat fragile. The questions in this section ask you to expand on its implementation in key ways.

- The LDJClient already handles the case in which a properly formatted JSON string is split over multiple lines. What happens if the incoming data is not a properly formatted JSON string?

- Write a test case that sends a data event that is not JSON. What do you think *should* happen in this case?

- What happens if the last data event completes a JSON message, but without the trailing newline?

- Write a case where the stream object sends a data event containing JSON but no newline, followed by a close event. A real Stream instance will emit a close event when going offline—update LDJClient to listen for close and process the remainder of the buffer.

- Should LDJClient emit a close event for its listeners? Under what circumstances?

CHAPTER 4

Connecting Robust Microservices

Any network is more than the sum of its parts—it's the sum of its parts and all of the interactions between parts.

This chapter focuses on those interactions. Specifically, you'll learn different ways that Node.js microservices communicate.

Connecting these services will expose you to the following aspects of Node.js development:

Node.js Core

Node.js is single-threaded, but you can still take advantage of multiple cores or processors by running more processes. In this chapter, you'll use Node.js's cluster module to create and manage a pool of Node.js workers.

Patterns

Microservice endpoints can have many roles and communicate in many ways. We'll explore powerful messaging patterns like publish/subscribe, request/reply, and push/pull. These patterns appear often in networked application design; you'll be a better programmer knowing when and how to apply them.

JavaScriptisms

Functions in JavaScript are variadic, meaning they can be called with any number of arguments, whether you planned to receive them or not. You'll learn how to use JavaScript's rest parameter syntax to capture arbitrary arguments passed to your functions.

Supporting Code

npm is an integral part of the Node.js ecosystem. You'll learn how to use and manage modules provided through npm. Sometimes modules have external dependencies beyond npm; you'll learn how to build those, too.

To connect our microservices in this chapter, we'll use a cross-platform library called ØMQ (pronounced "Zero-M-Q"). The MQ stands for *message queue*. ØMQ provides high-scalability, low-latency messaging. With its event-loop-based development model, ØMQ and Node.js go together like peanut butter and jelly.

After installing ØMQ, we'll take it for a spin by making improved versions of some of the services we developed in previous chapters. Then we'll quickly move on to new messaging patterns.

Let's get to it!

Installing ØMQ

It's fair to ask why we'd use ØMQ for connecting our microservices, as opposed to using sockets directly like we did last chapter. The answer is that the Node.js community believes in the Unix philosophy: "do one thing well." The committers keep the Node.js core small and tight, leaving everything else to the broader base of developers who publish their modules through npm.

Although the Node.js core has great, low-level support for binding and connecting to sockets, it leaves out higher-level messaging patterns. ØMQ's purpose is to expose higher-level messaging patterns and take care of many low-level networking concerns for you. Take the following examples:

- ØMQ endpoints automatically reconnect if they become unhitched for any reason—like if there's a hiccup in the network or if a process restarts.

- ØMQ delivers only whole messages, so you don't have to create buffers to deal with chunked data.

- ØMQ's low-overhead protocol takes care of many routing details, like sending responses back to the correct clients.

With ØMQ, like with any good library, your application can focus on what really matters.

You may be asking yourself why we'd start with the ØMQ library rather than diving right into the most widely used protocol, HTTP. My main reason is that ØMQ affords the exploration of several different messaging patterns all in one package. You don't have to piece together different solutions for your publish/subscribe and your request/reply patterns. ØMQ can do it all—and the exposure you'll gain here will transfer to HTTP and other protocols.

Another reason is that ØMQ gives you the flexibility to design your architecture your way. Other messaging protocols, such as MQTT and AMQP, require a dedicated message broker to act as a central hub of activity in your system. With ØMQ, you get to decide which parts of your architecture will be more permanent and which will be transitory.

And another thing: HTTP is hard! It's easy to overlook, but negotiating content between a client and a server over HTTP is a complex dance of headers and responses. The Node.js built-in http module has great low-level support, but you have to know what you're doing to make proper use of it. We'll explore HTTP in depth starting in Chapter 6, *Commanding Databases*, on page 111.

Lastly, Node.js is about more than just making web servers. Since 2015, releases of Raspbian, the OS for the Raspberry Pi, have included Node.js. Learning ØMQ's patterns and approach to distributed architecture will help you if you decide to venture into the realm of embedded Node.js systems and the Internet of Things.

With that preamble out of the way, let's get everything set up so we can build fast, robust microservices in Node.js with ØMQ.

Initializing Your package.json File

npm is your gateway to a large and growing pool of open source Node.js modules. They do everything from parsing streams to pooling connections to managing sessions.

To install a module from npm and save the dependency, you'll need a package.json file. Start by creating a directory called microservices and navigate to this directory on the command line.

Then generate an initial package.json file there with npm init:

```
$ npm init -y
Wrote to ./code/microservices/package.json:

{
  "name": "microservices",
  "version": "1.0.0",
  "description": "",
  "main": "index.js",
  "scripts": {
    "test": "echo \"Error: no test specified\" && exit 1"
  },
  "keywords": [],
  "author": "",
  "license": "ISC"
}
```

Take a look at the license attribute at the end. The default license that npm uses is ISC.[1] This is a permissive license written by the Internet Systems Consortium and is similar to the more familiar MIT license.[2]

Open Source Licenses and UNLICENSED

Though ISC is the default license produced by npm init, the MIT license is quite popular in the Node.js community. If you plan to publish your module on npm and you want widespread adoption, MIT is a good choice.

Another popular license, preferred by many companies, is the *Apache 2.0* license.[a] If you use Apache 2, remember to apply the boilerplate notice clause in a comment at the top of each source code file.[b]

If none of these suit your fancy, you can browse the Open Source Initiative's alphabetical list.[c] Or if you prefer, you can set license to the string *UNLICENSED* to indicate specifically that there is no license. But if you do, know that you're signalling to the community that they should not use your module.

---

a. https://www.apache.org/licenses/LICENSE-2.0
b. https://www.apache.org/licenses/LICENSE-2.0#apply
c. https://opensource.org/licenses/alphabetical

We'll discuss what the other package.json fields mean and how to configure them in future chapters. For now let's move on to installing the zeromq module.

Installing the zeromq Node.js Module

You'll rarely write a Node.js application that doesn't use at least one module from npm. We'll use many external modules in this book, and right now we're going to use zeromq, the official Node.js binding for ØMQ.

Modules managed by npm can be pure JavaScript or a combination of Java-Script and native *addon* code.[3]
Addons are dynamically linked shared objects—they provide the glue for working with native libraries written in C or C++.

The zeromq module should take care of building the necessary underlying libraries. Install zeromq like so:

```
$ npm install --save --save-exact zeromq@4.2.1
```

---

1. https://opensource.org/licenses/ISC
2. https://opensource.org/licenses/MIT
3. http://nodejs.org/api/addons.html

The --save flag tells npm to remember this dependency in your package.json under dependencies. These are runtime dependencies, in contrast to the development dependencies we used in *Installing Mocha with npm*, on page 43.

Just like when we installed Mocha, here we're using the --save-exact flag to explicitly depend on a particular version of the module. In your own projects you can choose to be less strict about which versions of modules you require, but in this book we're going to use exact versions.

There's nothing particularly special about version 4.2.1 of the zeromq module—it's simply the most recent version available at the time of this writing. For your own development purposes you could leave off the version number when you run the npm install command, in which case npm will figure out the most recent version for you.

Let's take a look at some of the output of npm install. This output has been truncated quite a bit for formatting reasons and to focus attention on the relevant parts.

```
$ npm install --save --save-exact zeromq@4.2.1

> zeromq@4.2.1 install ./code/microservices/node_modules/zeromq
> prebuild-install || (npm run build:libzmq && node-gyp rebuild)

prebuild-install info begin Prebuild-install version 2.1.2
prebuild-install info looking for local prebuild @ prebuilds/zeromq-v4.2.1-z...
prebuild-install info looking for cached prebuild @ ~/.npm/_prebuilds/https-...
prebuild-install http request GET https://github.com/zeromq/zeromq.js/releas...
prebuild-install http 200 https://github.com/zeromq/zeromq.js/releases/downl...
prebuild-install info downloading to @ ~/.npm/_prebuilds/https-github.com-ze...
prebuild-install info renaming to @ ~/.npm/_prebuilds/https-github.com-zerom...
prebuild-install info unpacking @ ~/.npm/_prebuilds/https-github.com-zeromq-...
prebuild-install info unpack resolved to ./code/microservices/node_modules/z...
prebuild-install info unpack required ./code/microservices/node_modules/zero...
prebuild-install info install Prebuild successfully installed!
microservices@1.0.0 ./code/microservices
└─┬ zeromq@4.2.1
  ├── nan@2.6.2
  └─┬ prebuild-install@2.1.2
    ├── ...

npm WARN microservices@1.0.0 No description
npm WARN microservices@1.0.0 No repository field
```

Notice the call to prebuild-install toward the top. This is a command-line utility for downloading and installing prebuilt binaries for Node.js. In my case, it's downloading the linux-x64 prebuilt binary, but the ØMQ team publishes binaries for Mac OS X and Windows as well.

If the prebuild-install fails, the fallback mechanism is to attempt to build the libzmq C library and then use node-gyp to rebuild the Node.js bindings for it. node-gyp is a cross-platform tool for compiling native addons. If anything went wrong with that build, the output should tell you, but remember that this is only a backup to the preferred prebuilt version.

When you run the preceding command, npm will download the zeromq module (and its dependencies) to a folder called node_modules under the current directory. To test that the module was installed successfully, run this command:

```
$ node -p -e "require('zeromq').version"
4.1.6
```

The -e flag tells Node.js to evaluate the provided string, and the -p flag tells it to print that output to the terminal. The zeromq module's .version property is a string containing the version of the ØMQ base library it found—i.e., the prebuilt binary.

You may notice that the version number logged here is different from the version number of the zeromq module you installed (4.1.6 vs. 4.2.1). This is OK! The reason is that the .version property of the module object (4.1.6) reflects the version of the underlying libzmq binary that powers the Node.js module, not the version of the zeromq npm module (4.2.1). If you get a version number, then you're all set. If you see an exception being thrown, then you might want to stop here and troubleshoot.

Now that the library and the Node.js module are installed, it's time to start programming Node.js with ØMQ!

Publishing and Subscribing to Messages

ØMQ supports a number of different message-passing patterns that work great in Node. We'll start with the publish/subscribe pattern (PUB/SUB).

Recall the code we wrote in Chapter 3, *Networking with Sockets*, on page 27, when we developed a networked file-watching service and a client to connect to it. They communicated over TCP by sending LDJ messages. The server would *publish* information in this format, and any number of client programs could *subscribe* to it.

We had to work hard to make our client code safely handle the message-boundary problem. And we created a separate module dedicated to buffering chunked data and emitting messages. Even so, we were left with questions like how to handle network interrupts and server restarts.

ØMQ makes all of this much simpler by taking care of low-level details like buffering and reconnecting. Let's see how much easier it is by implementing

Troubleshooting ØMQ Installation

In the previous edition of this book, getting the Node.js bindings for ØMQ to work was a significant pain point for some readers, especially those running Windows. This was in part because the code samples relied on the zmq module,[a] which required users to install the underlying libzmq C library and then compile the bindings using node-gyp.

By contrast, this edition uses the now-officially supported zeromq module, maintained by the ØMQ team. Since zeromq uses prebuilt binaries, I've found installation to be much smoother, and I hope you will too.

Please note, however, that this is the only chapter in the book that uses ØMQ. So if you have too much trouble getting it to work, I recommend you read through the chapter anyway to learn the concepts, and then resume following the examples in the next chapter.

If you'd like to try installing ØMQ and the Node.js bindings from source, the zeromq module page on the npm website has instructions for each platform.[b] Good luck!

---

a. https://www.npmjs.com/package/zmq
b. https://www.npmjs.com/package/zeromq#installation---from-source

a watcher that uses ØMQ PUB/SUB instead of naked TCP. This will get us used to the ØMQ way of doing things, and set us up to explore other messaging patterns with Node.js and ØMQ.

Publishing Messages over TCP

First, let's implement the PUB half of a PUB/SUB pair using the zeromq module. Open an editor and enter the following:

microservices/zmq-watcher-pub.js

```
'use strict';
const fs = require('fs');
const zmq = require('zeromq');
const filename = process.argv[2];

// Create the publisher endpoint.
const publisher = zmq.socket('pub');

fs.watch(filename, () => {

  // Send a message to any and all subscribers.
  publisher.send(JSON.stringify({
    type: 'changed',
    file: filename,
    timestamp: Date.now()
  }));

});
```

```
// Listen on TCP port 60400.
publisher.bind('tcp://*:60400', err => {
  if (err) {
    throw err;
  }
  console.log('Listening for zmq subscribers...');
});
```

Save the file as zmq-watcher-pub.js. This program is similar to ones we developed in previous chapters, with a few differences.

Instead of requiring the net module, now we're requiring zeromq and saving it as a variable called zmq for brevity. We use it to create a publisher endpoint by calling zmq.socket('pub').

Importantly, we have only one call to fs.watch(). Our servers from the last chapter would invoke watch() once for each connected client. Here we have just one filesystem watcher, which invokes the publisher's send() method.

Notice that the string we send to publisher.send() is the output of JSON.stringify(). ØMQ does not perform serialization of messages itself—it is interested only in pushing bytes down the wire. It's our job to serialize and deserialize any messages we send through ØMQ.

Finally, we call publisher.bind('tcp://*:60400') to tell ØMQ to listen on TCP port 60400 for subscribers. Let's get the publisher running:

```
$ node zmq-watcher-pub.js target.txt
Listening for zmq subscribers...
```

Even though this service uses TCP, we can't simply use nc like we did in the last chapter to get anything out of it. A ØMQ server requires a ØMQ client.

Now we'll implement the subscriber endpoint.

Subscribing to a Publisher

Implementing the SUB portion of the ØMQ PUB/SUB pair requires even less code than the publisher. Open an editor and enter this:

microservices/zmq-watcher-sub.js
```
'use strict';
const zmq = require('zeromq');

// Create subscriber endpoint.
const subscriber = zmq.socket('sub');

// Subscribe to all messages.
subscriber.subscribe('');

// Handle messages from the publisher.
```

```
subscriber.on('message', data => {
  const message = JSON.parse(data);
  const date = new Date(message.timestamp);
  console.log(`File "${message.file}" changed at ${date}`);
});

// Connect to publisher.
subscriber.connect("tcp://localhost:60400");
```

Save this file as zmq-watcher-sub.js. It uses zmq.socket('sub') to make a subscriber endpoint.

Calling subscriber.subscribe('') tells ØMQ that we want to receive all messages. If you only want certain messages, you can provide a string that acts as a prefix filter. You must call subscribe() at some point in your code—you won't receive any messages until you do.

The subscriber object inherits from EventEmitter. It emits a message event whenever it receives one from a publisher, so we use subscriber.on() to listen for them.

Lastly, we use subscriber.connect() to establish the connection.

Let's see how these pieces fit together. With the PUB program still running in one terminal, fire up zmq-watcher-sub in a second one:

```
$ node zmq-watcher-sub.js
```

Then, in a third terminal, touch the target file:

```
$ touch target.txt
```

In the subscriber terminal, you should see output something like this:

```
File "target.txt" changed at Tue Mar 01 2016 05:25:39 GMT-0500 (EST)
```

So far, things look pretty great. The publisher and subscriber programs are able to successfully communicate over the PUB/SUB socket pair.

But it gets even better. Keep those services running; next we'll cover how ØMQ handles network interruptions.

Automatically Reconnecting Endpoints

Let's see what happens when one of the endpoints gets disconnected unexpectedly. Try killing the publisher in its terminal via Ctrl-C.

Afterward, switch over to the subscriber terminal. You may notice that something strange happened—nothing. The subscriber keeps waiting for messages even though the publisher is down, as though nothing happened.

Start up the publisher again in the first terminal, then touch the target file. The subscriber should log a *File changed* message to the console. It's as though they were connected the whole time.

From ØMQ's perspective, it doesn't matter which endpoint starts up first. It automatically establishes and reestablishes the connection when either endpoint comes online. These characteristics add up to a robust platform that gives you stability without a lot of work on your part.

In our previous examples, both the PUB and SUB endpoints were made from zmq.socket(). This means they both have the power to either bind() or connect(). Our code had the publisher bind a TCP socket (as the server) and the subscriber connect (as the client), but ØMQ doesn't force you to do it this way. We could have flipped it around and had the subscriber bind a socket to which the publisher connects.

When you design a networked application, you'll typically have the more permanent parts of your architecture bind and have the transient parts connect to them. With ØMQ, you get to decide which parts of your system will come and go, and which messaging pattern best suits your needs. But you don't have to decide them at the same time, and it's easy to change your mind later. ØMQ provides flexible, durable pipes for constructing distributed applications.

Next we'll look at a different messaging pattern: request/reply (REQ/REP). Then we'll tie this in with Node.js's clustering support to manage a pool of worker processes.

Responding to Requests

The REQ/REP pattern is quite common in networked programming, particularly in Node. We'll use this pattern often in the next couple of chapters, and ØMQ has great support for it. As you'll see in a minute, this is where the "Q" of ØMQ becomes apparent.

In ØMQ, a REQ/REP pair communicates in lockstep. A request comes in, then a reply goes out. Additional incoming requests are *queued* and later dispatched by ØMQ. Your application, however, is aware of only one request at a time.

Let's see how this works, again using the filesystem as a source of information for building a microservice. In this scenario, a responder waits for a request for file data, then serves up the content when asked. We'll start with the responder—the REP (reply) part of the REQ/REP pair.

Implementing a Responder

Open an editor and enter the following:

microservices/zmq-filer-rep.js

```javascript
'use strict';
const fs = require('fs');
const zmq = require('zeromq');

// Socket to reply to client requests.
const responder = zmq.socket('rep');

// Handle incoming requests.
responder.on('message', data => {

  // Parse the incoming message.
  const request = JSON.parse(data);
  console.log(`Received request to get: ${request.path}`);

  // Read the file and reply with content.
  fs.readFile(request.path, (err, content) => {
    console.log('Sending response content.');
    responder.send(JSON.stringify({
      content: content.toString(),
      timestamp: Date.now(),
      pid: process.pid
    }));
  });

});

// Listen on TCP port 60401.
responder.bind('tcp://127.0.0.1:60401', err => {
  console.log('Listening for zmq requesters...');
});

// Close the responder when the Node process ends.
process.on('SIGINT', () => {
  console.log('Shutting down...');
  responder.close();
});
```

Save the file as zmq-filer-rep.js. The program creates a ØMQ REP socket and uses it to respond to incoming requests.

When a message event happens, we parse out the request from the raw data. Next we call fs.readFile() to asynchronously retrieve the requested file's content. When it arrives, we use the responder's send() method to reply with a JSON serialized response, including the file content and a timestamp. We also include the process ID (pid) of the Node.js process in the response.

The responder binds to TCP port 60401 of the loopback interface (IP 127.0.0.1) to wait for connections. This makes the responder the stable endpoint of the REP/REQ pair.

Since this service reads content from your filesystem and serves it to any requester, be sure to set the IP to 127.0.0.1 (localhost)! This is for demonstration purposes only.

Finally, we listen for SIGINT events on the Node.js process. This Unix signal indicates that the process has received an interrupt signal from the user—typically invoked by pressing Ctrl-C in the terminal. The clean thing to do in this case is ask the responder to gracefully close any outstanding connections.

Start the program in a terminal as usual:

```
$ node zmq-filer-rep.js
Listening for zmq requesters...
```

Looks like our responder is ready! But to connect to it, we'll need to develop a client, so let's put one together.

Issuing Requests

Creating a requester to work with our responder is pretty short. Open an editor and enter this:

microservices/zmq-filer-req.js
```
'use strict';
const zmq = require('zeromq');
const filename = process.argv[2];

// Create request endpoint.
const requester = zmq.socket('req');

// Handle replies from the responder.
requester.on('message', data => {
  const response = JSON.parse(data);
  console.log('Received response:', response);
});

requester.connect('tcp://localhost:60401');

// Send a request for content.
console.log(`Sending a request for ${filename}`);
requester.send(JSON.stringify({ path: filename }));
```

Save the file as zmq-filer-req.js.

This program starts off by creating a ØMQ REQ socket. Then we listen for incoming message events and interpret the data as a JSON serialized response (which we log to the console). The end of the program kicks off the request by connecting to the REP socket over TCP and finally calling requester.send(). The JSON request message contains the requested file's path as specified on the command line.

Let's see how these REQ and REP sockets work together. With the zmq-filer-rep program still running in one terminal, run this command in another:

```
$ node zmq-filer-req.js target.txt
Sending a request for target.txt
Received response: { content: '', timestamp: 1458898367933, pid: 24815 }
```

Success! The REP endpoint received the request, processed it, and sent back a response.

Trading Synchronicity for Scale

There is a catch to using ØMQ REP/REQ socket pairs with Node. Each end-point of the application operates on only one request or one response at a time. There is no parallelism.

We can see this in action by making a small change to the requester program. Open the zmq-filer-req.js file from last section. Find the code that sends the request and wrap it in a for loop like this:

```
for (let i = 1; i <= 5; i++) {
  console.log(`Sending request ${i} for ${filename}`);
  requester.send(JSON.stringify({ path: filename }));
}
```

Save this file as zmq-filer-req-loop.js. With the responder still running, invoke the new script:

```
$ node zmq-filer-req-loop.js target.txt
Sending request 1 for target.txt
Sending request 2 for target.txt
Received response: { content: '', timestamp: 1458902785998, pid: 24674 }
Sending request 3 for target.txt
Sending request 4 for target.txt
Sending request 5 for target.txt
Received response: { content: '', timestamp: 1458902786010, pid: 24674 }
Received response: { content: '', timestamp: 1458902786011, pid: 24674 }
Received response: { content: '', timestamp: 1458902786011, pid: 24674 }
Received response: { content: '', timestamp: 1458902786012, pid: 24674 }
```

We see that the requests were queued in the loop, and then we received the responses. The sending and receiving lines may be interleaved, depending on how quickly the responses become available.

This output shouldn't be too surprising, but let's take a look at the responder window:

```
$ node zmq-filer-rep.js
Listening for zmq requesters...
Received request to get: target.txt
Sending response content.
Received request to get: target.txt
Sending response content.
Received request to get: target.txt
Sending response content.
Received request to get: target.txt
Sending response content.
Received request to get: target.txt
Sending response content.
```

Notice that the responder program sent a response to each request before even becoming aware of the next queued request. This means Node.js's event loop was left spinning while the fs.readFile() for each request was being processed.

For this reason, a simple REQ/REP pair is probably not going to suit your high-performance Node.js needs. Next we'll construct a cluster of Node.js processes using more advanced ØMQ socket types to scale up our throughput.

Routing and Dealing Messages

The REQ/REP socket pair we explored makes request/reply logic easy to code by operating sequentially. The Node.js code for a given responder will only ever be aware of one message at a time.

For parallel message processing, ØMQ includes the more advanced socket types ROUTER and DEALER. Let's explore these a bit; then we'll be ready to construct our Node.js cluster.

Routing Messages

You can think of a ROUTER socket as a parallel REP socket. Rather than replying to only one message at a time, a ROUTER socket can handle many requests simultaneously. It remembers which connection each request came from and will route reply messages accordingly.

Recall from *Implementing a Messaging Protocol*, on page 32, that any time you do networked programming, you're working with one or more protocols. ØMQ uses the ZeroMQ Message Transport Protocol (ZMTP) for exchanging messages.[4] This protocol uses a sequence of low-overhead *frames* to compose messages. A ROUTER socket uses these frames to route each reply message back to the connection that issued the request.

Most of the time your Node.js programs can ignore the underlying details of ØMQ frames because the simpler socket types only need one frame per message. But the ROUTER socket type uses multiple frames.

Here's an example of how to create a ROUTER socket in Node.js, with a message handler that grabs all the incoming frames:

```
const router = zmq.socket('router');
router.on('message', (...frames) => {
  // Use frames.
});
```

Previously our message handlers would take a data parameter, but this handler takes an array of frames instead.

The three dots (...) introduce an ECMAScript 2015 feature called *rest parameters*. When used in a function declaration, this syntax allows you to collect any number of arguments passed into the function as an array.

Now that we can get all the frames, let's look at the DEALER socket type.

Dealing Messages

If a ROUTER socket is a parallel REP socket, then a DEALER is a parallel REQ. A DEALER socket can send multiple requests in parallel.

Let's see how a dealer and router work together in Node. Take a look at this code sample:

```
const router = zmq.socket('router');
const dealer = zmq.socket('dealer');

router.on('message', (...frames) => dealer.send(frames));
dealer.on('message', (...frames) => router.send(frames));
```

Here we create both a ROUTER socket and a DEALER socket. Whenever either receives a message, it sends the frames to the other socket.

This creates a passthrough relationship where incoming requests to the router will be passed off to the dealer to send out to its connections. Likewise, incoming replies to the dealer will be forwarded back to the router, which directs each reply back to the connection that requested it.

---

4. http://rfc.zeromq.org/spec:37

The following figure shows the structure we'll implement shortly, using the techniques we've just discussed.

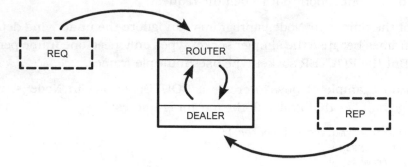

The box in the center of the figure is the Node.js program. An incoming REQ socket connects to the ROUTER. When the REQ socket issues a request, the ROUTER bounces it over to the DEALER. The DEALER then picks the next one of the REP sockets connected to it (round-robin style) and forwards the request.

When the REP connection produces a reply, it follows the reverse route. The DEALER receives the reply and bounces it back to the ROUTER. The ROUTER looks at the message's frames to determine its origin and sends the reply back to the connected REQ that sent the initial request.

From the perspective of the REQ and REP sockets, nothing has changed. Each still works on one message at a time. Meanwhile, the ROUTER/DEALER pair can distribute (round-robin) among the REQ and REP sockets connected on both ends.

Now we're ready to develop a clustered Node.js application on top of the REQ, REP, ROUTER, and DEALER sockets we've just explored.

Clustering Node.js Processes

In multithreaded systems, doing more work in parallel means spinning up more threads. But Node.js uses a single-threaded event loop, so to take advantage of multiple cores or multiple processors on the same computer, you have to spin up more Node.js processes.

This is called *clustering* and it's what Node.js's built-in cluster module does. Clustering is a useful technique for scaling up your Node.js application when there's unused CPU capacity available.

To explore how the cluster module works, we'll build up a program that manages a pool of worker processes to respond to ØMQ requests. This will be a drop-in replacement for our previous responder program. It will use ROUTER, DEALER, and REP sockets to distribute requests to workers.

In all, we'll end up with a short and powerful program that combines cluster-based, multiprocess work distribution and load-balanced message-passing.

Forking Worker Processes in a Cluster

Back in *Spawning a Child Process*, on page 16, we used the child_process module's spawn() function to fire up a process. This works great for executing non-Node.js processes from your Node.js program. But for spinning up copies of the same Node.js program, forking is a better option because fork() is a special case of spawn() that sets up an interprocess communication channel, as you'll see shortly.

Each time you call the cluster module's fork() method,[5] it creates a worker process running the same script as the original. To see what I mean, take a look at the following code snippet. It shows the basic framework for a clustered Node.js application.

```
const cluster = require('cluster');

if (cluster.isMaster) {
  // Fork some worker processes.
  for (let i = 0; i < 10; i++) {
    cluster.fork();
  }
} else {
  // This is a worker process; do some work.
}
```

First, we check whether the current process is the *master* process. If so, we use cluster.fork() to create additional processes. The fork method launches a new Node.js process running the same script, but for which cluster.isMaster is false.

The forked processes are called *workers*. They can intercommunicate with the master process through various events.

For example, the master can listen for workers coming online with code like this:

```
cluster.on('online', worker =>
    console.log(`Worker ${worker.process.pid} is online.`));
```

When the cluster module emits an online event, a worker parameter is passed along. One of the properties on this object is process—the same sort of process that you'd find in any Node.js program.

---

5. https://nodejs.org/api/cluster.html

Similarly, the master can listen for processes exiting:

```
cluster.on('exit', (worker, code, signal) =>
    console.log(`Worker ${worker.process.pid} exited with code ${code}`));
```

Like online, the exit event includes a worker object. It also includes the exit code of the process and what operating-system signal (like SIGINT or SIGTERM) was used to halt the process.

Building a Cluster

Now it's time to put everything together, harnessing Node.js clustering and the ØMQ messaging patterns we've been talking about. We'll build a program that distributes requests to a pool of worker processes.

Our master Node.js process will create ROUTER and DEALER sockets and spin up the workers. Each worker will create a REP socket that connects back to the DEALER.

The following figure illustrates how all these pieces fit together. As in previous figures, the rectangles represent Node.js processes. The ovals are the resources bound by ØMQ sockets, and the arrows show which sockets connect to which endpoints.

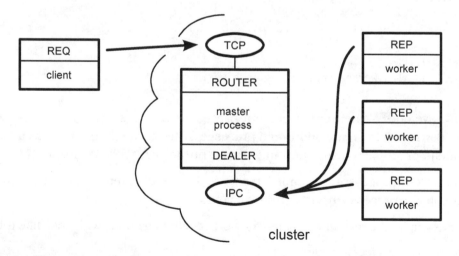

The master process is the most stable part of the architecture (it manages the workers), so it's responsible for doing the binding. The worker processes and clients of the service all connect to endpoints bound by the master. Remember that the flow of messages is decided by the socket *types*, not which socket happens to bind or connect.

Now let's get to the code. Open your favorite editor and enter the following:

```
microservices/zmq-filer-rep-cluster.js
'use strict';
const cluster = require('cluster');
const fs = require('fs');
const zmq = require('zeromq');

const numWorkers = require('os').cpus().length;

if (cluster.isMaster) {

  // Master process creates ROUTER and DEALER sockets and binds endpoints.
  const router = zmq.socket('router').bind('tcp://127.0.0.1:60401');
  const dealer = zmq.socket('dealer').bind('ipc://filer-dealer.ipc');

  // Forward messages between the router and dealer.
  router.on('message', (...frames) => dealer.send(frames));
  dealer.on('message', (...frames) => router.send(frames));

  // Listen for workers to come online.
  cluster.on('online',
      worker => console.log(`Worker ${worker.process.pid} is online.`));

  // Fork a worker process for each CPU.
  for (let i = 0; i < numWorkers; i++) {
    cluster.fork();
  }

} else {

  // Worker processes create a REP socket and connect to the DEALER.
  const responder = zmq.socket('rep').connect('ipc://filer-dealer.ipc');

  responder.on('message', data => {

    // Parse incoming message.
    const request = JSON.parse(data);
    console.log(`${process.pid} received request for: ${request.path}`);

    // Read the file and reply with content.
    fs.readFile(request.path, (err, content) => {
      console.log(`${process.pid} sending response`);
      responder.send(JSON.stringify({
        content: content.toString(),
        timestamp: Date.now(),
        pid: process.pid
      }));
    });

  });

}
```

Save this file as zmq-filer-rep-cluster.js. This program is a little longer than our previous Node.js programs, but it should look familiar to you since it's based entirely on snippets we've already discussed.

At the top, we use Node.js's built-in os module to look up the number of available CPUs.[6] Spinning up one worker per CPU is a good rule of thumb. Too few means you won't get maximum CPU utilization, and too many means more overhead for the OS to switch between them.

Next, notice that the ROUTER listens for incoming TCP connections on port 60401 on line 11. This allows the cluster to act as a drop-in replacement for the zmq-filer-rep.js program we developed earlier.

On line 12, the DEALER socket binds an interprocess connection (IPC) endpoint. This is backed by a Unix socket like the one we used in *Listening on Unix Sockets*, on page 32.

By convention, ØMQ IPC files should end in the file extension .ipc. In this case, the filer-dealer.ipc file will be created in the current working directory that the cluster was launched from (if it doesn't exist already). Let's run the cluster program to see how it works.

```
$ node zmq-filer-rep-cluster.js
Worker 10334 is online.
Worker 10329 is online.
Worker 10335 is online.
Worker 10340 is online.
```

So far so good—the master process has spun up the workers, and they've all reported in. In a second terminal, fire up our REQ loop program (zmq-filer-req-loop.js):

```
$ node zmq-filer-req-loop.js target.txt
Sending request 1 for target.txt
Sending request 2 for target.txt
Sending request 3 for target.txt
Sending request 4 for target.txt
Sending request 5 for target.txt
Received response: { content: '', timestamp: 1459330686647, pid: 10334 }
Received response: { content: '', timestamp: 1459330686672, pid: 10329 }
Received response: { content: '', timestamp: 1459330686682, pid: 10335 }
Received response: { content: '', timestamp: 1459330686684, pid: 10334 }
Received response: { content: '', timestamp: 1459330686685, pid: 10329 }
```

Just like our earlier reply program, this clustered approach answers each request in turn.

---

6. https://nodejs.org/api/os.html

But notice that the reported process ID (pid) is different for each response received. This shows that the master process is indeed load-balancing the requests to different workers.

Next, we'll examine one more messaging pattern offered by ØMQ before wrapping up the chapter.

Pushing and Pulling Messages

So far we've worked with two major message-passing patterns: publish/subscribe and request/reply. ØMQ offers one more pattern that's sometimes a good fit with Node.js—push/pull (PUSH/PULL).

Pushing Jobs to Workers

The PUSH and PULL socket types are useful when you have a queue of jobs that you want to assign among a pool of available workers.

Recall that with a PUB/SUB pair, each subscriber will receive all messages sent by the publisher. In a PUSH/PULL setup, only one puller will receive each message sent by the pusher.

A PUSH socket will distribute messages in a round-robin fashion to connected sockets, just like a DEALER. But unlike the DEALER/ROUTER flow, there is no backchannel. A message traveling from a PUSH socket to a PULL socket is one-way; the puller can't send a response back through the same socket.

Here's a quick example showing how to set up a PUSH socket and distribute 100 jobs. Note that the example is incomplete—it doesn't call bind() or connect() —but it does demonstrate the concept:

```
const pusher = zmq.socket('push');

for (let i = 0; i < 100; i++) {
  pusher.send(JSON.stringify({
    details: `Details about job ${i}.`
  });
}
```

And here's an associated PULL socket:

```
const puller = zmq.socket('pull');

puller.on('message', data => {
  const job = JSON.parse(data.toString());
  // Do the work described in the job.
});
```

Like other ØMQ sockets, either end of a PUSH/PULL pair can bind or connect. The choice comes down to which is the stable part of the architecture.

Using the PUSH/PULL pattern in Node.js brings up a couple of potential pitfalls hidden in these simple examples. Let's explore them, and what to do to avoid them.

The First-Joiner Problem

The *first-joiner problem* is the result of ØMQ being so fast at sending messages and Node.js being so fast at accepting them. Since it takes time to establish a connection, the first puller to successfully connect can often pull many or all of the available messages before the second joiner has a chance to get into the rotation.

To fix this problem, the pusher needs to wait until all of the pullers are ready to receive messages before pushing any. Let's consider a real-world scenario and how we'd solve it.

Say you have a Node.js cluster, and the master process plans to PUSH a bunch of jobs to a pool of worker processes. Before the master can start pushing, the workers need a way to signal back to the master that they're ready to start pulling jobs. They also need a way to communicate the results of the jobs that they'll eventually complete.

The following figure shows this scenario.

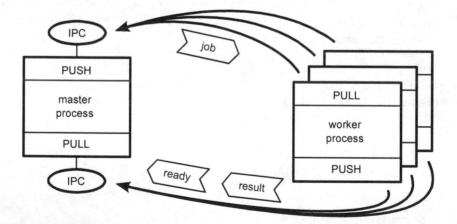

As in previous diagrams, rectangles are Node.js processes, ovals are resources, and heavy arrows point in the direction the connection is established. The job, ready, and result messages are shown as arrow boxes pointing in the direction they are sent.

In the top half of the figure, we have the main communication channel—the master's PUSH socket hooked up to the workers' PULL sockets. This is how jobs will be sent to workers.

In the bottom half of the figure, we have a backchannel. This time the master has a PULL socket connected to each worker's PUSH sockets. The workers can PUSH messages, such as their readiness to work or job results, back to the master.

The master process is the stable part of the architecture, so it binds while the workers connect. Since all of the processes are local to the same machine, it makes sense to use IPC for the transport.

The bonus challenge in *Bidirectional Messaging*, on page 77, will ask you to implement this PUSH/PULL cluster in Node.

The Limited-Resource Problem

The other common pitfall is the *limited-resource problem*. Node.js is at the mercy of the operating system with respect to the number of resources it can access at the same time. In Unix-speak, these resources are called *file descriptors*.

Whenever your Node.js program opens a file or a TCP connection, it uses one of its available file descriptors. When there are none left, Node.js will start failing to connect to resources when asked. This is a common problem for Node.js developers.

Strictly speaking, this problem isn't exclusive to the PUSH/PULL scenario, but it's very likely to happen there, and here's why: since Node.js is asynchronous, the puller process can start working on many jobs simultaneously. Every time a message event comes in, the Node.js process invokes the handler and starts working on the job. If these jobs require accessing system resources, then you're liable to exhaust the pool of available file descriptors. Then jobs will quickly start failing.

If your application starts to throw EMFILE or ECONNRESET errors under load, it means you've exhausted the pool of file descriptors.

A full discussion of how to manage the number of file descriptors available to your processes is outside the scope of this book, since it's mainly influenced by the operating system. But you can generally work around these limitations in a couple of ways.

One way is to keep a counter that tracks how many tasks your Node.js process is actively engaged in. The counter starts at zero, and when you get a new task you increment the counter. When a task finishes, you decrement the counter. Then, when a task pushes the counter over some threshold, pause listening for new tasks (stop pulling), then resume when one finishes.

Another way is to offload the handling of this problem to an off-the-shelf module. The graceful-fs module is a drop-in replacement for Node.js's built-in fs module.[7] Rather than choking when there are no descriptors left, graceful-fs will queue outstanding file operations until there are descriptors available.

Now it's time to wrap up this chapter so we can move on to working with data from the wild.

Wrapping Up

We covered a lot of ground in this chapter, so let's review.

Using ØMQ with Node.js gave us an opportunity to install and use a module from npm that included native addon code. This provided a basis for learning about three fundamental microservice messaging patterns: publish/subscribe, push/pull, and request/reply.

To overcome the lockstep nature of ØMQ's request/reply implementation, we learned how to parallelize requests using a dealer/router pair. This gave us a chance to use JavaScript's rest parameter syntax to capture variadic function arguments.

You also learned how to fork Node.js processes to create a cluster of cooperating processes. This introduced new challenges like the first-joiner problem and the limited-resource problem.

The following bonus tasks ask you to modify and create new Node.js and ØMQ programs using what you learned from the chapter.

Error Handling

The zmq-filer-rep.js program we created uses fs.readFile() to serve up file contents. However, it doesn't handle error cases at all.

- What should the program do in the case of an error?
- How would you change the JSON object structure of messages to support sending an error to the requester?

Later in this same program, we listen for the Unix signal SIGINT to detect the user's `Ctrl-C` in the terminal.

---

7. https://www.npmjs.com/package/graceful-fs

- What happens if the program ends in some other way, like SIGTERM (the termination signal)?

- What happens if there's an unhandled Node.js exception, and how should we deal with it? *Hint*: you can listen for the uncaughtException event on the process object.

Robustness

In *Building a Cluster*, on page 70, we created a Node.js cluster that spins up a pool of worker processes. In the master process, we listened for online events and logged a message when the workers came up. But we didn't specify what should happen when a worker process ends.

- What happens when you kill a worker process from the command line? *Hint*: use kill [pid] from the command line, where [pid] is the worker's process ID.

- How would you change the zmq-filer-rep-cluster.js program to fork a new worker whenever one dies?

Bidirectional Messaging

For this project, you'll need to use ØMQ PUSH/PULL sockets and the Node.js clustering techniques you learned in this chapter.

Your clustered program will spin up a pool of workers and distribute 30 jobs between them. Although this seems like a lot to do, the whole program should be fewer than 100 lines of code.

Create a Node.js program that uses the cluster and zmq modules and does the following:

The master process should

- Create a PUSH socket and bind it to an IPC endpoint—this socket will be for sending jobs to the workers.

- Create a PULL socket and bind to a different IPC endpoint—this socket will receive messages from workers.

- Keep a count of ready workers.

- Listen for messages on the PULL socket, and
    - if the message is a ready message, increment the ready counter, or
    - if the message is a result message, output it to the console.

- Spin up the worker processes.

- When the ready counter reaches 3, send 30 job messages out through the PUSH socket.

Each worker process should

- Create a PULL socket and connect it to the master's PUSH endpoint.

- Create a PUSH socket and connect it to the master's PULL endpoint.

- Listen for job messages on the PULL socket, and respond by sending a result message out on the PUSH socket.

- Send a ready message out on the PUSH socket.

Make sure your result messages include at least the process ID of the worker. This way you can inspect the console output and confirm that the workload is being balanced among the worker processes.

If you get completely stuck, consult the working example available in the downloadable code that accompanies this book. You can do it. Good luck!

Part II

Working with Data

No matter what you end up using Node.js for, you'll be working with data. It's what programs do!

Now that you're comfortable with Node.js's features and patterns, it's time to apply those skills to parse, process, organize, and transport data. You'll learn how to test and debug your Node.js programs and develop cogent command-line programs, too.

CHAPTER 5

Transforming Data
and Testing Continuously

Broadly speaking, there are two kinds of data: the kind that your own apps produce and the kind that comes from somewhere else. It would be nice if you only ever had to deal with data that you created. But the reality is that you'll almost certainly have to work with outside data sources during your career, perhaps frequently!

Between this chapter and the next, you'll use Node.js to take real data from the wild and put it into your own local datastore. This work can be neatly approached in two phases: transforming the raw data into an intermediate format, and importing that intermediate data into the datastore.

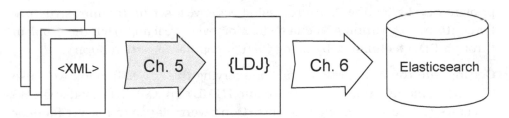

In this chapter, you'll learn how to use Node.js to transform XML data into the lingua franca of modern data formats, JSON and its close cousin line-delimited JSON (LDJ). Then, in the following chapter, you'll create a command-line tool to bring this LDJ content into Elasticsearch, a NoSQL database that indexes JSON objects.

While writing, testing, and debugging tools to transform raw XML data into LDJ, we'll investigate the following aspects of Node.js:

Node.js Core

Using Chrome DevTools, it's possible to inspect a running Node.js application. You'll learn how to set breakpoints, step through your running Node.js code, and interrogate scoped variables.

Patterns

Much of this chapter involves extracting data from XML files and transforming it into JSON for insertion into a document database. We'll use Cheerio for this, a DOM-based XML parser with a jQuery-like API. To use it effectively, you'll learn the basics of CSS selectors.

JavaScriptisms

In the Node.js ecosystem, it's fairly common to have modules that export a single stateless function rather than a collection of objects, classes, or methods. In this chapter, you'll develop such a module iteratively using behavior-driven development (BDD) techniques.

Supporting Code

We're going to double down on npm in this chapter, adding scripts to launch Mocha tests in standalone mode, continuous testing mode, and debug mode. You'll also learn to use Chai, an assertion library that pairs well with Mocha to write expressive, behavioral tests.

To kick off the chapter, we have to procure the data that we're going to be working with. Then we'll pick through it to get an understanding of the data format, as well as our desired output.

For processing data, it's quite useful to develop unit tests. For this reason, prior to developing the data-processing code we'll set up the infrastructure for continuously running Mocha tests. Moreover, we'll approach the problem through BDD techniques by using Chai, a popular assertion library.

Getting into the nitty-gritty details of querying the raw XML data, we'll use Cheerio, a module that lets you dive into HTML and XML data by using CSS selectors to find interesting elements. Don't worry if you're not yet familiar with writing CSS selectors—it's a useful skill, and we'll build up gradually.

In the final part of this chapter, you'll use the parsing code to roll through the raw data and produce new data that's ready for insertion into a database. You'll learn to walk down a directory tree sequentially, and how to step through your code using Chrome DevTools.

It's a lot to cover, but you can do it. Let's get started!

Procuring External Data

Before we can start manipulating data with Node.js, we have to get it. The data we'll be using comes from Project Gutenberg, which is dedicated to making public-domain works available as free ebooks.[1]

Project Gutenberg produces catalog download bundles that contain Resource Description Framework (RDF) files for each of its 53,000-plus books. (RDF is an XML-based format.) The bz2 compressed version of the catalog file is about 40 MB. Fully extracted, it contains a little over 1 GB of RDF files.

To begin, create two sibling directories on your machine, called databases and data.

```
$ mkdir databases
$ mkdir data
```

The databases project directory will hold all of the programs and configuration files you'll be developing in this chapter. Unless otherwise specified, commands you run will be from a terminal out of this directory.

The data directory will hold the raw data files that we'll be working with. If you want to put this directory somewhere else for storage reasons, that's fine, but the examples in this chapter will assume that it's a sibling of your databases project directory, so modify any paths accordingly.

With that out of the way, open a terminal to your data directory and run the following commands:

```
$ cd data
$ curl -O http://www.gutenberg.org/cache/epub/feeds/rdf-files.tar.bz2
$ tar -xvjf rdf-files.tar.bz2
x cache/epub/0/pg0.rdf
x cache/epub/1/pg1.rdf
x cache/epub/10/pg10.rdf
...
x cache/epub/9998/pg9998.rdf
x cache/epub/9999/pg9999.rdf
x cache/epub/999999/pg999999.rdf
```

This will create a cache directory that contains all the RDF files. Each RDF file is named after its Project Gutenberg ID and contains the metadata about one book. For example, book number 132 is Lionel Giles's 1910 translation of *The Art of War*, by Sunzi.

---

1. http://www.gutenberg.org

Here's a very stripped-down excerpt from cache/epub/132/pg132.rdf that shows only the fields that we care about and some surrounding detail:

```
<rdf:RDF>
  <pgterms:ebook rdf:about="ebooks/132">
    <dcterms:title>The Art of War</dcterms:title>
    <pgterms:agent rdf:about="2009/agents/4349">
      <pgterms:name>Sunzi, active 6th century B.C.</pgterms:name>
    </pgterms:agent>
    <pgterms:agent rdf:about="2009/agents/5101">
      <pgterms:name>Giles, Lionel</pgterms:name>
    </pgterms:agent>
    <dcterms:subject>
      <rdf:Description rdf:nodeID="N26bb21da0c924e5abcd5809a47f231e7">
        <dcam:memberOf rdf:resource="http://purl.org/dc/terms/LCSH"/>
        <rdf:value>Military art and science -- Early works to 1800</rdf:value>
      </rdf:Description>
    </dcterms:subject>
    <dcterms:subject>
      <rdf:Description rdf:nodeID="N269948d6ecf64b6caf1c15139afd375b">
        <rdf:value>War -- Early works to 1800</rdf:value>
        <dcam:memberOf rdf:resource="http://purl.org/dc/terms/LCSH"/>
      </rdf:Description>
    </dcterms:subject>
  </pgterms:ebook>
</rdf:RDF>
```

The important pieces of information that we'd like to extract are as follows:

- The Gutenberg ID (132)
- The book's title
- The list of authors (agents)
- The list of subjects

Ideally, we'd like to have all of this information formatted as a JSON document suitable for passing in to a document database. For this particular book, our desired JSON would be this:

```
{
  "id": 132,
  "title": "The Art of War",
  "authors": [
    "Sunzi, active 6th century B.C.",
    "Giles, Lionel"
  ],
  "subjects": [
    "Military art and science -- Early works to 1800",
    "War -- Early works to 1800"
  ]
}
```

To get this nice JSON representation, we'll have to parse the RDF file. On the way there, this provides a great opportunity to explore the BDD pattern.

Behavior-Driven Development with Mocha and Chai

It's a maxim of programming that testing is good for code health. One strategy for approaching testing is BDD, which advocates articulating your expected behaviors in tests even before you start writing the implementation.

Not all programming problems are equally well suited to the BDD approach, but data processing is one area where it makes a lot of sense. Since the inputs and outputs of the program are quite well defined, you can specify the desired behavior to a high degree even before implementing the functionality.

So in this chapter, let's take the opportunity to use BDD while parsing the RDF content. Along with Mocha, last seen back in *Developing Unit Tests with Mocha,* on page 43, we'll use Chai, a popular assertion library.

Of course, you can use Mocha, or any test framework, without an assertion library, so why use one? The answer comes down to expressiveness. Using an assertion library like Chai, you can express your test conditions in a way that's more readable and maintainable.

Chai supports several different styles of assertions, each with their own pros and cons. Here I'll show you how to use Chai's *expect* style. It offers a readable syntax without too much magic, making it a good balance between the other two Chai styles: *assert* and *should*.

I'll give you an example, first using Node.js's built-in assert module, and the same using Chai's expect style:

```
assert.ok(book.authors, 'book should have authors');
assert.ok(Array.isArray(book.authors), 'authors should be an array');
assert.equal(book.authors.length, 2, 'authors length should be 2');
```

If you read the code carefully, you can deconstruct that it's confirming that the book object has a property called authors that is an Array of length 2. By contrast, check out this example using Chai's expect() method:

```
expect(book).to.have.a.property('authors')
  .that.is.an('array').with.lengthOf(2);
```

By comparison to the native Node.js assert code, this reads like poetry. Let's get Mocha and Chai set up for this project, then we'll dig further into how to make good use of expect().

Setting Up Tests with Mocha and Chai

First you need to install Mocha and Chai as development dependencies. Open a terminal to your databases project directory and create a minimal package.json, then use npm to install Mocha and Chai.

```
$ cd databases
$ npm init -y
$ npm install --save-dev --save-exact mocha@2.4.5 chai@3.5.0
```

Next, open your package.json for editing. Find the scripts section and update the test entry to look like this:

```
"scripts": {
  "test": "mocha"
}
```

The test entry invokes Mocha with all its default arguments. This provides good output for running all the unit tests once with npm test.

By default, Mocha will look for a directory called test in which to find tests to execute. Create a test dir now.

```
$ mkdir test
```

Now let's run npm test and see what happens. Open a terminal to your databases project directory and give it a try.

```
$ npm test

> @ test ./databases
> mocha


  0 passing (2ms)
```

Unsurprisingly, Mocha successfully runs, but since we have no tests we see 0 passing. Let's change that by adding a test.

Declaring Expectations with Chai

Now that Mocha is ready to run your tests, open a text editor and enter the following:

databases/test/parse-rdf-test.js
```
'use strict';

const fs = require('fs');
const expect = require('chai').expect;

const rdf = fs.readFileSync(`${__dirname}/pg132.rdf`);
```

```
describe('parseRDF', () => {
  it('should be a function', () => {
    expect(parseRDF).to.be.a('function');
  });
});
```

Save this file as parse-rdf-test.js in your databases/test directory.

Stepping through this code, first we pull in the fs module and Chai's expect function. expect() will be the basis of our assertions going forward.

Next, we load *The Art of War*'s RDF content via fs.readFileSync(). Most of the time in Node.js, you want to avoid synchronous I/O, but in this case the proper execution of the test absolutely depends on it loading, so it's OK.

With the setup out of the way, we use Mocha's describe() and it() functions to declare behavior we want from the as-yet-unwritten parseRDF function. Using expect(), we can state our requirements in a very sentence-like form. So far all we require is that parseRDF is a function, but we'll add more requirements soon.

Before you run npm test again, you will need to copy pg132.rdf into the test directory. Run the following command from your databases project directory to take care of it:

```
$ cp ../data/cache/epub/132/pg132.rdf test/
```

Now we're ready to run npm test again.

```
$ npm test

> @ test ./databases
> mocha


  parseRDF
    1) should be a function


  0 passing (11ms)
  1 failing

  1) parseRDF should be a function:
     ReferenceError: parseRDF is not defined
      at Context.it (test/parse-rdf-test.js:14:12)



npm ERR! Test failed.  See above for more details.
```

As expected, we now have one failing test. Since parseRDF is not defined, it cannot be a function.

Now we're ready to create the parse-rdf library, which will define the function and make the test pass.

Developing to Make the Tests Pass

To start, create a new directory called lib in your databases project directory. Putting your modules in a lib directory is a strong convention in the Node.js community.

Open your text editor and enter the following:

```
databases/lib/parse-rdf.js
'use strict';

module.exports = rdf => {
};
```

Save this file as parse-rdf.js in your databases/lib directory.

At this point, all the library does is assign a function to module.exports. This function takes a single argument called rdf and returns nothing, but it should be good enough to make the test pass, so let's pull it in and find out.

Back in your parse-rdf-test.js, add a require() to the top of the file—right after Chai's require line—to pull in the module you just created:

```
databases/test/parse-rdf-test.js
const parseRDF = require('../lib/parse-rdf.js');
```

Here we're taking the anonymous function that we assigned to module.exports in parse-rdf.js and placing it in a constant called parseRDF.

After you save the file, rerun npm test.

```
$ npm test

> @ test ./databases
> mocha


  parseRDF
    ✓ should be a function

  1 passing (8ms)
```

Great! With our test harness in place, we're now in position to iteratively improve the RDF parser library as we add tests and then make them pass.

Enabling Continuous Testing with Mocha

Head back to your parse-rdf-test.js file; it's time to add some more assertions. Insert the following into the describe() callback after our original it('should be a function'):

```
databases/test/parse-rdf-test.js
it('should parse RDF content', () => {
  const book = parseRDF(rdf);
  expect(book).to.be.an('object');
});
```

This test asserts that when we call the parseRDF function, we get back an object. Since the function currently returns nothing (undefined), it's no surprise that our test now fails when we run npm test:

```
$ npm test

> @ test ./databases
> mocha


  parseRDF
    ✓ should be a function
    1) should parse RDF content

  1 passing (45ms)
  1 failing

  1) parseRDF should parse RDF content:
     AssertionError: expected undefined to be an object
      at Context.it (test/parse-rdf-test.js:24:24)


npm ERR! Test failed.  See above for more details.
```

No problem—to make the test pass, we just have to add code to the parseRDF function so it will create and return an object. In your parse-rdf.js file, expand the exported function to this:

```
databases/lib/parse-rdf.js
module.exports = rdf => {
  const book = {};
  return book;
};
```

And now when you run npm test, it should pass again:

```
$ npm test

> @ test ./databases
> mocha


  parseRDF
    ✓ should be a function
    ✓ should parse RDF content (38ms)

  2 passing (46ms)
```

You may have noticed by now that by going back and forth between the test and the implementation, we have established a pretty strong development pattern:

1. Add new criteria to the test.

2. Run the test and see that it fails.

3. Modify the code being tested.

4. Run the test and see that it passes.

We can significantly speed up the running of the tests in steps 2 and 4 above by running the tests continuously, rather than having to invoke npm test from the command line each time.

Mocha can help us here. When you invoke Mocha with the --watch flag, it will continuously monitor any files ending in .js that it can find, and then rerun the tests whenever they change.

Let's add another script to our package.json to run Mocha in this way:

```
"scripts": {
  "test": "mocha",
  "test:watch": "mocha --watch --reporter min"
}
```

Now, instead of executing npm test to run the tests just once, you can use npm run test:watch to begin continuous monitoring. By using the --reporter min option, every time Mocha runs it will clear the screen and provide only minimal output for passing tests. Failing tests will still show their full output.

Try this command in your terminal:

```
$ npm run test:watch
```

If everything is working properly, the terminal screen should be cleared and you should see only this:

```
2 passing (44ms)
```

Mocha has a number of other built-in reporters with various pros and cons that you can explore on the Mocha website.[2]

With Mocha still running and watching files for changes, let's begin another round of development.

---

2. https://mochajs.org/#reporters

Extracting Data from XML with Cheerio

At this point, you should have two successfully passing tests in test/parse-rdf-test.js that are powered by your module in lib/parse-rdf.js. In this section, we'll expand the tests to cover all of our requirements for parsing Project Gutenberg RDF files, and implement the library code to make them pass.

To extract the data attributes we desire, we'll need to parse the RDF (XML) file. As with everything in the Node.js ecosystem, there are multiple valid approaches to parsing, navigating, and querying XML files.

Let's discuss some of the options, then move on to installing and using Cheerio.

Considering XML Data Extraction Options

In this chapter, we will be treating the RDF files like regular, undifferentiated XML files for parsing and for data extraction. The benefit to you (as opposed to addressing them specifically as RDF/XML) is that the skills and techniques you learn will transfer to parsing other kinds of XML and HTML documents.

For situations like this, where the documents are relatively small, I prefer to use Cheerio, a fast Node.js module that provides a jQuery-like API for working with HTML and XML documents.[3] Cheerio's big advantage is that it offers a convenient way to use CSS selectors to dig into the document, without the overhead of setting up a browser-like environment.

Cheerio isn't the only DOM-like XML parser for Node.js—far from it. Other popular options include xmldom and jsdom,[4] [5] both of which are based on the W3C's DOM specification.

In your own projects, if the XML files that you're working with are quite large, then you're probably going to want a streaming SAX parser instead. SAX, which stands for *Simple API for XML*, treats XML as a stream of tokens that your program digests in sequence. Unlike a DOM parser, which considers the document as a whole, a SAX parser operates on only a small piece at a time.

Compared to DOM parsers, SAX parsers can be quite fast and memory-efficient. But the downside of using a SAX parser is that your program will have to keep track of the document structure in flight. I've had good experiences using the sax Node.js module for parsing large XML files.[6]

---

3. https://www.npmjs.com/package/cheerio
4. https://www.npmjs.com/package/xmldom
5. https://www.npmjs.com/package/jsdom
6. https://www.npmjs.com/package/sax

Speaking of RDF/XML in particular, it's a rich data format for which custom tooling is available. If you find yourself working with linked data in the wild, you may find it more convenient to convert it to JSON for Linked Data (JSON-LD) and then perform additional operations from there.

JSON-LD is to JSON as RDF is to XML.[7] With JSON-LD, you can express relationships between entities, not just a hierarchical structure like JSON allows. The jsonld module would be a good place to start for this.[8]

Which of these approaches is best for you really comes down to your use case and personal taste. If your documents are large, then you'll probably want a SAX parser. If you need to preserve the structured relationships in the data, then JSON-LD may be best. Do you need to fetch remote documents? Some modules have this capability built in (Cheerio does not).

Our task at hand is to extract a small amount of data from relatively small files that are readily available locally. I find Cheerio to be an excellent fit for this particular kind of task, and I hope you will too!

Getting Started with Cheerio

To get started with Cheerio, install it with npm and save the dependency.

```
$ npm install --save --save-exact cheerio@0.22.0
```

Please be careful with the version number here. Cheerio has not historically followed the semantic versioning convention, introducing breaking changes in minor releases. If you install any version other than 0.22.0, the examples in this book may not work.

Before we start using Cheerio, let's create some BDD tests that we can make pass by doing so. If Mocha is not already running continuously, open a terminal to your databases project directory and run the following:

```
$ npm run test:watch
```

It should clear the screen and report two passing tests:

```
2 passing (44ms)
```

Great; now let's require that the book object returned by parseRDF() has the correct numeric ID for *The Art of War*. Open your parse-rdf-test.js file and expand the second test by adding a check that the book object has an id property containing the number 132.

---

7.   https://json-ld.org/spec/latest/json-ld/
8.   https://www.npmjs.com/package/jsonld

```
databases/test/parse-rdf-test.js
it('should parse RDF content', () => {
  const book = parseRDF(rdf);
  expect(book).to.be.an('object');
  expect(book).to.have.a.property('id', 132);
});
```

This code takes advantage of Chai's sentence-like BDD API, which we'll use in increasing doses as we add more tests.

Since we have not yet implemented the code to include the 'id' in the returned 'book' object, as soon as you save the file, your Mocha terminal should report this:

```
1 passing (4ms)
1 failing

1) parseRDF should parse RDF content:
    AssertionError: expected {} to have a property 'id'
      at Context.it (test/parse-rdf-test.js:32:28)
```

Good! The test is failing exactly as we expect it should.

Now it's time to use Cheerio to pull out the four fields we want: the book's ID, the title, the authors, and the subjects.

Reading Data from an Attribute

The first piece of information we hope to extract using Cheerio is the book's ID. Recall that we're trying to grab the number 132 out of this XML tag:

```
<pgterms:ebook rdf:about="ebooks/132">
```

Open your lib/parse-rdf.js file and make it look like the following:

```
databases/lib/parse-rdf.js
'use strict';
const cheerio = require('cheerio');

module.exports = rdf => {
  const $ = cheerio.load(rdf);

  const book = {};

  book.id = +$('pgterms\\:ebook').attr('rdf:about').replace('ebooks/', '');

  return book;
};
```

This code adds three things to the version listed in *Enabling Continuous Testing with Mocha,* on page 88:

- At the top, we now require Cheerio.

- Inside the exported function, we use Cheerio's load() method to parse the rdf content. The $ function that's returned is very much like jQuery's $ function.

- Using Cheerio's APIs, we extract the book's ID and, finally, format it.

The line where we set book.id is fairly dense, so let's break it down. Here's the same line, but split out and commented so we can dissect it:

```
book.id =                        // Set the book's id.
  +                              // Unary plus casts the result as a number.
  $('pgterms\\:ebook')           // Query for the <pgterms:ebook> tag.
    .attr('rdf:about')           // Get the value of the rdf:about attribute.
    .replace('ebooks/', '');     // Strip off the leading 'ebooks/' substring.
```

In CSS, the colon character (:) has special meaning—it is used to introduce *pseudo selectors* like :hover for links that are hovered over. In our case, we need a literal colon character for the <pgterms:ebook> tag name, so we have to escape it with a backslash. But since the backslash is a special character in JavaScript string literals, that too needs to be escaped-. Thus, our query selector for finding the tag is pgterms\\:ebook.

Once we have selected the pgterms:ebook tag, we pull out the rdf:about attribute value and strip off the leading ebooks/ substring, leaving only the string "132". The leading unary plus (+) at the start of the line ensures that this gets cast as a number.

If all has gone well so far, your terminal running Mocha's continuous testing should again read 2 passing.

Reading the Text of a Node

Next, let's add a test for the title of the book. Insert the following code right after the test for the book's ID.

databases/test/parse-rdf-test.js
```
expect(book).to.have.a.property('title', 'The Art of War');
```

Your continuous testing terminal should read as follows:

```
1 passing (3ms)
1 failing

1) parseRDF should parse RDF content:
   AssertionError: expected { id: 132 } to have a property 'title'
     at Context.it (test/parse-rdf-test.js:35:28)
```

Now let's grab the title and add it to the returned book object. Recall that the XML containing the title looks like this:

```
<dcterms:title>The Art of War</dcterms:title>
```

Getting this content is even easier than extracting the ID. Add the following to your parse-rdf.js file, after the line where we set book.id:

databases/lib/parse-rdf.js
```
book.title = $('dcterms\\:title').text();
```

Using Cheerio, we select the tag named dcterms:title and save its text content to the book.text property. Once you save this file, your tests should pass again.

Collecting an Array of Values

Moving on, let's add tests for the array of book authors. Open your parse-rdf-test.js file and add these lines:

databases/test/parse-rdf-test.js
```
expect(book).to.have.a.property('authors')
  .that.is.an('array').with.lengthOf(2)
  .and.contains('Sunzi, active 6th century B.C.')
  .and.contains('Giles, Lionel');
```

Here we really start to see the expressive power of Chai assertions. This line of code reads almost like an English sentence.

> Expect book to have a property called authors that is an array of length two and contains "Sunzi, active 6th century B.C." and "Giles, Lionel".

In Chai's language-chaining model, words like and, that, and which are largely interchangeable. This lets you write clauses like .and.contains('X') or .that.contains('X'), depending on which version reads better in your test case.

Once you save this change, your continuous testing terminal should again report a test failure:

```
1 passing (11ms)
1 failing

1) parseRDF should parse RDF content:
   AssertionError: expected { id: 132, title: 'The Art of War' } to have a
   property 'authors'
    at Context.it (test/parse-rdf-test.js:39:28)
```

To make the test pass, recall that we will need to pull out the content from these tags:

```
<pgterms:agent rdf:about="2009/agents/4349">
  <pgterms:name>Sunzi, active 6th century B.C.</pgterms:name>
</pgterms:agent>
<pgterms:agent rdf:about="2009/agents/5101">
  <pgterms:name>Giles, Lionel</pgterms:name>
</pgterms:agent>
```

We're looking to extract the text of each <pgterms:name> tag that's a child of a <pgterms:agent>. The CSS selector *pgterms:agent pgterms:name* finds the elements we need, so we can start with this:

```
$('pgterms\\:agent pgterms\\:name')
```

You might be tempted to grab the text straight away like this:

```
book.authors = $('pgterms\\:agent pgterms\\:name').text();
```

But unfortunately, this won't give us what we want, because Cheerio's text() method returns a single string and we need an array of strings. Instead, add the following code to your parse-rdf.js file, after the book.title piece, to correctly extract the authors:

databases/lib/parse-rdf.js
```
book.authors = $('pgterms\\:agent pgterms\\:name')
  .toArray().map(elem => $(elem).text());
```

Calling Cheerio's .toArray() method converts the collection object into a true JavaScript Array. This allows us to use the native map() method to create a new array by calling the provided function on each element and grabbing the returned value.

Unfortunately, the collection of objects that comes out of toArray() doesn't consist of Cheerio-wrapped objects, but rather document nodes. To extract the text using Cheerio's text(), we need to wrap each node with the $ function, then call text() on it. The resulting mapping function is elem => $(elem).text().

Traversing the Document

Finally, we're down to just one more piece of information we wanted to pull from the RDF file—the list of subjects.

```
<dcterms:subject>
  <rdf:Description rdf:nodeID="N26bb21da0c924e5abcd5809a47f231e7">
    <dcam:memberOf rdf:resource="http://purl.org/dc/terms/LCSH"/>
    <rdf:value>Military art and science -- Early works to 1800</rdf:value>
  </rdf:Description>
</dcterms:subject>
```

```
<dcterms:subject>
  <rdf:Description rdf:nodeID="N269948d6ecf64b6caf1c15139afd375b">
    <rdf:value>War -- Early works to 1800</rdf:value>
    <dcam:memberOf rdf:resource="http://purl.org/dc/terms/LCSH"/>
  </rdf:Description>
</dcterms:subject>
```

As with previous examples, let's start by adding a test. Insert the following code into your parse-rdf-test.js after the other tests.

databases/test/parse-rdf-test.js
```
expect(book).to.have.a.property('subjects')
  .that.is.an('array').with.lengthOf(2)
  .and.contains('Military art and science -- Early works to 1800')
  .and.contains('War -- Early works to 1800');
```

Unfortunately, these subjects are a little trickier to pull out than the authors were. It would be nice if we could use the tag structure to craft a simple CSS selector like this:

```
$('dcterms\\:subject rdf\\:value')
```

However, this selector would match another tag in the document, which we don't want.

```
<dcterms:subject>
  <rdf:Description rdf:nodeID="Nfb797557d91f44c9b0cb80a0d207eaa5">
    <dcam:memberOf rdf:resource="http://purl.org/dc/terms/LCC"/>
    <rdf:value>U</rdf:value>
  </rdf:Description>
</dcterms:subject>
```

To spot the difference, look at the <dcam:memberOf> tags' rdf:resource URLs. The ones we want end in LCSH, which stands for Library of Congress Subject Headings.[9] These headings are a collection of rich indexing terms used in bibliographic records.

Contrast that with the tag we don't want to match, which ends in LCC. This stands for Library of Congress Classification.[10] These are codes that divide all knowledge into 21 top-level classes (like U for Military Science) with many subclasses. These could be interesting in the future, but right now we only want the Subject Headings.

With your continuous test still failing, here's the code you can add to your parse-rdf.js to make it pass:

---

9. https://en.wikipedia.org/wiki/Library_of_Congress_Subject_Headings
10. https://en.wikipedia.org/wiki/Library_of_Congress_Classification

```
databases/lib/parse-rdf.js
book.subjects = $('[rdf\\:resource$="/LCSH"]')
  .parent().find('rdf\\:value')
  .toArray().map(elem => $(elem).text());
```

Let's break this down. First, we select the <dcam:memberOf> tags of interest with the CSS selector [rdf\:resource$="/LCSH"]. The brackets introduce a CSS *attribute selector*, and the $= indicates that we want elements whose rdf:resource attribute ends with /LCSH.

Next, we use Cheerio's .parent() method to traverse up to our currently selected elements' parents. In this case, those are the <rdf:Description> tags. Then we traverse back down using .find() to locate all of their <rdf:value> tags.

Lastly, just like with the book authors, we convert the Cheerio selection object into a true Array and use .map() to get each element's text. And that's it! At this point your tests should be passing, meaning your parseRDF() function is correctly extracting the data we want.

Anticipating Format Changes

One quick note before we move on—an older version of the Project Gutenberg RDF format had its subjects listed like this:

```
<dcterms:subject>
  <rdf:Description>
    <dcam:memberOf rdf:resource="http://purl.org/dc/terms/LCSH"/>
    <rdf:value>Military art and science -- Early works to 1800</rdf:value>
    <rdf:value>War -- Early works to 1800</rdf:value>
  </rdf:Description>
</dcterms:subject>
```

Instead of finding each subject's <rdf:value> living in its own <dcterms:subject> tag, we find them bunched together under a single one. Now consider the traversal code we just wrote. By finding the /LCSH tag, going up to its parent <rdf:Description>, and then searching down for <rdf:value> tags, our code would work with both this earlier data format and the current one (at the time of this writing, anyway).

Whenever you work with third-party data, there's a chance that it could change over time. When it does, your code may or may not continue to work as expected. There's no hard and fast rule to tell you when to be more or less specific with your data-processing code, but I encourage you to stay vigilant to these kinds of issues in your work.

The beauty of testing in these scenarios is that when a data format changes, you can add more tests. This gives you confidence that you're meeting the new demands of the updated data format while still honoring past data.

Recapping Data Extraction with Cheerio

After all of the incremental additions of the last several sections, here's what your final parse-rdf-test.js should look like:

databases/test/parse-rdf-test.js

```
'use strict';

const fs = require('fs');
const expect = require('chai').expect;
const parseRDF = require('../lib/parse-rdf.js');

const rdf = fs.readFileSync(`${__dirname}/pg132.rdf`);

describe('parseRDF', () => {
  it('should be a function', () => {
    expect(parseRDF).to.be.a('function');
  });

  it('should parse RDF content', () => {
    const book = parseRDF(rdf);

    expect(book).to.be.an('object');
    expect(book).to.have.a.property('id', 132);
    expect(book).to.have.a.property('title', 'The Art of War');

    expect(book).to.have.a.property('authors')
      .that.is.an('array').with.lengthOf(2)
      .and.contains('Sunzi, active 6th century B.C.')
      .and.contains('Giles, Lionel');

    expect(book).to.have.a.property('subjects')
      .that.is.an('array').with.lengthOf(2)
      .and.contains('Military art and science -- Early works to 1800')
      .and.contains('War -- Early works to 1800');
  });
});
```

And here's the parse-rdf.js itself:

databases/lib/parse-rdf.js

```
'use strict';
const cheerio = require('cheerio');

module.exports = rdf => {
  const $ = cheerio.load(rdf);

  const book = {};

  book.id = +$('pgterms\\:ebook').attr('rdf:about').replace('ebooks/', '');

  book.title = $('dcterms\\:title').text();

  book.authors = $('pgterms\\:agent pgterms\\:name')
    .toArray().map(elem => $(elem).text());
```

```
  book.subjects = $('[rdf\\:resource$="/LCSH"]')
    .parent().find('rdf\\:value')
    .toArray().map(elem => $(elem).text());

  return book;
};
```

Using this, we can now quickly put together a command-line program to explore some of the other RDF files. Open your editor and enter this:

databases/rdf-to-json.js

```
#!/usr/bin/env node
const fs = require('fs');
const parseRDF = require('./lib/parse-rdf.js');
const rdf = fs.readFileSync(process.argv[2]);
const book = parseRDF(rdf);
console.log(JSON.stringify(book, null, '  '));
```

Save this file as rdf-to-json.js in your databases project directory. This program simply takes the name of an RDF file, reads its contents, parses them, and then prints the resulting JSON to standard output.

Previously when calling JSON.stringify(), we passed only one argument, the object to be serialized. Here we're passing three arguments to get a prettier output. The second argument (null) is an optional replacer function that can be used for filtering (this is almost never used in practice). The last argument (' ') is used to indent nested objects, making the output more human-readable.

Let's try it! Open a terminal to your databases project directory and run this:

```
$ node rdf-to-json.js ../data/cache/epub/11/pg11.rdf
{
  "id": 11,
  "title": "Alice's Adventures in Wonderland",
  "authors": [
    "Carroll, Lewis"
  ],
  "subjects": [
    "Fantasy"
  ]
}
```

If you see this, great! It's time to start performing these conversions in bulk.

Processing Data Files Sequentially

By now your lib/parse-rdf.js is a robust module that can reliably convert RDF content into JSON documents. All that remains is to walk through the Project Gutenberg catalog directory and collect all the JSON documents.

More concretely, we need to do the following:

1. Traverse down the data/cache/epub directory looking for files ending in .rdf.

2. Read each RDF file.

3. Run the RDF content through parseRDF().

4. Collect the JSON serialized objects into a single, bulk file for insertion.

The NoSQL database we'll be using is Elasticsearch, a document datastore that indexes JSON objects. Soon, in Chapter 6, *Commanding Databases*, on page 111, we'll dive deep into Elasticsearch and how to effectively use it with Node.js. You'll learn how to install it, configure it, and make the most of its HTTP-based APIs.

For now, though, our focus is just on transforming the Gutenberg data into an intermediate form for bulk import.

Conveniently, Elasticsearch has a bulk-import API that lets you pull in many records at once. Although we could insert them one at a time, it is significantly faster to use the bulk-insert API.

The format of the file we need to create is described on Elasticsearch's Bulk API page.[11] It's an LDJ file consisting of actions and the source objects on which to perform each action.

In our case, we're performing *index* operations—that is, inserting new documents into an index. Each source object is the book object returned by parseRDF(). Here's an example of an action followed by its source object:

```
{"index":{"_id":"pg11"}}
{"id":11,"title":"Alice's Adventures in Wonderland","authors":...}
```

And here's another one:

```
{"index":{"_id":"pg132"}}
{"id":132,"title":"The Art of War","authors":...}
```

In each case, an action is a JSON object on a line by itself, and the source object is another JSON object on the next line. Elasticsearch's bulk API allows you to chain any number of these together like so:

```
{"index":{"_id":"pg11"}}
{"id":11,"title":"Alice's Adventures in Wonderland","authors":...}
{"index":{"_id":"pg132"}}
{"id":132,"title":"The Art of War","authors":...}
```

---

11. https://www.elastic.co/guide/en/elasticsearch/reference/5.2/docs-bulk.html

The _id field of each index operation is the unique identifier that Elasticsearch will use for the document. Here I've chosen to use the string pg followed by the Project Gutenberg ID. This way, if we ever wanted to store documents from another source in the same index, they shouldn't collide with the Project Gutenberg book data.

To find and open each of the RDF files under the data/cache/epub directory, we will use a module called node-dir. Install and save it as usual. Then we will begin like this:

```
$ npm install --save --save-exact node-dir@0.1.16
```

This module comes with a handful of useful methods for walking a directory tree. The method we'll use is readFiles(), which sequentially operates on files as it encounters them while walking a directory tree.

Let's use this method to find all the RDF files and send them through our RDF parser. Open a text editor and enter this:

databases/rdf-to-bulk.js
```
'use strict';

const dir = require('node-dir');
const parseRDF = require('./lib/parse-rdf.js');

const dirname = process.argv[2];

const options = {
  match: /\.rdf$/,        // Match file names that in '.rdf'.
  exclude: ['pg0.rdf'],  // Ignore the template RDF file (ID = 0).
};
dir.readFiles(dirname, options, (err, content, next) => {
  if (err) throw err;
  const doc = parseRDF(content);
  console.log(JSON.stringify({ index: { _id: `pg${doc.id}` } }));
  console.log(JSON.stringify(doc));
  next();
});
```

Save the file as rdf-to-bulk.js in your databases project directory. This short program walks down the provided directory looking for files that end in .rdf, but excluding the template RDF file called pg0.rdf.

As the program reads each file's content, it runs it through the RDF parser. For output, it produces JSON serialized actions suitable for Elasticsearch's bulk API.

Run the program, and let's see what it produces.

```
$ node rdf-to-bulk.js ../data/cache/epub/ | head
```

If all went well, you should see 10 lines consisting of interleaved actions and documents—like the following, which has been truncated to fit on the page.

```
{"index":{"_id":"pg1"}}
{"id":1,"title":"The Declaration of Independence of the United States of Ame...
{"index":{"_id":"pg10"}}
{"id":10,"title":"The King James Version of the Bible","authors":[],"subject...
{"index":{"_id":"pg100"}}
{"id":100,"title":"The Complete Works of William Shakespeare","authors":["Sh...
{"index":{"_id":"pg1000"}}
{"id":1000,"title":"La Divina Commedia di Dante: Complete","authors":["Dante...
{"index":{"_id":"pg10000"}}
{"id":10000,"title":"The Magna Carta","authors":["Anonymous"],"subjects":["M...
```

Because the head command closes the pipe after echoing the beginning lines, this can sometimes cause Node.js to throw an exception, sending the following to the standard error stream:

```
events.js:160
      throw er; // Unhandled 'error' event
      ^

Error: write EPIPE
    at exports._errnoException (util.js:1022:11)
    at WriteWrap.afterWrite [as oncomplete] (net.js:804:14)
```

To mitigate this error, you can capture error events on the process.stdout stream. Try adding the following line to rdf-to-bulk.js and rerunning it.

```
process.stdout.on('error', err => process.exit());
```

Now, when head closes the pipe, the next attempt to use console.log() will trigger the error event listener and the process will exit silently. If you're worried about output errors other than EPIPE, you can check the err object's code property and take action as appropriate.

```
process.stdout.on('error', err => {
  if (err.code === 'EPIPE') {
    process.exit();
  }
  throw err;  // Or take any other appropriate action.
});
```

At this point we're ready to let rdf-to-bulk.js run for real. Use the following command to capture this LDJ output in a new file called bulk_pg.ldj.

```
$ node rdf-to-bulk.js ../data/cache/epub/ > ../data/bulk_pg.ldj
```

This will run for quite a while, as rdf-to-bulk.js traverses the epub directory, parses each file, and tacks on the Elasticsearch action for it. When it's finished, the bulk_pg.ldj file should be about 11 MB.

Debugging Tests with Chrome DevTools

The examples so far in this chapter may have given you an overly harmonious view of what it's like to develop a data-transformation program in Node.js. The reality is that as you learn the APIs and explore the data, you'll frequently make mistakes and want to track down where you went wrong.

Fortunately, it's possible to attach Chrome's DevTools to Node.js, bringing the full power of Chrome's debugging features with it. If you've done any serious web programming, then you're probably already familiar with Chrome's DevTools—if so, this will be a refresher on how to use them.

In this section, you'll learn how to start up your continuous test suite with Mocha in such a way that you can attach Chrome DevTools and step through the code at your own pace. You'll also be able to execute commands interactively through the console, set breakpoints, and expect variables.

Running Mocha in Debug Mode with npm

So far, to run Mocha tests we've used npm test and npm run test:watch, both of which trigger scripts defined in the project's package.json. Now we'll add a new script called test:debug that runs Mocha in a way that allows the Chrome Dev-Tools to become attached.

Unfortunately, the mocha command we've been using doesn't make it easy, because it spawns a child Node.js process to carry out the tests. So we need to go one level deeper.

When you use npm to install Mocha, it puts two command-line programs into node_modules/mocha/bin: mocha (which we've been using) and _mocha (note the leading underscore). The former invokes the latter in a newly spawned child Node.js process when you use mocha from the command line or through npm.

To attach the Node.js debugger, we have to cut out the middleman and invoke _mocha directly. Open your package.json, and add the following test:debug script to the scripts section.

```
"scripts": {
  "test": "mocha",
  "test:watch": "mocha --watch --reporter min",
  "test:debug":
    "node --inspect node_modules/mocha/bin/_mocha --watch --no-timeouts"
},
```

The --inspect flag tells Node.js that we intend to run in debug mode, which will output a special URL you can open in Chrome to attach DevTools to the process. The --watch flag you're already familiar with—it tells Mocha to watch files for changes and rerun the tests when they happen.

Finally, the --no-timeouts flag tells Mocha that we don't care how long tests take to complete. By default, Mocha will time out asynchronous tests and call them failing after two seconds. But if you're engaged in step-through debugging, it may take significantly longer.

After you save the file, try out npm run test:debug to see what happens.

```
$ npm run test:debug

> databases@1.0.0 test:debug ./code/databases
> node --inspect node_modules/mocha/bin/_mocha --watch --no-timeouts

Debugger listening on ws://127.0.0.1:9229/06a172b5-2bee-475d-b069-0da65d1ea2af
For help see https://nodejs.org/en/docs/inspector


  parseRDF
    ✓ should be a function
    ✓ should parse RDF content


  2 passing (35ms)
```

The special URL beginning with ws:// is a WebSocket that Chrome can connect to for debugging. Open a Chrome browser and navigate to chrome://inspect. This will take you to the Devices page of Chrome DevTools.

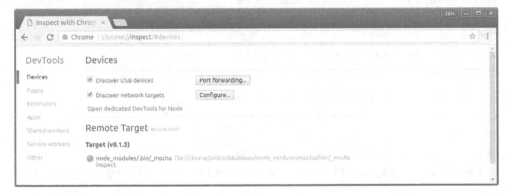

Under the heading Remote Target #LOCALHOST, you should see an entry for your Node.js process running Mocha. Click the blue *inspect* link to launch the debugger.

Using Chrome DevTools to Step Through Your Code

At this point, you should have your Chrome browser running, with a DevTools window open and connected to your Node.js debugging session. When you press `Enter`, Chrome should bring up Chrome DevTools attached to your process. Then make sure you have the Sources tab selected.

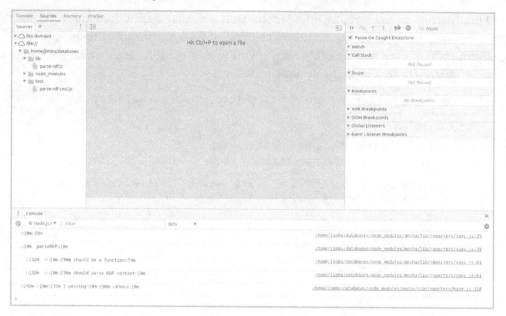

In the left pane, under the file:// heading, you will find the hierarchy of directories and files we have been working on. Under the lib directory you should see parse-rdf.js, and under test there should be the parse-rdf-test.js file.

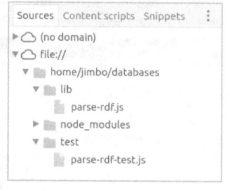

Select the parse-rdf.js file to bring up its contents in the center panel. You can set breakpoints by clicking on the line numbers. Set one now, inside but near the top of the module's exported function (as shown in the first figure on page 107).

Since Mocha is running in watch mode, any time a file changes it will rerun the tests, hitting the breakpoint. So to trigger a test run, open a terminal to your databases project directory and touch either file.

```
$ touch test/parse-rdf-test.js
```

Back in Chrome DevTools, the test run should now be paused at your breakpoint (as shown in the second figure on page 107).

```
1  (function (exports, require, module, __filename, __dirname) { 'use strict';
2  const cheerio = require('cheerio');
3
4  module.exports = rdf => {
5    const $ = cheerio.load(rdf);
6
7    const book = {};
8
9    book.id = +$('pgterms\\:ebook').attr('rdf:about').replace('ebooks/', '');
10
11   book.title = $('dcterms\\:title').text();
12
13   book.authors = $('pgterms\\:agent pgterms\\:name')
14     .toArray().map(elem => $(elem).text());
15
16   book.subjects = $('[rdf\\:resource$="/LCSH"]')
17     .parent().find('rdf\\:value')
18     .toArray().map(elem => $(elem).text());
19
20   return book;
21  };
22
23  });
```

You can use the clickable icons at the top of the right-hand sidebar to step through your code.

As you step forward through the code, DevTools will decorate the source view with information about the current state. You can also explore the available variables and their contents in the Scope section of the right-hand sidebar (as shown in the figure on page 108).

At the time of this writing, a few important features are missing from the Node.js DevTools experience. Most notably, although DevTools appears to allow you to make changes to the source files locally in the browser, it doesn't give you a way to save those changes to disk. And without the ability to save, your Node.js process (Mocha) won't be able to see the changes and run the tests.

Wrapping Up

In this first chapter of Part II of the book, we started working with data from external sources. Acquiring, transforming, storing, and querying data are crucial skills in modern software development with Node.js.

Using Project Gutenberg's catalog data, you iteratively developed the code and tests to parse and make sense of RDF (XML) files. This allowed us to use Mocha and to harness the expressive power of Chai, an assertion library that facilitates for BDD.

For the nuts and bolts of parsing and querying the XML documents, you used Cheerio, a Node.js module that provides a jQuery-like API. Although we didn't use a lot of CSS, we used some sophisticated selectors to pick out specific elements, then we walked the DOM using Cheerio's methods to extract data.

Once this robust parsing library was complete, we used it in combination with the node-dir module to create rdf-to-bulk.js. This program walks down a directory tree looking for RDF files, parses each one, and collects the resulting output objects. You'll use this intermediate, bulk data file in the following chapter to populate an Elasticsearch index.

Finally, you learned how to launch a Node.js program in debug mode and attach Chrome DevTools for interactive, step-through debugging. While there are certainly some kinks that need to be worked out, it sure beats debugging by gratuitous console.log()!

Whereas this chapter was all about manipulating input data and transforming it into a usable form, the next chapter is about storing this data and querying it from a database. In particular, we're going to use Elasticsearch, a full-text indexing, JSON-based document datastore. With its RESTful, HTTP-based API, working with Elasticsearch will let us use Node.js in new and interesting ways.

In case you'd like to have more practice with the techniques we used in this chapter, the following tasks ask you to think about how you would pull out even more data from the RDF files we've been looking at. Good luck!

Extracting Classification Codes

When extracting fields from the Project Gutenberg RDF (XML) files, in *Traversing the Document*, on page 96, we specifically selected the Library of Congress Subject Headings (LCSH) and stored them in an array called subjects. At that time, we carefully avoided the Library of Congress Classification (LCC) single-letter codes. Recall that the LCC portion of an RDF file looks like this:

```
<dcterms:subject>
  <rdf:Description rdf:nodeID="Nfb797557d91f44c9b0cb80a0d207eaa5">
    <dcam:memberOf rdf:resource="http://purl.org/dc/terms/LCC"/>
    <rdf:value>U</rdf:value>
  </rdf:Description>
</dcterms:subject>
```

Using your BDD infrastructure built on Mocha and Chai, implement the following:

- Add a new assertion to parse-rdf-test.js that checks for book.lcc. It should be of type string and it should be at least one character long. It should start with an uppercase letter of the English alphabet, but not I, O, W, X, or Y.

- Run the tests to see that they fail.

- Add code to your exported module function in parse-rdf.js to make the tests pass.

Hint: When working on the code, use Cheerio to find the <dcam:memberOf> element with an rdf:resource attribute that ends with /LCC. Then traverse up to its parent <rdf:Description>, and read the text of the first descendent <rdf:value> tag. You may want to refer to Chai's documentation when crafting your new assertions.[12]

---

12. http://chaijs.com/api/bdd/

Extracting Sources

Most of the metadata in the Project Gutenberg RDF files describes where each book can be downloaded in various formats. For example, here's the part that shows where to download the plain text of *The Art of War*:

```
<dcterms:hasFormat>
  <pgterms:file rdf:about="http://www.gutenberg.org/ebooks/132.txt.utf-8">
    <dcterms:isFormatOf rdf:resource="ebooks/132"/>
    <dcterms:modified rdf:datatype="http://www.w3.org/2001/XMLSchema#dateTime">
        2016-09-01T01:20:00.437616</dcterms:modified>
    <dcterms:format>
      <rdf:Description rdf:nodeID="N2293d0caa918475e922a48041b06a3bd">
        <dcam:memberOf rdf:resource="http://purl.org/dc/terms/IMT"/>
        <rdf:value
            rdf:datatype="http://purl.org/dc/terms/IMT">text/plain</rdf:value>
      </rdf:Description>
    </dcterms:format>
    <dcterms:extent rdf:datatype="http://www.w3.org/2001/XMLSchema#integer">
        343691</dcterms:extent>
  </pgterms:file>
</dcterms:hasFormat>
```

Suppose we wanted to include a list of download sources in each JSON object we create from an RDF file. To get an idea of what data you might want, take a look at the Project Gutenberg page for *The Art of War*.[13]

Consider these questions:

- Which fields in the raw data would we want to capture, and which could we discard?

- What structure would make the most sense for this data?

- What information would you need to be able to produce a table that looked like the one on the Project Gutenberg site?

Once you have an idea of what data you'll want to extract, try creating a JSON object by hand for this one download source. When you're happy with your data representation, use your existing continuous testing infrastructure and add a test that checks for this new information.

Finally, extend the book object produced in parse-rdf.js to include this data to make the test pass. You can do it!

---

13. http://www.gutenberg.org/ebooks/132

CHAPTER 6

Commanding Databases

In this chapter you'll be crafting a rich command-line utility program for interacting with Elasticsearch—a schema-free, RESTful, NoSQL database that stores and indexes JSON documents over HTTP. Your program will be configurable through many options, and will support advanced query capabilities. Importantly, it will be able to import documents in bulk, like the corpus of Project Gutenberg documents produced in the preceding chapter. The following image shows where we're headed.

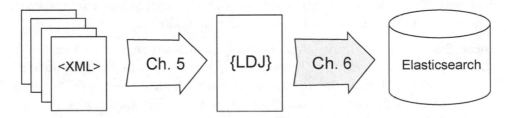

With the experience you gain here, you'll be able to develop your own richly featured Node.js command-line programs, as well as communicate with other RESTful, JSON-based services. You'll also be in a good position to judge whether Elasticsearch is the right database for your future Node.js projects.

Doing this work will introduce you to these aspects of Node.js development:

Node.js Core
In this chapter, we'll revisit piping streams of data, but this time in the context of communicating with remote services over HTTP. We'll also use npm to interactively create a package.json file, the cornerstone of a Node.js project.

Patterns

You'll use the Commander module's method-chaining pattern for building out command-line programs. And you'll use the Request module for performing HTTP requests.

JavaScriptisms

In JavaScript, a caller can invoke your function without providing all the arguments that the function expects. To compensate for missing arguments, when defining a function, you can supply a default parameter value that is evaluated at runtime. You'll use this technique, as well as some useful Array methods such as filter() and join().

Supporting Code

Outside of Node.js proper, this chapter will introduce you to Elasticsearch, a JSON-based document datastore. In addition, to manipulate JSON you'll use an exciting command-line tool called jq.

Over the course of this book, you've already been briefly exposed to a couple of domain-specific languages (DSLs) like RDF (XML), as well as CSS selectors and how to make good use of them with Node.js. In this chapter we'll touch on a few more. You'll learn Elasticsearch's query syntax, which is needed to find matching documents. In addition, you'll learn how to use jq's filter expressions to manipulate JSON on the command line.

These DSLs could warrant whole books in their own right, but I can only afford partial coverage in this book. It is my sincere goal to provide you with the best footing on your way to becoming a great Node.js developer. For that reason, I feel it's necessary to introduce you to these topics, even if you'll have to take the rest of the journey on your own.

At the outset of this chapter, you'll install Elasticsearch and confirm that it's running. After that, for the rest of the chapter, you'll be developing a program called esclu from the ground up. This process will provide a rough blueprint of what it's like to develop a featureful command-line program in Node.js.

Rather than dive deep on Elasticsearch features at the outset, we'll explore them as we go, meeting each one as we expand the capabilities of the command-line program. Let's get to it!

Introducing Elasticsearch

Elasticsearch is a distributed, document-oriented, NoSQL database. In recent years, Elasticsearch has been gaining in popularity relative to other JSON-based document datastores, and for good reason. Built on Apache

Lucene,[1] Elasticsearch provides a rich suite of querying capabilities, including full-text search, stemming, and fuzzy search. With Elasticsearch you can also execute a variety of aggregation queries, apply filters, and perform numeric comparisons.

No one tool is best for all jobs, of course, and Elasticsearch is no exception. But given that our Project Gutenberg documents are textual in nature—including titles of books, author names, and subject strings—Elasticsearch is a natural fit. Once the documents are stored in Elasticsearch, we'll be able to develop our own specific RESTful APIs on top, starting in the next chapter.

The scalability and reliability of Elasticsearch comes from its clustered architecture. By sharding indices and replicating the shards, an Elasticsearch cluster guards against outages and can often parallelize the execution of queries. Proper configuring and tuning of an Elasticsearch cluster are huge topics, and are outside the scope of this book. Fortunately, the default configuration settings are sufficient for our exploratory use case.

As for interacting with Elasticsearch, it's all about making proper HTTP requests. Doing this will give us the opportunity to talk about HTTP and RESTful practices—information that will be handy in Chapter 7, *Developing RESTful Web Services*, on page 147, when we'll implement our own RESTful web services on top of Elasticsearch. And the techniques you'll use here apply to any other RESTful APIs you use with Node.js, as well.

Of course, to do anything with Elasticsearch, you'll need to install it. Let's do that now.

Installing Prerequisites

Elasticsearch is built on Java 8, which means you'll need to install a Java Runtime Environment if you haven't already. For production use, Elastic recommends using Oracle's Java Development Kit (JDK) version 1.8.0_73 or higher. Instructions on how to install Java 8 are available on Oracle's website.[2]

You can run java -version from the command line to confirm that Java is installed and ready.

```
$ java -version
openjdk version "1.8.0_91"
OpenJDK Runtime Environment (build 1.8.0_91-8u91-b14-3ubuntu1~16.04.1-b14)
OpenJDK 64-Bit Server VM (build 25.91-b14, mixed mode)
```

---

1. http://lucene.apache.org/
2. http://docs.oracle.com/javase/8/docs/technotes/guides/install/install_overview.html

Once you have Java installed, it's time to download and install Elasticsearch.

Installing Elasticsearch

We'll be using version 5.2 of Elasticsearch, available from Elastic's download page.[3] Once you download the archive, unzip it and run bin/elasticsearch from the command line. You should see a lot of output containing something like the following (much of the output is omitted here for brevity).

```
$ bin/elasticsearch
[INFO ][o.e.n.Node               ] [] initializing ...
... many lines omitted ...
[INFO ][o.e.h.HttpServer         ] [kAh7Q7Z] publish_address {127.0.0.1:9200},
    bound_addresses {[::1]:9200}, {127.0.0.1:9200}
[INFO ][o.e.n.Node               ] [kAh7Q7Z] started
[INFO ][o.e.g.GatewayService     ] [kAh7Q7Z] recovered [0] indices into
    cluster_state
```

Notice the publish_address and bound_addresses listed toward the end of the output. By default, Elasticsearch binds TCP port 9200 for its HTTP endpoint.

You can specify a lot of settings when setting up an Elasticsearch cluster. We haven't specified any here, which means it's running in development mode. A full discussion of the Elasticsearch cluster settings is outside the scope of this book, but you can read about them on Elastic's Important System Configuration page.[4]

With Elasticsearch running, we can now implement a command-line utility program for it.

Creating a Command-Line Program in Node.js with Commander

In this section, you'll produce the outline of a command-line program that provides access to some features of Elasticsearch. You'll start by creating a package.json, then build up from there.

To begin, open a terminal and create a directory called esclu that will house our Elasticsearch Command Line Utilities project. From inside the esclu directory, run npm init to start the interactive package.json creation wizard. All of the defaults are fine except for description, for which you should provide a short sentence describing the project.

---

3.   https://www.elastic.co/downloads/past-releases/elasticsearch-5-2-2
4.   https://www.elastic.co/guide/en/elasticsearch/reference/5.2/system-config.html

```
‹ $ npm init
  This utility will walk you through creating a package.json file.
  It only covers the most common items, and tries to guess sensible defaults.

  See `npm help json` for definitive documentation on these fields
  and exactly what they do.

  Use `npm install <pkg> --save` afterward to install a package and
  save it as a dependency in the package.json file.

  Press ^C at any time to quit.
  name: (esclu)
  version: (1.0.0)
  description:
⇒ Elasticsearch Command Line Utilities
‹ entry point: (index.js)
  test command:
  git repository:
  keywords:
  author:
  license: (ISC)
  About to write to ./code/esclu/package.json:

  {
    "name": "esclu",
    "version": "1.0.0",
    "description": "Elasticsearch Command Line Utilites",
    "main": "index.js",
    "scripts": {
      "test": "echo \"Error: no test specified\" && exit 1"
    },
    "author": "",
    "license": "ISC"
  }

  Is this ok? (yes)
```

Once you're happy with the basic structure of your package, it's time to move on to installing the modules we'll depend on.

Introducing the Commander and Request Modules

So far in this book, you've implemented a number of command-line programs. These have been relatively simple in terms of the variety of options and arguments they can accept. To take it to the next level, we're going to use a module called Commander, which makes it easy to construct elaborate and powerful command-line tools in Node.js.

Likewise, while Node.js supplies rudimentary support for HTTP requests with its built-in http module,[5] it can take a lot of finagling to get it right. Using a higher-level module like Request simplifies the process of issuing HTTP requests and handling the asynchronous responses.

Given their power to reduce tedious boilerplate code while providing useful functionality, the Commander module and the Request module will provide the backbone of the Elasticsearch command-line program. Install them using npm as follows:

```
$ npm install --save --save-exact commander@2.9.0 request@2.79.0
```

With these two crucial Node.js modules installed, it's time to lay out the fundamental structure of the Elasticsearch command-line program.

Alternatives to Commander and Request

The Commander module is not the only module in npm that aims to help you create command-line programs. For example, yargs is another command-line utility module with many of the same features as Commander.[a] With yargs, you don't have to explicitly spell out each option in advance; instead you layer in checks such as required options and data types as you develop.

Likewise, while the Request module isn't the only one that aims to simplify the making of HTTP requests, it is the most popular (at the time of this writing). Another module worth pointing out is superagent,[b] which has a very similar API but aims to function compatibly in browsers as well as Node.js. Although superagent has some streaming support, I had trouble using it to POST a large file in a streaming fashion while also streaming the response body.

One more alternative to Request worth mentioning is node-fetch.[c] This module implements the Fetch API, a recent addition to modern browsers to replace the aging XMLHttpRequest.[d] You'll use fetch() in Chapter 8, *Creating a Beautiful User Experience*, on page 185, to interact with the Node.js services you develop on top of Elasticsearch.

Your mileage may vary. As you explore different modules for achieving different goals, always be open to the idea that there may be another similar module that more closely matches your objectives and development philosophy.

---

a. https://www.npmjs.com/package/yargs
b. https://www.npmjs.com/package/superagent
c. https://www.npmjs.com/package/node-fetch
d. https://developer.mozilla.org/en-US/docs/Web/API/WindowOrWorkerGlobalScope/fetch

---

5. https://nodejs.org/api/http.html

Creating a Basic Command-Line Program with Commander

The Commander module handles a variety of details: enforcing required parameters, parsing command-line options, interpreting alternative short names for flags called aliases, and so on. To take advantage of these features, you should follow a basic structure to your program. We'll set that up in this section a step at a time.

For starters, we'll want an extensionless executable file called esclu that we'll be able to execute directly, without explicitly running Node.js. Recall back in *Creating Read and Write Streams*, on page 21, that using #! nomenclature in the first line of your Node.js file is an acceptable Unix convention when making a file executable. We'll use that again here, but separate the working JavaScript into its own file. Start by making a file called esclu with these contents:

esclu/esclu
```
#!/usr/bin/env node
require('./index.js');
```

As you can see, all this file does is execute the code in index.js by way of the require() method.

Once you save the file, use chmod to make it executable from the command line.

```
$ chmod +x esclu
```

Next, open your text editor and enter this code, which you should save as index.js:

esclu/index.js
```
'use strict';

const fs = require('fs');
const request = require('request');
const program = require('commander');
const pkg = require('./package.json');

program
  .version(pkg.version)
  .description(pkg.description)
  .usage('[options] <command> [...]')
  .option('-o, --host <hostname>', 'hostname [localhost]', 'localhost')
  .option('-p, --port <number>', 'port number [9200]', '9200')
  .option('-j, --json', 'format output as JSON')
  .option('-i, --index <name>', 'which index to use')
  .option('-t, --type <type>', 'default type for bulk operations');

program.parse(process.argv);

if (!program.args.filter(arg => typeof arg === 'object').length) {
  program.help();
}
```

In the intro section at the top of the file, notice how we pull package.json into a constant called pkg. Node.js's require() method can read JSON files as well as modules written in JavaScript. By pulling in the package.json we can reference configuration parameters therein.

Next, we start setting up the command-line program object provided by Commander. After setting the version, description, and usage strings, we enumerate some flags and their default values. Exactly which flags your program needs is up to you, but these are the one we'll use in chatting with Elasticsearch.

With that out of the way, we call program.parse() on the Node.js process's command-line arguments. This causes flags to be interpreted as such.

Lastly, we check whether the program's args array contains any objects, as opposed to just strings. Commander fills the program.args array with the user-supplied arguments as strings, except those arguments that match a named command. We don't have any commands defined yet; those will come shortly. But this block of code ensures that if users enter arguments that we don't recognize, they see the same thing as if they'd asked for help with -h.

Once you save the file with this content, open a terminal to your esclu project directory and try running the script:

```
$ ./esclu
  Usage: esclu [options] <command> [...]

  Elasticsearch Command Line Utilites

  Options:

    -h, --help               output usage information
    -V, --version            output the version number
    -o, --host <hostname>    hostname [localhost]
    -p, --port <number>      port number [9200]
    -j, --json               format output as JSON
    -i, --index <name>       which index to use
    -t, --type <type>        default type for bulk operations
```

As you can see, the help is already working. You can also try out the version option and confirm that it gives you the same value as specified in the package.json.

```
$ ./esclu -V
1.0.0
```

Now that you have the basic structure of your program ready, it's time to start adding commands.

Adding a Command to Your Program

Throughout the rest of this chapter, we're going to be adding commands to esclu for interacting with Elasticsearch. Since Elasticsearch is primarily a RESTful datastore, interacting with it begins with composing the correct URLs to achieve our goals.

REST is an acronym that stands for *Representational State Transfer*. When an API is RESTful, it is HTTP-based and its resources are identified by their URLs. Requesting or making a change to a resource comes down to issuing an HTTP request using the particular method that matches your intent. For example, the HTTP GET method retrieves a resource, and HTTP PUT sends a resource to be saved.

In Elasticsearch, the RESTful resources are JSON documents. Each document lives in an index and has a *type*, which defines a class of related documents. To construct a URL for an Elasticsearch document, first you append which index you're interested in (if any) and then optionally the *type* of object you're interested in, separated by slashes. To get information about your whole cluster, you could make an HTTP GET request to the root: http://localhost:9200/.

In a bit, we'll create an index to store the book metadata we created in Chapter 5, *Transforming Data*, on page 81. To request information about the index named books, you would GET http://localhost:9200/books.

No matter what URL we end up hitting, we'll want to incorporate the user-provided index and type information. To do that, add this fullUrl() to your esclu program after the require() lines and before setting up the program:

esclu/index.js

```
const fullUrl = (path = '') => {
  let url = `http://${program.host}:${program.port}/`;
  if (program.index) {
    url += program.index + '/';
    if (program.type) {
      url += program.type + '/';
    }
  }
  return url + path.replace(/^\/*/, '');
};
```

The fullUrl() function takes a single parameter, path, and returns the full URL to Elasticsearch based on the program parameters. Note that here we're taking advantage of ECMAScript's *default parameter* feature to a set path to the empty string if one isn't provided.

Constructing the URL consists of appending the index (if specified) and the type (if both it and the index were specified) and, finally, appending the path. If the path includes a leading forward slash, we strip it off using a short regular expression to avoid double slashes in the final URL.

With the fullUrl() method ready, now we can add a *command* to log it to the console. Add the following code to your index.js, before the program.parse() line.

esclu/index.js
```
program
  .command('url [path]')
  .description('generate the URL for the options and path (default is /)')
  .action((path = '/') => console.log(fullUrl(path)));
```

Adding a command to your program consists of three things: specifying the command name and parameters, providing a description, and setting up an action callback. The string you provide to the command() tells Commander the name of the command an any arguments it takes. Required arguments should be surrounded by angle brackets (like <this>) and optional arguments should use square brackets (like [this]).

The function you provide to action() is the callback that will be invoked when the command is run. It will be called with the same list of arguments specified when setting up the command. In this case, we expect an optional variable called path with the default value of /.

Inside the body of the action callback, all we do here is use the console to output the result of calling fullUrl() with the path.

Head back to the terminal and try it out. First, just run esclu with no arguments to see that the new url command was added.

```
$ ./esclu

  Usage: esclu [options] <command> [...]

  Commands:

    url [path]   generate the URL for the options and path (default is /)

  Elasticsearch Command Line Utilities

  Options:

    -h, --help              output usage information
    -V, --version           output the version number
    -o, --host <hostname>   hostname [localhost]
    -p, --port <number>     port number [9200]
    -j, --json              format output as JSON
    -i, --index <name>      which index to use
    -t, --type <type>       default type for bulk operations
```

As you can see, url is now listed under Commands, including the description string. When you execute esclu url, you should see the default root URL of your local Elasticsearch cluster.

```
$ ./esclu url
http://localhost:9200/
```

If you provide various options, those should be constructed appropriately too.

```
$ ./esclu url 'some/path' -p 8080 -o my.cluster
http://my.cluster:8080/some/path
```

Next we'll add a command to perform an HTTP GET request for the URL and output the results. This will unlock a lot of utility by itself, so it's a good place to start.

Using request to Fetch JSON over HTTP

The Request module aims to simplify making HTTP requests, particularly when it comes to streaming data. It's true that Node.js ships with a built-in module called http, which has APIs for creating low-level HTTP servers and making client requests. But using the Request module cuts past many of the details so you can focus on the job being done.

As an introduction to using the Request module, open your text editor to your index.js file and insert the following code after the url command.

```
esclu/index.js
program
  .command('get [path]')
  .description('perform an HTTP GET request for path (default is /)')
  .action((path = '/') => {
    const options = {
      url: fullUrl(path),
      json: program.json,
    };
    request(options, (err, res, body) => {
      if (program.json) {
        console.log(JSON.stringify(err || body));
      } else {
        if (err) throw err;
        console.log(body);
      }
    });
  });
```

Like the url command from the previous section, this code adds a command called get that takes a single optional parameter called path. Inside the action() callback, we're using the request() function provided by the module of the same name to execute an asynchronous HTTP request and call a callback when it's done.

The options for request() can include many settings, but here we're providing only the URL and the Boolean flag json. When set to true, the json flag indicates that the request should include an HTTP header asking the server for a JSON-formatted response. It also ensures that the returned content will be parsed as JSON.

The callback function to request takes three parameters: the error if any, the response object, and the response body. If esclu was invoked with the --json flag, then we want to output the JSON stringified error or response body. Without the JSON flag, we want to throw an exception on error and otherwise output the response verbatim.

Once you save the file, head back to the terminal and we'll give the get command a try. To start, run get without specifying a path, and without any other flags to give us a baseline.

```
$ ./esclu get
{
  "name" : "kAh7Q7Z",
  "cluster_name" : "elasticsearch",
  "cluster_uuid" : "_kRYwEXISDKtcPXeihPwZw",
  "version" : {
    "number" : "5.2.2",
    "build_hash" : "f9d9b74",
    "build_date" : "2017-02-24T17:26:45.835Z",
    "build_snapshot" : false,
    "lucene_version" : "6.4.1"
  },
  "tagline" : "You Know, for Search"
}
```

Recall that the default path is the root of the server: /. This response tells us that Elasticsearch is up and running, and gives us some additional information about the current running version.

If Elasticsearch is not up and running, you'll see something quite different:

```
$ ./esclu get
./code/esclu/esclu:51
        if (err) throw err;
              ^

Error: connect ECONNREFUSED 127.0.0.1:9200
    at Object.exports._errnoException (util.js:1022:11)
    at exports._exceptionWithHostPort (util.js:1045:20)
    at TCPConnectWrap.afterConnect [as oncomplete] (net.js:1090:14)
```

Presuming your Elasticsearch is up and responding, you can start poking around to get more info. For example, the _cat endpoint offers a human-readable (non-JSON) API for assessing the health and status of your cluster. Start with get '_cat' for a list of options.

```
$ ./esclu get '_cat'
=^.^=
/_cat/pending_tasks
/_cat/snapshots/{repository}
/_cat/templates
/_cat/health
/_cat/segments
/_cat/segments/{index}
/_cat/aliases
/_cat/aliases/{alias}
/_cat/repositories
/_cat/allocation
/_cat/indices
/_cat/indices/{index}
/_cat/shards
/_cat/shards/{index}
/_cat/thread_pool
/_cat/thread_pool/{thread_pools}/_cat/plugins
/_cat/nodeattrs
/_cat/tasks
/_cat/count
/_cat/count/{index}
/_cat/fielddata
/_cat/fielddata/{fields}
/_cat/master
/_cat/recovery
/_cat/recovery/{index}
/_cat/nodes
```

Since we haven't inserted any documents yet—or even created any indexes, for that matter—the responses to these commands will be pretty boring at this point. But keep in mind that you can use get with the _cat API to explore your cluster later.

Speaking of adding an index, let's add a command to do that next.

Creating an Elasticsearch Index

To create an index, Elasticsearch expects an incoming HTTP PUT request to the index you wish to create.

Open your text editor and fill in the action callback as follows:

```
esclu/index.js
const handleResponse = (err, res, body) => {
  if (program.json) {
    console.log(JSON.stringify(err || body));
  } else {
    if (err) throw err;
    console.log(body);
  }
};

program
  .command('create-index')
  .description('create an index')
  .action(() => {
    if (!program.index) {
      const msg = 'No index specified! Use --index <name>';
      if (!program.json) throw Error(msg);
      console.log(JSON.stringify({error: msg}));
      return;
    }

    request.put(fullUrl(), handleResponse);
  });
```

First, let's factor out the handling of the response to the HTTP request. The way we handled the request for the get command is common to the rest of the requests we'll be making, so it makes sense to turn this into a named function.

Next, take a look at the create-index command. Inside the action callback, we start by checking that the user specified an index with the --index flag. If not, we'll either throw an exception or output an error as JSON if the --json flag is in use.

Then we use request.put() to issue an HTTP PUT request using the handler we just defined.

You may already be familiar with the HTTP method POST, which is widely used for submitting HTML forms. The difference between POST and PUT is subtle but important. In cases where you know the full URL for the RESTful thing you're working on, use PUT; otherwise, use POST. So if you're updating an existing resource, PUT is always correct, but to create a new resource you use PUT only if you know the full URL to where that resource will be.

In the case of Elasticsearch, each index lives at a unique URL specified by its name under the server root. So to create a new index, we use PUT, pointing to the path. For the books index, the URL will be http://localhost:9200/books/. The fullUrl() function we created earlier handles this URL construction already.

Save this file, then run esclu with no command-line arguments to confirm that create-index shows up.

```
$ ./esclu

  Usage: esclu [options] <command> [...]

  Commands:

    url [path]      generate the URL for the options and path (default is /)
    get [path]      perform an HTTP GET request for path (default is /)
    create-index    create an index
```

Great! Now let's try to create the books index using the create-index command.

```
$ ./esclu create-index --index books
{"acknowledged":true,"shards_acknowledged":true}
```

It looks like Elasticsearch acknowledged the request. To see if the index is there, let's list the indices using _cat/indices?v. The v stands for verbose, and adds a header row to the output table.

```
$ ./esclu get '_cat/indices?v'
health status index uuid    pri rep docs.count store.size pri.store.size
yellow open    books n9...sQ  5   1           0       650b           650b
```

(Some values were omitted or truncated for brevity.)

Listing indices seems like a useful command, so let's add it to esclu.

Listing Elasticsearch Indices

Insert the following code after the create-index command.

esclu/index.js
```
program
  .command('list-indices')
  .alias('li')
  .description('get a list of indices in this cluster')
  .action(() => {
    const path = program.json ? '_all' : '_cat/indices?v';
    request({url: fullUrl(path), json: program.json}, handleResponse);
  });
```

As before, we use the program object to add a command, but this time we're adding an alias using the alias() method. This will allow us to invoke the list-indices command by typing only li instead of the full command name.

Inside the action callback method, first we determine the path to request. This will be _all if the user has specified JSON mode with the --json flag; otherwise it'll be_cat/indices?v like we just used with the get command.

The question mark and colon (?:) constitute the *ternary operator*. This is an inline if statement that evaluates the first parameter then returns the second parameter if the first is true; otherwise it returns the third parameter. For example, if a and b are two numbers, you could find the greater of the two with a > b ? a : b.

Once we have the path, we run its full URL through request() as before. Rather than setting up a separate options object to house the url and json properties, this time we're specifying it inline.

Let's try it out. Back on the command line, run esclu with the list-indices command (or li for short). You should see the same table as before.

```
$ ./esclu li
health status index uuid    pri rep docs.count store.size pri.store.size
yellow open   books n9...sQ  5   1           0       650b           650b
```

Now let's try it with the --json or -j flag.

```
$ ./esclu li -j
{"books":{"aliases":{},"mappings":{},"settings":{"index":{"creation_date":"1484
650920414","number_of_shards":"5","number_of_replicas":"1","uuid":"3t4pwCBmTwyV
KMe_0j26kg","version":{"created":"5010199"},"provided_name":"books"}}}}
```

When you GET /_all, Elasticsearch returns an object whose keys are the names of the indices, and values contain information about each index. The JSON contains some useful information, but is difficult to read on the command line. This is a good time to introduce a useful command-line tool for manipulating JSON, called jq.

Shaping JSON with jq

jq is a command-line program for querying and manipulating JSON objects. Technically speaking, it's not a Node.js thing, but it's so useful for working with JSON (and JSON is so prevalent in Node.js development) that it's absolutely worth knowing. You'll be a better developer knowing how to use jq to explore and manipulate your JSON data.

You can find instructions for downloading and installing jq on the jq website,[6] or use the package manager of your choice. Once you have it installed, you should be able to see the version number on the command line if you run it with the -V option.

```
$ jq -V
jq-1.5-1-a5b5cbe
```

The examples in this book assume you're using version 1.5.x.

---

6. https://stedolan.github.io/jq/

jq reads JSON from standard input and operates on it according to a query string you provide. This string uses jq's custom domain-specific language for articulating transformations (more on this in a bit).

The simplest query is the string containing a single dot (.), which means output the object as is. To try it out, pipe the output from your esclu command into jq with that string argument.

```
$ ./esclu li -j | jq '.'
{
  "books": {
    "aliases": {},
    "mappings": {},
    "settings": {
      "index": {
        "creation_date": "1484650920414",
        "number_of_shards": "5",
        "number_of_replicas": "1",
        "uuid": "3t4pwCBmTwyVKMe_0j26kg",
        "version": {
          "created": "5010199"
        },
        "provided_name": "books"
      }
    }
  }
}
```

Already it's looking better, because by default jq will format its output using pretty indentation. Now let's try another jq function, keys, which extracts the keys of an object as an array.

```
$ ./esclu li -j | jq 'keys'
[
  "books"
]
```

You may have noticed that while the JSON and non-JSON outputs of the list-indices command both contain interesting information, it's not quite the same. For example, two interesting fields from the non-JSON output are doc.count (the number of documents), and store.size (the number of bytes on disk used by this index).

We can get the same information in JSON form, but we have to go to Elastic-search's _stats API endpoint to get it. Be warned, though; _stats provides a lot of information we'll have to troll through to find what we need.

To start, let's take a peek at the first few lines of _stats output after nicely formatting it with jq. For the purpose of this book, these examples use the program head to show only the first *N* lines of output. In your own terminal, you could use an interactive paging program like less instead.

```
$ ./esclu get _stats | jq '.' | head -n 20
{
  "_shards": {
    "total": 10,
    "successful": 5,
    "failed": 0
  },
  "_all": {
    "primaries": {
      "docs": {
        "count": 0,
        "deleted": 0
      },
      "store": {
        "size_in_bytes": 650,
        "throttle_time_in_millis": 0
      },
      "indexing": {
        "index_total": 0,
        "index_time_in_millis": 0,
        "index_current": 0,
```

OK, from this output we can tell a couple of things. First, the return value of _stats is an object with at least two keys: _shards and _all. In Elasticsearch, leading underscores are reserved, and in particular _all usually means all indices.

We can also see that under _all the path primaries.docs.count is a number (currently zero since we have inserted no documents). And primary.store.size_in_bytes is 650.

To see what else is in this object, let's use a jq *function* called keys,[7] which, like JavaScript's Object.keys(), returns an array containing the keys of an object.

```
$ ./esclu get _stats | jq 'keys'
[
  "_all",
  "_shards",
  "indices"
]
```

In addition to _all and _shards, there is also indices. We can take a look at that by using a jq *filter*,[8] which is a string that describes a path into an object. The filter .indices will return the value for the key indices. We'll have to use head again to truncate the output.

---

7.   https://stedolan.github.io/jq/manual/v1.5/#Builtinoperatorsandfunctions
8.   https://stedolan.github.io/jq/manual/v1.5/#Basicfilters

```
$ ./esclu get _stats | jq '.indices' | head -n 20
{
  "books": {
    "primaries": {
      "docs": {
        "count": 0,
        "deleted": 0
      },
      "store": {
        "size_in_bytes": 650,
        "throttle_time_in_millis": 0
      },
      "indexing": {
        "index_total": 0,
        "index_time_in_millis": 0,
        "index_current": 0,
        "index_failed": 0,
        "delete_total": 0,
        "delete_time_in_millis": 0,
        "delete_current": 0,
        "noop_update_total": 0,
```

The keys of the indices object are the names of the indices we've created. So far, the only key is books. Under each index, the structure looks roughly the same as the _all object we inspected earlier.

Using jq, we can combine filters and functions by piping one expression into another using the *pipe operator* (|). For example, we can see what keys the books object has by piping the output of the .indices.books filter into the keys function. Try this:

```
$ ./esclu get _stats | jq '.indices.books | keys'
[
  "primaries",
  "total"
]
```

With jq, you can also compose new objects using filters and functions. For example, we could create a custom JSON report containing the total number of all documents in Elasticsearch and the total size in bytes for those documents.

```
$ ./esclu get _stats | \
jq '._all.primaries | { count: .docs.count, size: .store.size_in_bytes }'
{
  "count": 0,
  "size": 650
}
```

The expression here tells jq to start by applying the filter ._all.primaries. The resulting object is piped into an *object constructor*, which is a set of curly braces wrapping the desired content. In this case, we want to construct an object with a count key containing the value under .docs.count, and a size key with the value under .store.size_in_bytes.

You can do more than this, of course, but that's enough jq for now. Keep this tool in mind as you deal with JSON data in the future—it makes it easy to poke around, and the jq manual does a superb job of explaining the tool's features.[9]

Inserting Elasticsearch Documents in Bulk

We need one more big feature from the esclu command-line tool, and that's to allow us to bulk-upload documents. Recall that in *Processing Data Files Sequentially*, on page 100, we developed an LDJ data file containing interleaved commands and documents for Elasticsearch's bulk API.

Here's a truncated sample to refresh your memory:

```
{"index":{"_id":"pg11"}}
{"id":11,"title":"Alice's Adventures in Wonderland","authors":...}
{"index":{"_id":"pg132"}}
{"id":132,"title":"The Art of War","authors":...}
```

Open your index.js file and insert this new command, again before the program.parse() line.

```
esclu/index.js
program
  .command('bulk <file>')
  .description('read and perform bulk options from the specified file')
  .action(file => {
    fs.stat(file, (err, stats) => {
      if (err) {
        if (program.json) {
          console.log(JSON.stringify(err));
          return;
        }
        throw err;
      }

      const options = {
        url: fullUrl('_bulk'),
        json: true,
        headers: {
          'content-length': stats.size,
          'content-type': 'application/json',
        }
      };
```

---

9. https://stedolan.github.io/jq/manual/v1.5/

```
    const req = request.post(options);

    const stream = fs.createReadStream(file);
    stream.pipe(req);
    req.pipe(process.stdout);
  });
});
```

This command takes a bit more code than the previous ones, but it's mostly stuff you've seen before.

Unlike the get and url commands that took an optional parameter, the bulk command's <file> parameter is required. You can try running esclu bulk without a file parameter to see how the Commander module handles this situation.

Inside the action callback, the first thing we do is use fs.stat() to asynchronously check on the provided file. This asserts that the file exists and can be reached by the user running the process. If for any reason the stat() call was unsuccessful, we produce the correct response—either outputting a JSON object or throwing an exception, depending on whether the user specified the --json flag.

Next, we construct the options for the request. Elasticsearch's _bulk API endpoint expects to receive JSON and we expect to receive JSON back, so we set the json option to true as well as provide a content-type header of application/json.

Using the size information from the stat() call, we can specify the HTTP header content-length. This is important because we'll be streaming the file content to the server rather than handing all the content to the Request module at once.

Using request.post(), we initialize an HTTP POST request to Elasticsearch, capturing the returned object in a variable called req. This object can be used as a writable stream (stream.Writable) for sending content, and also as a readable stream (stream.Readable) for receiving the server's response.

This means we can pipe() content into and out of it, according to Node.js's stream APIs.[10] Here, we're piping the bulk file content from the filesystem into it, and piping the output directly to standard output. The upshot of this approach is that neither the bulk file nor the response from Elasticsearch needs to be wholly resident in the Node.js process's memory.

Lastly, we open a read stream to the file using fs.createReadStream() and pipe that into the request object. As for the server's response, we pipe the request object's output directly to process.stdout.

---

10. https://nodejs.org/api/stream.html

Let's try out the _bulk command, first by failing to supply a file path to see how Commander responds.

```
$ ./esclu bulk
  error: missing required argument `file'
```

No surprise here: esclu knows that the file parameter is required.

Now let's try performing a bulk file insertion. Since the bulk file we created does not list an index or type for each document to insert, we should provide defaults using the --index and --type flags, respectively. Also, since the output will be large, we'll capture it in a file then explore it with jq.

Here's the command you should run:

```
$ ./esclu bulk ../data/bulk_pg.ldj -i books -t book > ../data/bulk_result.json
```

This command assumes that you've been following along, with a data directory that's a sibling of the esclu project directory, and that you've created or downloaded the bulk_pg.ldj as described in Chapter 5, *Transforming Data*, on page 81. If your file is somewhere else, or you'd like to store the result JSON somewhere else, adjust your paths accordingly.

That command may take a while to finish, depending on a variety of factors. For me, on my Ubuntu laptop with an SSD, it takes only a few seconds, but it's hard to tell if that's typical. When the command is finished, take a peek at the JSON using jq.

```
$ cat ../data/bulk_result.json | jq '.' | head -n 20
{
  "took": 3410,
  "errors": false,
  "items": [
    {
      "index": {
        "_index": "books",
        "_type": "book",
        "_id": "pg1",
        "_version": 1,
        "result": "created",
        "_shards": {
          "total": 2,
          "successful": 1,
          "failed": 0
        },
        "created": true,
        "status": 201
      }
    },
```

Three keys are immediately visible in the response JSON object:

- took—How long the request took in milliseconds
- errors—An array of errors that occurred (if any); otherwise false
- items—An array that reports on successfully executed operations

Each object in the items array describes one of the bulk commands. Here we can see just the first such command, whose index key tells the story of the operation.

Note that the status key of the index object has the value 201. You may already be familiar with the HTTP status code 200 OK. Like 200 OK, the HTTP status code 201 Created is also an affirmative code, but it means that an object on the server was created as a result of the request.

Using jq's length function, we can count how many total operations there were.

```
$ cat ../data/bulk_result.json | jq '.items | length'
53212
```

Of course, the number of items you see may be different. Project Gutenberg is adding new books to its catalog all the time.

Now, using our list-indices command, let's check how many documents the books index has:

```
$ ./esclu li
health status index uuid    pri rep docs.count store.size pri.store.size
yellow open    books n9...sQ  5   1     53212     24.5mb         24.5mb
```

Wonderful! As you can see under the docs.count column, all 53,212 documents have been successfully added to the books index.

Implementing an Elasticsearch Query Command

Now that the documents are in the index, we can start querying for them. First we'll take a look around using the existing get command, and then we'll implement a specific command just for querying.

The Elasticsearch API endpoint we want to hit is /_search. We can already hit this endpoint using the get command. Let's try that now.

```
$ ./esclu get '_search' | jq '.' | head -n 20
{
  "took": 3,
  "timed_out": false,
  "_shards": {
    "total": 5,
    "successful": 5,
    "failed": 0
  },
```

```
"hits": {
  "total": 53212,
  "max_score": 1,
  "hits": [
    {
      "_index": "books",
      "_type": "book",
      "_id": "pg100",
      "_score": 1,
      "_source": {
        "id": 100,
        "title": "The Complete Works of William Shakespeare",
```

Peeking at the head of the JSON response gives a good idea of what's in it. As with the bulk API response, we see a took field, which indicates how long the request took to execute in milliseconds.

The results of the query are in the hits object, which contains three fields: total, max_score, and hits. The total field shows that all documents matched the query (we'll perform more specific queries in a bit). The max_score field indicates the score value of the highest-scoring match. And the internal hits key points to an array of individual results.

Note that by default the _search API will return only the top 10 results. This can be increased by specifying the size URL parameter.

To dig into the results further, let's again use the handy command-line tool jq.

Digging into Elasticsearch Results with jq

Using jq, we can dig down into the hits result from a query and see that the _source object is the original document. Try out the following command, which contains a fairly deep filter expression.

```
$ ./esclu get '_search' | jq '.hits.hits[]._source' | head -n 20
{
  "id": 100,
  "title": "The Complete Works of William Shakespeare",
  "authors": [
    "Shakespeare, William"
  ],
  "subjects": [
    "English drama -- Early modern and Elizabethan, 1500-1600"
  ]
}
```

```
{
  "id": 1000,
  "title": "La Divina Commedia di Dante: Complete",
  "authors": [
    "Dante Alighieri"
  ],
  "subjects": []
}
{
  "id": 10000,
```

Here, the jq expression .hits.hits[]._source is a compact way of describing the following steps:

- .hits—Start at the root object and traverse into the object under the key hits.
- .hits—Do this again.
- []—Return each element of the array individually.
- ._source—For each element, return the object under the key _source.

The output is a stream of JSON objects, one after the other. To get a true JSON array instead, we can wrap the whole jq expression in brackets.

```
$ ./esclu get '_search' | jq '[ .hits.hits[]._source ]' | head -n 20
[
  {
    "id": 100,
    "title": "The Complete Works of William Shakespeare",
    "authors": [
      "Shakespeare, William"
    ],
    "subjects": [
      "English drama -- Early modern and Elizabethan, 1500-1600"
    ]
  },
  {
    "id": 1000,
    "title": "La Divina Commedia di Dante: Complete",
    "authors": [
      "Dante Alighieri"
    ],
    "subjects": []
  },
  {
```

Through the _search API, if you pass a query parameter, q, Elasticsearch will use its value to find documents. For example, say we were interested in books by Mark Twain. We could search for documents whose authors array includes the substring Twain using the query expression authors:Twain, like this:

```
$ ./esclu get '_search/?q=authors:Twain' | jq '.' | head -n 30
{
  "took": 3,
  "timed_out": false,
  "_shards": {
    "total": 5,
    "successful": 5,
    "failed": 0
  },
  "hits": {
    "total": 229,
    "max_score": 6.302847,
    "hits": [
      {
        "_index": "books",
        "_type": "book",
        "_id": "pg1837",
        "_score": 6.302847,
        "_source": {
          "id": 1837,
          "title": "The Prince and the Pauper",
          "authors": [
            "Twain, Mark"
          ],
          "subjects": [
            "London (England) -- Fiction",
            "Historical fiction",
            "Boys -- Fiction",
            "Poor children -- Fiction",
            "Social classes -- Fiction",
            "Impostors and imposture -- Fiction",
```

Elasticsearch's query string syntax is a DSL with many useful features like wildcards, Boolean AND/OR operators, negation, and even regular expressions. We'll explore some of these in future chapters, but a full treatment is outside the scope of this book. You can read about these options on Elasticsearch's query string syntax page.[11]

Sometimes when you query Elasticsearch, you may not be interested in retrieving the whole source document for each match. Continuing the previous example, say we wanted to find just the title of each book by Mark Twain. For this, Elasticsearch supports another DSL for specifying a *source filter*.[12] Here we could use the source filter expression _source=title.

---

11. https://www.elastic.co/guide/en/elasticsearch/reference/5.2/query-dsl-query-string-query.html#query-string-syntax

12. https://www.elastic.co/guide/en/elasticsearch/reference/current/search-request-source-filtering.html

```
$ ./esclu get '_search?q=authors:Twain&_source=title' | jq '.' | head -n 30
{
  "took": 2,
  "timed_out": false,
  "_shards": {
    "total": 5,
    "successful": 5,
    "failed": 0
  },
  "hits": {
    "total": 229,
    "max_score": 6.302847,
    "hits": [
      {
        "_index": "books",
        "_type": "book",
        "_id": "pg1837",
        "_score": 6.302847,
        "_source": {
          "title": "The Prince and the Pauper"
        }
      },
      {
        "_index": "books",
        "_type": "book",
        "_id": "pg19987",
        "_score": 6.302847,
        "_source": {
          "title": "Chapters from My Autobiography"
        }
      },
```

Now the _source objects contain only the title key. As you might imagine, this pairs well again with jq, which lets you extract just those specific strings.

(Note the trailing backslash to indicate a continuing line.)

```
$ ./esclu get '_search?q=authors:Twain&_source=title' | \
    jq '.hits.hits[]._source.title'
"The Prince and the Pauper"
"Chapters from My Autobiography"
"The Awful German Language"
"Personal Recollections of Joan of Arc — Volume 1"
"Personal Recollections of Joan of Arc — Volume 2"
"In Defence of Harriet Shelley"
"The Innocents Abroad"
"The Mysterious Stranger, and Other Stories"
"The Curious Republic of Gondour, and Other Whimsical Sketches"
"Jenkkejä maailmalla I\nHeidän toivioretkensä Pyhälle Maalle"
```

Now that we've covered a bit of what you can do with the _search API, let's add a final command to esclu to issue these kinds of queries.

Implementing an Elasticsearch Query Command

Using your understanding of Elasticsearch's _search API endpoint, it's time to add one final command to esclu before closing out the chapter. The command will be called query, with the alias q for short. It will take any number of optional query parts, so the user won't have to wrap the query in quotes.

Here's an example usage of the q command that we'll be adding:

```
$ ./esclu q authors:Twain AND subjects:children
```

As before, we'll want it to understand the --index flag to limit the query to a particular index. But additionally, it would be nice if we could specify an optional source filter expression to limit the output documents.

Begin by adding the --filter option alongside the other options during the initial program setup stanza toward the top of the file.

esclu/index.js
```
program
  // Other options...
  .option('-f, --filter <filter>', 'source filter for query results');
```

Finally, add this new query command just before the program.parse() line at the bottom.

esclu/index.js
```
program
  .command('query [queries...]')
  .alias('q')
  .description('perform an Elasticsearch query')
  .action((queries = []) => {
    const options = {
      url: fullUrl('_search'),
      json: program.json,
      qs: {},
    };

    if (queries && queries.length) {
      options.qs.q = queries.join(' ');
    }

    if (program.filter) {
      options.qs._source = program.filter;
    }

    request(options, handleResponse);
  });
```

This code sets up a query command in much the same fashion as other commands you've created while going through this chapter. The parameter declaration [queries...] tells Commander that we expect any number of arguments to this command (even zero).

Inside the action callback, virtually all of the work focuses on building out the query string for the URL by adding properties to options.qs. request() will take the properties of options.qs and encode them into query string parameters to append to the URL.

If the user provided any query parameters on the command line (using the -q flag), then we would concatenate them with spaces and assign the result to the q parameter. For example, if the user entered esclu -q "Mark" "Twain", then the q parameter would become the string "Mark Twain". When request() encodes options.qs, this would become ?q=Mark%20Twain, appended to the end of the URL. Elasticsearch would then use this q parameter to search for matching documents. Likewise, if the user provided a filter on the command line with the -f flag, we would convert this to a _source parameter for the query string.

Now, continuing with the previous example, if the user only wanted to get back the title field of matching documents, then the thing to do is add -f title to the command line. request() would then encode both options together as ?q=Mark%20Twain&_source=title.

After you save the file, give the new query command a try. The simplest query is the empty query, which matches all documents.

```
$ ./esclu q | jq '.' | head -n 30
{
  "took": 4,
  "timed_out": false,
  "_shards": {
    "total": 5,
    "successful": 5,
    "failed": 0
  },
  "hits": {
    "total": 53212,
    "max_score": 1,
    "hits": [
      {
        "_index": "books",
        "_type": "book",
        "_id": "pg100",
        "_score": 1,
        "_source": {
```

```
              "id": 100,
              "title": "The Complete Works of William Shakespeare",
              "authors": [
                "Shakespeare, William"
              ],
              "subjects": [
                "English drama -- Early modern and Elizabethan, 1500-1600"
              ]
          }
      },
      {
        "_index": "books",
```

To abbreviate output, we can focus on just the title and author fields.

```
$ ./esclu q -f title,authors | jq '.' | head -n 30
{
  "took": 5,
  "timed_out": false,
  "_shards": {
    "total": 5,
    "successful": 5,
    "failed": 0
  },
  "hits": {
    "total": 53212,
    "max_score": 1,
    "hits": [
      {
        "_index": "books",
        "_type": "book",
        "_id": "pg100",
        "_score": 1,
        "_source": {
          "title": "The Complete Works of William Shakespeare",
          "authors": [
            "Shakespeare, William"
          ]
        }
      },
      {
        "_index": "books",
        "_type": "book",
        "_id": "pg1000",
        "_score": 1,
        "_source": {
```

Now using jq we can focus on just the source objects.

```
$ ./esclu q -f title,authors | jq '.hits.hits[]._source' | head -n 30
{
  "title": "The Complete Works of William Shakespeare",
  "authors": [
    "Shakespeare, William"
  ]
}
{
  "title": "La Divina Commedia di Dante: Complete",
  "authors": [
    "Dante Alighieri"
  ]
}
{
  "title": "The Magna Carta",
  "authors": [
    "Anonymous"
  ]
}
{
  "title": "My First Years as a Frenchwoman, 1876-1879",
  "authors": [
    "Waddington, Mary King"
  ]
}
{
  "title": "A Voyage to the Moon\r\nWith Some Account of the Manners and ...
  "authors": [
    "Tucker, George"
  ]
}
```

Taking advantage of the joining of query parts, you can specify a complex query without wrapping it in quotes.

```
$ ./esclu q authors:Shakespeare AND subjects:Drama -f title |\
jq '.hits.hits[]._source.title'
"The Tragedy of Othello, Moor of Venice"
"The Tragedy of Romeo and Juliet"
"The Tempest"
"The Comedy of Errors"
"Othello"
"As You Like It"
"The Two Gentlemen of Verona"
"The Merchant of Venice"
"Two Gentlemen of Verona"
"All's Well That Ends Well"
```

Be aware that if you need any characters that your shell treats as special, you should wrap the whole query in quotes. For example, to do a multiword query with Elasticsearch you can wrap the expression in double quotes (q title:"United States"). But your shell may strip out these quotes unless they're wrapped in another set of quotes (q 'title:"United States"').

Wrapping Up

In this chapter, you learned how to use Node.js to interact with the popular document-oriented datastore Elasticsearch. Elasticsearch stores JSON documents over HTTP and provides a rich search API, making it a great example to learn from as you start to think about creating your own RESTful APIs.

By taking advantage of the Commander module, you developed a command-line utility program with a number of useful commands for getting information into and out of Elasticsearch. In turn, this allowed us to discuss default parameters for JavaScript functions, and the useful Array methods filter() and join().

As for DSLs, you learned the basics of Elasticsearch's query language, which we'll utilize more in upcoming chapters. And, importantly, you used jq to dig into and reshape JSON messages. JSON over HTTP is ubiquitous in Node.js development, and knowing how to quickly dive into an unfamiliar dataset or API is a valuable skill.

Using the Request module made it relatively painless to issue GET, PUT, and POST requests to HTTP endpoints. It even made it easy to stream content from a file to the server, and from the server response to standard output.

Although the Request module follows the Node.js core convention of taking a single callback handler, it can be used with Promises for more fluid handling of asynchronous responses. We'll cover how to do this in upcoming chapters.

The next chapter will build on your knowledge of RESTful/JSON APIs as we use Node.js and Express to develop HTTP endpoints that operate on your Elasticsearch indices. But before we get to that, the following bonus tasks invite you to add more functionality to the incomplete esclu program. See you again soon!

Deleting an Index

Any database you work with will offer at least the following four operations: Create, Read, Update, and Delete (CRUD). RESTful datastores like Elasticsearch use a different HTTP method (or *verb*) for each operation. You use POST to create, GET to read, PUT to update, and DELETE to (you guessed it) delete records.

In this chapter, you've already used three of these four verbs. You used PUT to create an index, GET to query for documents, and POST to upload documents in bulk.

For this task, implement a new command called delete-index, which checks for an index specified with the --index flag and issues an HTTP DELETE request to remove it. (Hint: request.del() issues a DELETE request.)

Adding a Single Document

When creating the esclu program, we made the bulk command, which provided a way for the user to perform bulk operations on Elasticsearch. However, we did not provide a command for performing a single action, such as inserting a new document.

For this task, you'll add a new command called put, which inserts a new document for indexing (or overwrites the existing document if there's a collision).

With the get command, you can already retrieve a book by its _id. For example, here's how to look up *The Art of War* by its ID:

```
$ ./esclu get pg132 --index books --type book | jq '.'
{
  "_index": "books",
  "_type": "book",
  "_id": "pg132",
  "_version": 1,
  "found": true,
  "_source": {
    "id": 132,
    "title": "The Art of War",
    "authors": [
      "Sunzi, active 6th century B.C.",
      "Giles, Lionel"
    ],
    "subjects": [
      "Military art and science -- Early works to 1800",
      "War -- Early works to 1800"
    ]
  }
}
```

Putting a document into Elasticsearch is roughly the opposite maneuver, but the API should be quite similar. For example, say we save the document part of the above response to a file, like so:

```
$ ./esclu get pg132 -i books -t book | jq '._source' > ../data/art_of_war.json
```

Ideally, we should be able to reinsert the document from the file using the following command:

```
$ ./esclu put ../data/art_of_war.json -i books -t book --id pg132
```

To make this work, you'll need to do the following:

- Add a new, optional, --id flag.

- Update the fullUrl() function to append the ID in the returned URL.

- Add a new command called put that takes a single required parameter called file (same as the bulk command).

- Inside the action() callback of your new command, assert that an ID was specified, or fail loudly.

- Stream the contents of the file to Elasticsearch through the request object and stream the results to standard output.

For a reference on the expectation of the Elasticsearch API, see the Index documentation.[13]

If you get all of this working, great! Next, think about how you might relax the requirement that the document came from an actual file. For example, could you make the file part of the put command optional? If the file wasn't specified, how would you read the JSON document content from standard input instead?

---

13. https://www.elastic.co/guide/en/elasticsearch/reference/5.2/docs-index_.html

Part III

Creating an Application from the Ground Up

On top of the infrastructure born out of previous chapters on working with data, we'll craft a web application end to end.

We begin by developing web services that provide bidirectional access to the databases and messaging infrastructure. Using these services, we'll develop a web-based user interface and then harden it for deployment.

Developing RESTful Web Services

Creating web services is what Node.js was made for, and that's still a dominant use case for it. In this chapter, we'll continue the multipart journey to build out a web application, this time by implementing RESTful web services.

It's a long chapter, not because the code is particularly verbose, but because the concepts deserve particular attention. We'll cover all of these topics on the way:

Node.js Core

Node.js 8 is the first long-term support (LTS) version to include async functions, a recent ECMAScript feature. Unlike regular functions that run to completion, async functions allow you to effectively suspend execution to await an asynchronous result. You'll use async functions to dramatically simplify programming sequences of asynchronous events.

Patterns

You'll develop RESTful APIs using Express, backed by Elasticsearch. You'll learn about Express middleware, how to write route handlers, and how to harness Elasticsearch's query APIs. We'll also review and reinforce HTTP methods and status codes for communicating to your services' users.

JavaScriptisms

A Promise is a special kind of object that presents a unified way of dealing with synchronous and asynchronous code flows. You'll use Promise-producing factory methods for issuing HTTP requests. You'll take advantage of destructuring assignment and computed property names to streamline data definitions.

Supporting Code

Configuring your service shouldn't be an exercise in frustration. You'll learn how to use the nconf module for organizing configuration options.

You'll also use nodemon to monitor Node.js programs and automatically restart them when the source changes.

Node.js comes with support for low-overhead HTTP servers out of the box using the http module.[1] But writing services against the low-level http module directly can be a lot of work. So we'll use Express for developing our web services.[2]

Advantages of Express

Express is a web application framework for Node.js, modeled after the Ruby project Sinatra.[3] Express provides a lot of the plumbing code that you'd otherwise end up writing yourself. To see why, let's take a look at a basic Node.js server using only the http module.

```
web-services/server.js
'use strict';
const http = require('http');
const server = http.createServer((req, res) => {
  res.writeHead(200, {'Content-Type': 'text/plain'});
  res.end('Hello World\n');
});
server.listen(60700, () => console.log('Ready!'));
```

This is quite similar to creating a basic TCP server using the net module like you did way back in Chapter 3, *Networking with Sockets*, on page 27. We bring in the http module, call its createServer() method with a callback, and finally use server.listen() to bind a TCP socket for listening. The callback function uses information from the incoming HTTP request (req) to send an appropriate response (res).

What's remarkable about this example isn't what it does, but rather what it doesn't do. A typical web server would take care of lots of little jobs that this code doesn't touch. Here are some examples:

- Routing based on URL paths
- Managing sessions via cookies
- Parsing incoming requests (such as form data or JSON)
- Rejecting malformed requests

The Express framework helps with these and myriad other tasks.

---

1. http://nodejs.org/api/http.html
2. http://expressjs.com/
3. http://www.sinatrarb.com/

Serving APIs with Express

In this section, you'll develop a minimal Hello World application using Express to cover the basics, then we'll move on to something more substantial. Since this project will be short-lived, we won't bother with creating a package.json file.

To begin, create a directory called hello to hold the application, and open a terminal to this directory. Next, install Express and Morgan (a logging utility).

```
$ npm install express@4.14.1 morgan@1.8.1
```

With those modules installed, open a text editor and enter the following:

web-services/hello/server.js
```
'use strict';
const express = require('express');
const morgan = require('morgan');

const app = express();

app.use(morgan('dev'));

app.get('/hello/:name', (req, res) => {
  res.status(200).json({'hello': req.params.name});
});

app.listen(60701, () => console.log('Ready.'));
```

Save this file as server.js in your hello project directory. First, this program brings in the Express module and the Morgan module. Morgan provides HTTP request logging.

Like the Request module we worked with in the last chapter, the Express module is itself a function. When you call this function, Express creates an application context for you. By strong convention, we name this variable app.

Express functionality is provided through *middleware*, which are functions that manipulate the request and response objects. To specify middleware for your app, you call app.use(), passing in the middleware you want. In our case, we're using the morgan middleware set to dev mode, which will log to the console all requests coming in.

Next we use app.get() to tell Express how we want to handle HTTP GET requests to the /hello/:name path. The :name chunk in the path is called a *named route parameter*. When the API is hit, Express will grab that part of the URL and make it available in req.params.

In addition to get(), Express has put(), post(), and delete() methods to register handlers for HTTP PUT, POST, and DELETE requests, respectively. In our case, we tell the response object, res, to send back as JSON an object whose hello key is set to the name parameter.

Finally, this program listens on TCP port 60701 for incoming HTTP requests, and logs a message to the console when it's ready to receive connections. Let's run the app to see what it does.

Open a terminal to the hello directory and run node server.js.

```
$ node server.js
Ready.
```

With the Hello server running, let's try it out in a separate terminal using curl, an extremely useful off-the-shelf command-line program for issuing HTTP requests.

Most popular operating systems come with curl bundled in, but if yours doesn't, pause here and install it. We'll be using curl frequently in this chapter to try out our various APIs.

Now, try hitting the /hello/:name path with curl, supplying your own name in the URL.

```
$ curl -i localhost:60701/hello/jimbo
HTTP/1.1 200 OK
X-Powered-By: Express
Content-Type: application/json; charset=utf-8
Content-Length: 17
ETag: W/"11-vrDYBORw9smBgTMv0r99rA"
Date: Tue, 14 Feb 2017 10:34:13 GMT
Connection: keep-alive

{"hello":"jimbo"}
```

Adding the -i flag tells curl that it should output the HTTP headers in addition to the response body. Note that the HTTP response code was 200 OK, as expected.

Back in the server terminal, you should see something like this (thanks to the Morgan middleware):

```
GET /hello/jimbo 200 3.013 ms - 17
```

By default, curl will display information in the terminal describing the progress of the request. This is useful for large requests, but it can be distracting for smaller requests, especially when you intend to pipe the response into another program, such as jq. To disable this progress output, use the -s flag, meaning silent.

```
$ curl -s localhost:60701/hello/jimbo | jq '.'
{
  "hello": "jimbo"
}
```

Now that we've got the basic outline of an Express REST/JSON service under control, let's build something with a bit more bite to it.

Writing Modular Express Services

Throughout the remainder of the chapter, we're going to build a RESTful web service with Express for creating and managing *book bundles*. These are basically named reading lists. Here's an example of a book bundle:

```
{
  "name": "light reading",
  "books": [{
    "id": "pg132",
    "title": "The Art of War"
  },{
    "id": "pg2680",
    "title": "Meditations",
  },{
    "id": "pg6456",
    "title": "Public Opinion"
  }]
}
```

The name field is a user-defined string to identify the list. Names do not have to be unique. The books field contains a list of the books in that bundle. Each book is identified by its document ID and includes the title of the book.

Our app will be called Better Book Bundle Builder (or B4 for short).

We'll work extensively with the books index that we set up in Chapter 6, *Commanding Databases*, on page 111, as well as a second Elasticsearch index called b4. The application will work roughly as follows:

- It will communicate with two indices: the books index and the b4 index.

- To the B4 application, the books index is read-only (we will not add, delete, or overwrite any documents in it).

- The b4 index will store user data, including the book bundles that users make.

To create the b4 index, make sure Elasticsearch is running, then open a terminal to the esclu directory from the last chapter. Use esclu to create the b4 index:

```
$ ./esclu create-index -i b4
{"acknowledged":true,"shards_acknowledged":true}
```

Now we're ready to create our modular, RESTful web services.

Separating Server Code into Modules

Just like our Hello World example, the main entry point for the b4 service is the server.js file. But instead of assigning a handler with app.get() directly, now we'll specify some configuration parameters and then pull in API modules.

To start, create a directory called b4 to house the B4 project. Next, use npm init to create the basic outline of a package.json. All of the default values are fine.

```
$ mkdir b4
$ cd b4
$ npm init
```

Now install the Express, Morgan, and nconf modules. We'll use the nconf module to manage configuration settings like the hostname and port of the Elasticsearch server.

```
$ npm install --save --save-exact express@4.14.1 morgan@1.8.1 nconf@0.8.4
```

OK, next comes the configuration settings. Open your text editor and enter the following:

web-services/b4/config.json

```json
{
  "port": 60702,
  "es": {
    "host": "localhost",
    "port": 9200,
    "books_index": "books",
    "bundles_index": "b4"
  }
}
```

Save this file as config.json. It contains the port number that Express will listen on as well as information about where to find the Elasticsearch service.

Finally, let's put together the shell of the server.js. Open your editor and enter this:

web-services/b4/server.js

```js
'use strict';
const express = require('express');
const morgan = require('morgan');
const nconf = require('nconf');
const pkg = require('./package.json');
```

```
nconf.argv().env('__');
nconf.defaults({conf: `${__dirname}/config.json`});
nconf.file(nconf.get('conf'));

const app = express();

app.use(morgan('dev'));

app.get('/api/version', (req, res) => res.status(200).send(pkg.version));

app.listen(nconf.get('port'), () => console.log('Ready.'));
```

Aside from the nconf setup, the content of this file should seem pretty familiar to you. Putting the nconf part aside for just a moment, let's step through the rest of the code.

First, as usual, we pull in the modules we depend on. We'll also pull in the package.json contents so we can put out a simple version endpoint.

After setting up nconf, we invoke express() to create the app object. With it, we add Morgan for logging, then establish a simple endpoint at the path /api/version that reports the version listed in package.json.

Finally, we instruct the Express app to listen on our configured port (60702). Let's start this up and try it out; then we'll return to nconf.

```
$ npm start

> b4@1.0.0 start ./code/web-services/b4
> node server.js

Ready.
```

To test it, use curl to hit the /api/version endpoint.

```
$ curl -s "http://localhost:60702/api/version"
1.0.0
```

Great! Looks like everything is working so far. Now let's dig into how nconf manages configuration settings.

The nconf module manages configuration settings through a customizable hierarchy of config files, environment variables, and command-line arguments. The order in which you load a source of configuration determines its precedence. Earlier values stick, meaning that later values will not overwrite them. Here again is the first line of the server.js file that handles setting up nconf:

```
nconf.argv().env('__');
```

This first line means that nconf should load argument variables first, then environment variables. The double underscore string passed to env() means that two underscores should be used to denote object hierarchy when reading from environment variables. This is because many shell programs do not allow colon characters in variable names.

An example should help clarify. In the config.json file, recall that we set es.host to localhost. nconf uses the colon character by default to flatten the object hierarchy, so to get the value of this configuration parameter, we would call nconf.get('es:host') in Node.

Now, we've set it up so that nconf gives us the option to override es:host either as an argument variable or as an environment variable since these are loaded first. To override es:host as a command-line argument, we would invoke server.js from the command line like this:

```
$ node server.js --es:host=some.other.host
```

On the other hand, to override es:host with an environment variable, we would invoke server.js like so:

```
$ es__host=some.other.host node server.js
```

Now let's move on to the second line of the nconf setup code.

```
nconf.defaults({conf: `${__dirname}/config.json`});
```

This line establishes a default value for the conf parameter. This is the path to the configuration file we created earlier. But since we're prioritizing environment variables and command-line arguments, the user could employ either of those mechanisms to override the configuration file path.

For example, to override the config file path using a command-line argument, you could do this:

```
$ node server.js --conf=/path/to/some.other.config.json
```

Finally, in the last line of the nconf setup stanza, we tell nconf to load the file defined in the conf path.

```
nconf.file(nconf.get('conf'));
```

Any values in that file will take effect only if they haven't been set already in the command-line arguments or environment variables.

These three lines give you some pretty amazing flexibility right out of the gate. Of course, you could choose to call the argv(), env(), file(), and other methods in a different order to achieve different effects. Check out the nconf npm page for more info.[4]

---

4.   https://www.npmjs.com/package/nconf

Keeping Services Running with nodemon

Especially during development, it's useful to have your Node.js application automatically restart when files change on disk. We saw a similar technique work well when running tests using Mocha back in *Enabling Continuous Testing with Mocha*, on page 88.

Short for *Node Monitor*, nodemon runs a Node.js program and then automatically restarts it whenever the source code changes or if the process terminates. To use it, first we have to install and save the dependency.

```
$ npm install --save --save-exact nodemon@1.11.0
```

Next, open your package.json file and add a new start command to the scripts section to override the default.

```
"scripts": {
  "start": "nodemon server.js",
  "test": "echo \"Error: no test specified\" && exit 1"
},
```

After you save the package.json file, run npm start again from your terminal.

```
$ npm start
```

```
> b4@1.0.0 start ./code/web-services/b4
> nodemon server.js

[nodemon] 1.11.0
[nodemon] to restart at any time, enter `rs`
[nodemon] watching: *.*
[nodemon] starting `node server.js`
Ready.
```

From here out, you shouldn't have to stop and rerun npm start as you make changes to the files in the B4 project. nodemon will faithfully watch for file changes and restart the process for you.

Adding Search APIs

With the basic structure of the web services project in place, it's time to start adding some APIs. First we'll add APIs for searching the books index, and then we'll add APIs for creating and manipulating book bundles.

To begin, open a terminal to your b4 project directory and add a new subdirectory called lib. This will house the individual modules that contribute API code for the service.

Next, open a text editor and enter the following skeleton code for the search APIs.

web-services/b4/lib/search.js
```
/**
 * Provides API endpoints for searching the books index.
 */
'use strict';
const request = require('request');
module.exports = (app, es) => {

  const url = `http://${es.host}:${es.port}/${es.books_index}/book/_search`;

};
```

Save this file as lib/search.js. At the top, we pull in the Request module, which you may recall from Chapter 6, *Commanding Databases*, on page 111, where it was central to the development of the esclu program.

Next, we assign a function to module.exports that takes two parameters. The app parameter will be the Express application object, and es will contain the configuration parameters relevant to Elasticsearch, as provided through nconf.

Inside the function, all we're doing currently is establishing the URL that will be key to performing searches against the books index. Shortly we'll be adding additional code to this file to implement the APIs.

To use the Request module with this project, go ahead and install it.

```
$ npm install --save --save-exact request@2.79.0
```

Finally, let's wire this new module up in server.js. Open that file now, and add the following in the space between the app.get() line and the app.listen() line:

web-services/b4/server.js
```
require('./lib/search.js')(app, nconf.get('es'));
```

This code brings in the lib/search.js module, then immediately invokes the module function by passing in the Express application object and the Elasticsearch configuration. When you call nconf.get('es'), nconf returns an object that includes all of the settings from es on down.

Once you save the server.js file, nodemon should automatically restart the service. If it fails to start back up for any reason, you should see the relevant exception printed to the console.

However, since lib/search.js currently doesn't do anything with the Express app, there's nothing to test with curl. We'll fix that next.

Using Request with Express

Open lib/search.js using your text editor. Inside the exported module function, after setting up the Elasticsearch url constant, add the following code:

```
web-services/b4/lib/search.js
/**
 * Search for books by matching a particular field value.
 * Example: /api/search/books/authors/Twain
 */
app.get('/api/search/books/:field/:query', (req, res) => {

});
```

This shell establishes an endpoint for the field-search API. The code inside will proceed in two parts.

In the first part we'll construct a request body—an object that will be serialized as JSON and sent to Elasticsearch. In the second part, we'll fire off the request to Elasticsearch, handle the eventual response, and forward the results to the upstream requester that hit the API.

Since we'll be making a request to Elasticsearch, there will be two distinct request/reply pairs that this code will deal with. The first pair is the Express request and response objects called req and res, respectively. To distinguish the Elasticsearch variables from the Express pair, we'll prefix the Elasticsearch variables with es, as in esReq and esRes.

Add the following code to construct the Elasticsearch request body, esReqBody.

```
web-services/b4/lib/search.js
const esReqBody = {
  size: 10,
  query: {
    match: {
      [req.params.field]: req.params.query
    }
  },
};
```

The Elasticsearch request body that we're constructing conforms to Elasticsearch's Request Body Search API.[5] It includes a size parameter that limits the number of documents that will be sent back, and a query object describing what kinds of documents we want to find.

Take a moment to observe how the esReqBody.query.match object is created.

---

5. https://www.elastic.co/guide/en/elasticsearch/reference/5.2/search-request-body.html

```
match: {
  [req.params.field]: req.params.query
}
```

When a JavaScript object literal key is surrounded with brackets, like [req.params.field] is here, this is called a *computed property name*. The expression inside the brackets is evaluated at runtime, and the result is used as the key. In this case, since the expression in brackets is req.params.field, the key used in the match object will be whatever the :field param of the incoming request contained.

For example, say the incoming URL is /api/search/books/authors/Twain. Then the query.match object will have a property called authors whose value is Twain.

With the request body ready to go, add this code underneath to issue the request to Elasticsearch and handle the response:

web-services/b4/lib/search.js
```
const options = {url, json: true, body: esReqBody};
request.get(options, (err, esRes, esResBody) => {

  if (err) {
    res.status(502).json({
      error: 'bad_gateway',
      reason: err.code,
    });
    return;
  }

  if (esRes.statusCode !== 200) {
    res.status(esRes.statusCode).json(esResBody);
    return;
  }

  res.status(200).json(esResBody.hits.hits.map(({_source}) => _source));
});
```

This use of request() is similar to what we first explored back in *Using request to Fetch JSON over HTTP*, on page 121. Here we pass two arguments to request(): an options object and a callback to handle the response. Inside the callback function, most of the code covers potential error conditions.

In the first error-handling block, we deal with the case where the connection couldn't be made at all. If the err object is not null, this means that the connection to Elasticsearch failed before a response could be retrieved. Typically this would be because the Elasticsearch cluster is unreachable—maybe it's down, or the hostname has been misconfigured. It could also be that the server has run out of file descriptors, but this is less common. For whatever reason, if we couldn't get a response from Elasticsearch, then the correct HTTP code to send back to the caller is 502 Bad Gateway.

In the second error-handling block, we've received a response from Elastic-search, but it came with some HTTP status code other than 200 OK. This could be for any of a variety of reasons, such as a 404 Not Found if, say, the books index has not been created. Or during development, while you're experimenting to get the right request body for Elasticsearch, you may receive a 400 Bad Request. In any of these cases, we just pass the response more or less straight through to the caller with the same status code and response body.

Finally, if there were no errors, we extract just the _source objects (the underlying documents) from the Elasticsearch response, and report these to the caller as JSON. The _source extraction code deserves a little extra attention. Here it is again:

```
resBody.hits.hits.map(({_source}) => _source)
```

Note that the repetition of hits.hits is not an accident. This is in fact how Elasticsearch structures query responses (recall the in-depth exploration of these from the last chapter).

The tiny, anonymous callback method passed here into the map() method uses a technique called *destructuring assignment*. The pair of curly braces in the parameter to the anonymous function, ({_source}), indicates that we expect an object with a property named _source, and that we want to create a local variable of the same name with the same value.

You can use destructuring assignment when declaring variables, as well. The following code is identical in effect to the code we've been discussing.

```
resBody.hits.hits.map(hit => {
  const {_source} = hit;
  return _source;
})
```

If you've been following along, the new search API code you've been filling in should look like the following:

```
web-services/b4/lib/search.js
/**
 * Search for books by matching a particular field value.
 * Example: /api/search/books/authors/Twain
 */
app.get('/api/search/books/:field/:query', (req, res) => {

  const esReqBody = {
    size: 10,
    query: {
      match: {
```

```
      [req.params.field]: req.params.query
    }
  },
};

const options = {url, json: true, body: esReqBody};
request.get(options, (err, esRes, esResBody) => {

  if (err) {
    res.status(502).json({
      error: 'bad_gateway',
      reason: err.code,
    });
    return;
  }

  if (esRes.statusCode !== 200) {
    res.status(esRes.statusCode).json(esResBody);
    return;
  }

  res.status(200).json(esResBody.hits.hits.map(({_source}) => _source));
});

});
```

Save your search.js file if you haven't already. Provided nodemon is still running, your server should automatically restart and you can try out the API immediately.

Now let's use curl and jq to list some of Shakespeare's works.

```
$ curl -s localhost:60702/api/search/books/authors/Shakespeare | jq '.[].title'
"Venus and Adonis"
"The Second Part of King Henry the Sixth"
"King Richard the Second"
"The Tragedy of Romeo and Juliet"
"A Midsummer Night's Dream"
"Much Ado about Nothing"
"The Tragedy of Julius Caesar"
"As You Like It"
"The Tragedy of Othello, Moor of Venice"
"The Tragedy of Macbeth"
```

Using this API, you can search other fields, as well. For example, you could search for books with *Sawyer* in the title:

```
$ curl -s localhost:60702/api/search/books/title/sawyer | jq '.[].title'
"Tom Sawyer Abroad"
"Tom Sawyer, Detective"
"The Adventures of Tom Sawyer"
"Tom Sawyer\nKoulupojan historia"
"Tom Sawyer Abroad"
"Tom Sawyer, Detective"
"The Adventures of Tom Sawyer, Part 3."
```

```
"De Lotgevallen van Tom Sawyer"
"The Adventures of Tom Sawyer"
"Les Aventures De Tom Sawyer"
```

If you're getting results like these, great! It's time to move on to the next API, which returns suggestions based on a search term.

Simplifying Code Flows with Promises

In this section, you'll add another API to your lib/search.js file. Like the /search/books API from last section, this /suggest API will hit your Elasticsearch cluster for information, but this time we'll use Promises rather than callbacks to manage asynchronous control flow.

Fulfilling Promises

To understand Promises, it helps to start with a brief review of JavaScript code flow and the mechanisms for structuring it. Whenever a regular JavaScript function starts executing, it will finish in one of two ways: either it will run to completion (success) or it will throw an exception (failure).

For synchronous code this is good enough, but for asynchronous code we need a bit more. The Node.js core module callbacks use two arguments to reflect these two cases; e.g., (err, data) => {...}. And EventEmitters use different event types (like data and error) to distinguish success and failure modes.

Promises offer yet another way to manage asynchronous results. A *Promise* is an object that encapsulates these two possible results (success and failure) for an operation. Once the associated operation has completed, the Promise will either be *resolved* (success case) or *rejected* (error case). When using a Promise, you attach callback functions for these cases using .then() and .catch(), respectively.

Let's take a look at a quick example.

```
const promise = new Promise((resolve, reject) => {
  // If successful:
  resolve(someSuccessValue);
  // Otherwise:
  reject(someErrorValue);
});
```

Here we're creating a new Promise, passing in an anonymous callback function that is invoked immediately. The resolve and reject parameters are callback functions you should invoke to resolve or reject the Promise, respectively. The value you pass to these functions will be sent forward to any .then() or .catch() handlers.

Let's add those next.

```
promise.then(someSuccessValue => { /* Do something on success. */ });
promise.catch(someErrorValue => { /* Do something on failure. */ });
```

Now, whenever the Promise is *settled*, the appropriate callback will be invoked. Importantly, it doesn't matter whether the Promise has already been settled when you attach handlers with .then() and .catch(). If the Promise has already been settled, those handlers will be called right away. But if the Promise has yet to be settled, then those handlers will wait to be called when it is. Contrast this with a typical EventEmitter—if you attached your .on('error') handler too late, you'll simply miss out on handling the event.

A Promise can only ever be settled once. That is, once a Promise has been resolved or rejected, it can't be resolved or rejected again. This doesn't stop you from attaching more callbacks using .then() or .catch(), but it does guarantee that any particular callback added this way will be invoked at most once. Once again, contrast this with a typical EventEmitter, which may emit many data or error events.

That's enough theory for now. Let's see Promises in action.

Using a Promise with request

Start by adding the following shell code to your lib/search.js below the previous /search/books API to create the /suggest API endpoint.

web-services/b4/lib/search.js
```
/**
 * Collect suggested terms for a given field based on a given query.
 * Example: /api/suggest/authors/lipman
 */
app.get('/api/suggest/:field/:query', (req, res) => {
});
```

As with the /searchi/books API, this API takes two parameters: the :field for which we want suggestions and the :query to suggest from.

Now, inside the shell we need to construct the Elasticsearch request body and the rest of the options to send through request().

web-services/b4/lib/search.js
```
const esReqBody = {
  size: 0,
  suggest: {
    suggestions: {
      text: req.params.query,
      term: {
        field: req.params.field,
```

```
        suggest_mode: 'always',
      },
    }
  }
};
```

```
const options = {url, json: true, body: esReqBody};
```

This request body is designed to trigger Elasticsearch's Search Suggesters feature.[6] Setting the size parameter to zero informs Elasticsearch that we don't want any matching documents returned, just the suggestions.

Elasticsearch's Suggest API allows you to request multiple kinds of suggestions in the same request, but here we're submitting only one. If the request succeeds, we expect to get back a JSON object that contains something like the following, which resulted from an authors search for the string *lipman*:

```
{
  "suggest": {
    "suggestions": [
      {
        "text": "lipman",
        "offset": 0,
        "length": 6,
        "options": [
          {
            "text": "lilian",
            "score": 0.6666666,
            "freq": 26
          },
          {
            "text": "lippmann",
            "score": 0.6666666,
            "freq": 5
          },
          // ...
        ]
      }
    ]
  }
}
```

To get this result, let's use request() like we did for the /search/books API, but this time we'll use a Promise. Add the following code after creating the options object.

web-services/b4/lib/search.js
```
const promise = new Promise((resolve, reject) => {
  request.get(options, (err, esRes, esResBody) => {
```

---

6. https://www.elastic.co/guide/en/elasticsearch/reference/5.2/search-suggesters.html

```
  if (err) {
    reject({error: err});
    return;
  }

  if (esRes.statusCode !== 200) {
    reject({error: esResBody});
    return;
  }

  resolve(esResBody);
  });
});

promise
  .then(esResBody => res.status(200).json(esResBody.suggest.suggestions))
  .catch(({error}) => res.status(error.status || 502).json(error));
```

This code proceeds in two parts. First we create the Promise, then we attach callbacks to it.

In the Promise-creation part, we call out to request() just like in the previous API. But this time, instead of handling the results directly, we either reject or resolve the Promise.

The two rejection cases are the same as before. If the Elasticsearch cluster is unreachable, then the err object will be populated. On the other hand, if the request is malformed, then the err object will be null but the statusCode will be something other than 200 OK. In both cases, we want to reject the Promise so that any .catch() handlers are invoked.

Notice that the object passed to reject() has a single key called error that includes the error details. This is a design choice that I'll explain in a bit. When calling reject() for a Promise, you're free to give it any value you like (or none at all).

In the event that Elasticsearch was reachable and returned a 200 OK status code, we resolve the Promise.

Once the Promise has been created, we attach a .then() and a .catch() handler. The .then() handler sets the Express response status to 200, then extracts and serializes the suggest.suggestions object returned from Elasticsearch.

The .catch() handler extracts the .error property of the object provided. It does this using the destructuring assignment technique we used earlier when extracting the _source documents in the /search/books API. Inside the callback, we use the error object to set the response status code and body.

Save your lib/search.js if you haven't already. To review, your /suggest API code should look like the following:

web-services/b4/lib/search.js

```
/**
 * Collect suggested terms for a given field based on a given query.
 * Example: /api/suggest/authors/lipman
 */
app.get('/api/suggest/:field/:query', (req, res) => {

  const esReqBody = {
    size: 0,
    suggest: {
      suggestions: {
        text: req.params.query,
        term: {
          field: req.params.field,
          suggest_mode: 'always',
        },
      }
    }
  };

  const options = {url, json: true, body: esReqBody};

  const promise = new Promise((resolve, reject) => {
    request.get(options, (err, esRes, esResBody) => {

      if (err) {
        reject({error: err});
        return;
      }

      if (esRes.statusCode !== 200) {
        reject({error: esResBody});
        return;
      }

      resolve(esResBody);
    });
  });

  promise
    .then(esResBody => res.status(200).json(esResBody.suggest.suggestions))
    .catch(({error}) => res.status(error.status || 502).json(error));
```

Once you save the file, nodemon should pick up the changes and restart the service automatically. Now we can hit the service with curl and jq.

First, let's try finding author suggestions for the string *lipman*.

```
$ curl -s localhost:60702/api/suggest/authors/lipman | jq '.'
[
  {
    "text": "lipman",
    "offset": 0,
    "length": 6,
    "options": [
      {
        "text": "lilian",
        "score": 0.6666666,
        "freq": 26
      },
      {
        "text": "lippmann",
        "score": 0.6666666,
        "freq": 5
      },
      {
        "text": "lampman",
        "score": 0.6666666,
        "freq": 3
      },
      {
        "text": "lanman",
        "score": 0.6666666,
        "freq": 3
      },
      {
        "text": "lehman",
        "score": 0.6666666,
        "freq": 3
      }
    ]
  }
]
```

If you see this, great! Things are working as expected.

Of course, you can use jq to extract just the text of the suggestions if you like.

```
$ curl -s localhost:60702/api/suggest/authors/lipman | jq '.[].options[].text'
"lilian"
"lippmann"
"lampman"
"lanman"
"lehman"
```

Next, let's look at a module called request-promise, which streamlines the use of Promises with the request() module for issuing requests.

Replacing request with request-promise

Recall in the last section, where we created a Promise to abstract out the fulfillment of the asynchronous request from the handling of the success and failure cases. In practice, you won't usually use new Promise() to create a Promise for a bit of asynchronous functionality. It's considerably more common for Promises to be created by factory methods.

For example, you can use the static method Promise.resolve() to create a new Promise and immediately resolve it.

```
Promise.resolve("exampleValue")
  .then(val => console.log(val));  // Logs "exampleValue".
```

In the case of request(), there's a module called request-promise that wraps the various request methods to return Promises instead of taking a callback. To use it, start by installing it with npm.

```
$ npm install --save --save-exact request-promise@4.1.1
```

Next, add a require() line to the top of your lib/search.js to pull it in as a constant named rp.

web-services/b4/lib/search.js
```
const rp = require('request-promise');
```

Now it's a drop-in replacement for the Promise-creating code we used in the previous section. This simplifies the whole block down to just this:

web-services/b4/lib/search.js
```
rp({url, json: true, body: esReqBody})
  .then(esResBody => res.status(200).json(esResBody.suggest.suggestions))
  .catch(({error}) => res.status(error.status || 502).json(error));
```

This is the reason that I elected to wrap the rejection value in an object whose .error property contained the error—so that we could use request-promise as a replacement.

For the rest of the APIs in this chapter, we'll use request-promise rather than regular request(). Now let's move on to building out the API endpoints for working with book bundles. Unlike the /search/books and /suggest APIs, which only retrieved data from Elasticsearch, the bundle APIs will need to create, update, and delete records as well.

Manipulating Documents RESTfully

In the first half of this chapter, you developed APIs for discovering and returning books based on a variety of search criteria. In this second half, you'll be creating APIs for manipulating book bundles. Recall that a book bundle has a name and maintains a collection of related books.

Here's an example of a book bundle:

```
{
  "name": "light reading",
  "books": [{
    "id": "pg132",
    "title": "The Art of War"
  },{
    "id": "pg2680",
    "title": "Meditations",
  },{
    "id": "pg6456",
    "title": "Public Opinion"
  }]
}
```

Creating these APIs will be programmatically more intensive than creating the search APIs because they require more back-and-forth between your Node.js service and the underlying datastore. For example, consider an API to update the name of a bundle. Roughly speaking, your Node.js code will need to do the following:

1. Retrieve the bundle from Elasticsearch.

2. Update the name field on the object in memory.

3. Put the updated object back into Elasticsearch.

In addition to handling these asynchronously and in order, you'll have to deal with various failure modes. What if Elasticsearch is down? What if the bundle doesn't exist? What if the bundle changed between the time Node.js downloaded it and the time it reuploaded it? What if Elasticsearch fails to update for some other reason?

Some of these considerations were already covered while creating the search APIs, but you get the point. There are a lot of ways a sequence of asynchronous events could fail midstride, and it's important to think about what kind of response you should provide to users of your API. What HTTP status code is closest to explaining the situation? What kind of error message should you present?

We'll cover much of this as we go along, so let's get to it. To begin, create a file called lib/bundle.js.

```
web-services/b4/lib/bundle.js
/**
 * Provides API endpoints for working with book bundles.
 */
'use strict';
const rp = require('request-promise');

module.exports = (app, es) => {

  const url = `http://${es.host}:${es.port}/${es.bundles_index}/bundle`;

};
```

Next, open your server.js and use require() to bring in the bundle API.

```
web-services/b4/server.js
require('./lib/bundle.js')(app, nconf.get('es'));
```

To create a new resource using a RESTful API, the right HTTP method to use is POST. Recall that POST is good for creating a resource when you don't know the URL where that resource will reside.

This is the case for the book bundles. Although each bundle has a name parameter, these are not guaranteed to be unique, and so they don't make good identifiers. It's better to let Elasticsearch automatically generate an identifier for each bundle as it's created.

Add this code to your module.exports function for creating a book bundle:

```
web-services/b4/lib/bundle.js
/**
 * Create a new bundle with the specified name.
 * curl -X POST http://<host>:<port>/api/bundle?name=<name>
 */
app.post('/api/bundle', (req, res) => {
  const bundle = {
    name: req.query.name || '',
    books: [],
  };

  rp.post({url, body: bundle, json: true})
    .then(esResBody => res.status(201).json(esResBody))
    .catch(({error}) => res.status(error.status || 502).json(error));
});
```

To begin, we're using app.post() rather than app.get() as with previous APIs. This means Express will use this handler only when the incoming HTTP request is using the POST method. This API does not take any named route parameters, but docs expect one optional query parameter called name.

Inside the callback, first we construct the bundle object, which consists of a name field (which may be the empty string), and an initially empty list to hold the books that will be added to the bundle.

Next, we use rp.post() to fire off a POST request to Elasticsearch, passing it the JSON-encoded bundle object we just created. rp.post() returns a Promise, to which we attach success and failure callbacks using .then() and .catch(). This is the same pattern we used in the /suggest API earlier, but instead of 200 OK we return a 201 Created HTTP status code. Once you save the lib/bundle.js file, it should be ready to try out. Open a terminal and use curl to create a bundle.

```
$ curl -s -X POST localhost:60702/api/bundle?name=light%20reading | jq '.'
{
  "_index": "b4",
  "_type": "bundle",
  "_id": "AVuFkyXcpWVRyMBC8pgr",
  "_version": 1,
  "result": "created",
  "_shards": {
    "total": 2,
    "successful": 1,
    "failed": 0
  },
  "created": true
}
```

Note the _id field. This is automatically generated by Elasticsearch for the new bundle document that was just created. Copy this string, as you'll need it for the remaining examples in this chapter. It may help to put it in an environment variable for easy retrieval.

```
$ BUNDLE_ID=AVuFkyXcpWVRyMBC8pgr
$ echo $BUNDLE_ID
AVuFkyXcpWVRyMBC8pgr
```

Using curl, we can hit Elasticsearch directly to check on this bundle document.

```
$ curl -s localhost:9200/b4/bundle/$BUNDLE_ID | jq '.'
{
  "_index": "b4",
  "_type": "bundle",
  "_id": "AVuFkyXcpWVRyMBC8pgr",
  "_version": 1,
  "found": true,
  "_source": {
    "name": "light reading",
    "books": []
  }
}
```

In the next section, we'll add an API to perform exactly this kind of lookup so we don't have to go to Elasticsearch directly. While doing that, we'll explore one of the most exciting new features of Node.js 8: async functions.

Emulating Synchronous Style with async and await

One of the most powerful new features in Node.js 8 is the introduction of *async functions*. Part of the 2017 ECMAScript draft specification, async functions allow you reap the benefits of Promises for simplifying code flow while structuring your code in a more natural way.

The key is that unlike a regular function, which always runs to completion, an async function can be intentionally suspended midexecution to wait on the resolution of a Promise. Note that this does not violate the central maxim that JavaScript is single-threaded. It's not that some other code will preempt your async function, but rather that you choose to unblock the event loop to *await* a Promise.

An example should clarify. Consider this contrived function that returns a Promise.

```
const delay = (timeout = 0, success = true) => {
  const promise = new Promise((resolve, reject) => {
    setTimeout(() => {
      if (success) {
        resolve(`RESOLVED after ${timeout} ms.`);
      } else {
        reject(`REJECTED after ${timeout} ms.`);
      }
    }, timeout);
  });
  return promise;
};
```

The delay() function takes two arguments, a timeout in milliseconds and a success Boolean value that indicates whether the returned Promise should be resolved (true) or rejected (false) after the specified amount of time. Using the delay() function is pretty straightforward—you call its .then() and .catch() methods to assign callback handlers. Here's an example:

```
const useDelay = () => {
  delay(500, true)
    .then(msg => console.log(msg))     // Logs "RESOLVED after 500 ms."
    .catch(err => console.log(err));   // Never called.
};
```

The useDelay() function invokes the delay() to get a Promise that's scheduled to be resolved after 500 milliseconds. Whether the Promise is resolved or rejected, the result is logged to the console.

Now, let's see what useDelay() would look like as an async function.

```
const useDelay = async () => {
  try {
    const msg = await delay(500, true);
    console.log(msg);  // Logs "RESOLVED after 500 ms."
  } catch (err) {
    console.log(err);  // Never called.
  }
};
```

First, notice the addition of the async keyword in the function declaration. This signals that the function can use the await keyword to suspend while resolving a Promise.

Next, check out the await keyword inside the try{} block, right before the call to delay(). Inside of an async function, await suspends execution until the Promise has been settled. If the Promise is resolved, then the await expression evaluates to the resolved value and the async function picks up where it left off.

On the other hand, if the Promise is rejected, then the rejection value gets thrown as an exception. In this case, we use the catch{} block to handle it.

Using async functions together with Promises presents a consistent, synchronous coding style for both synchronous and asynchronous operations. To practice, we'll use async functions for the remaining bundle APIs that we'll be adding.

Providing an Async Handler Function to Express

Open your lib/bundle.js and add the following inside the module.exports function, after the bundle-creation API you added previously.

web-services/b4/lib/bundle.js
```
/**
 * Retrieve a given bundle.
 * curl http://<host>:<port>/api/bundle/<id>
 */
app.get('/api/bundle/:id', async (req, res) => {
  const options = {
    url: `${url}/${req.params.id}`,
    json: true,
  };
```

```
  try {
    const esResBody = await rp(options);
    res.status(200).json(esResBody);
  } catch (esResErr) {
    res.status(esResErr.statusCode || 502).json(esResErr.error);
  }
});
```

This code block sets up a handler for the /bundle/:id route, which will allow us to retrieve a book bundle by its ID. Note the use of async before the function parameters in the opening line to indicate that we're using an async function. Inside the async function, like with other route handlers, the code proceeds in two parts: the setup of options and the request to Elasticsearch.

After setting up the options, we use a try/catch block to handle the success and failure modes of the Elasticsearch request. We issue the Elasticsearch request itself with the expression await rp(options). This causes the async function to suspend while waiting for the Promise to be settled.

If the Promise is resolved, then the return value of the await expression will be the Elasticsearch response body. In this case, we send it onward with a 200 OK status via the Express response object, res.

If the Promise is rejected, then the await expression throws the rejection value as an exception, which we catch and process. In this case, the rejection value is an object with rich information about the nature of the failure. We use that object's .statusCode and .error properties to close out the Express response.

Let's try this out using curl and jq. Open the terminal where you saved the BUNDLE_ID earlier and run the following command:

```
$ curl -s localhost:60702/api/bundle/$BUNDLE_ID | jq '.'
{
  "_index": "b4",
  "_type": "bundle",
  "_id": "AVuFkyXcpWVRyMBC8pgr",
  "_version": 1,
  "found": true,
  "_source": {
    "name": "light reading",
    "books": []
  }
}
```

The bundle object itself is in the _source property of this object. You can also try getting a bundle for a nonexistent ID to see what that returns.

```
$ curl -s localhost:60702/api/bundle/no-such-bundle | jq '.'
{
  "_index": "b4",
  "_type": "bundle",
  "_id": "no-such-bundle",
  "found": false
}
```

Back in your terminal that's running Node.js, you should see lines like the following:

```
GET /api/bundle/AVuFkyXcpWVRyMBC8pgr 200 60.512 ms - 133
GET /api/bundle/no-such-bundle 404 40.986 ms - 69
```

You should know one quick thing about the try/catch block before we move on. Consider this bad implementation that omits the try/catch block:

web-services/b4/lib/bundle.js
```
// BAD IMPLEMENTATION! async Express handler without a try/catch block.
app.get('/api/bundle/:id', async (req, res) => {
  const options = {
    url: `${url}/${req.params.id}`,
    json: true,
  };

  const esResBody = await rp(options);
  res.status(200).json(esResBody);
});
```

What would happen if the Promise returned by the rp() call was rejected instead of resolved? Do you have a guess?

Let's try it out. Comment out the try/catch lines from your async function, then save the file. Then try again to access a nonexistent bundle with curl using the verbose flag.

```
$ curl -v localhost:60702/api/bundle/no-such-bundle
*   Trying 127.0.0.1...
* Connected to localhost (127.0.0.1) port 60702 (#0)
> GET /api/bundle/no-such-bundle HTTP/1.1
> Host: localhost:60702
> User-Agent: curl/7.47.0
> Accept: */*
>
```

You should notice two things. First, the curl call never seems to terminate. It just hangs there after sending the request but receiving no response.

The second thing to notice is the warning messages in the Node.js terminal.

```
(node:16075) UnhandledPromiseRejectionWarning: Unhandled promise rejection
    (rejection id: 1): StatusCodeError: 404 - {"_index":"b4","_type":"bundle",
    "_id":"no-such-bundle","found":false}
(node:16075) DeprecationWarning: Unhandled promise rejections are deprecated.
    In the future, Promise rejections that are not handled will terminate the
    Node.js process with a nonzero exit code.
```

It turns out that indeed the await clause triggers the rejection object to be thrown, but since it's not caught inside the async function, it bubbles up to a Promise returned by the async function itself. That Promise is rejected, but since its rejection wasn't handled, we get warnings.

The moral of the story is always provide a try/catch block when using an async function as an Express route handler. More generally, it'll depend on the purpose of your async function, but as a rule of thumb you should consider the consequence of rejected Promises and take action accordingly.

Now let's move on to adding a few more APIs.

Setting the Bundle Name with PUT

Now we'll use an async function to implement an API endpoint that allows setting the name property of a book bundle.

Open your lib/bundle.js and add the following, after the GET bundle API.

```
web-services/b4/lib/bundle.js
/**
 * Set the specified bundle's name with the specified name.
 * curl -X PUT http://<host>:<port>/api/bundle/<id>/name/<name>
 */
app.put('/api/bundle/:id/name/:name', async (req, res) => {
  const bundleUrl = `${url}/${req.params.id}`;

  try {
    const bundle = (await rp({url: bundleUrl, json: true}))._source;

    bundle.name = req.params.name;

    const esResBody =
      await rp.put({url: bundleUrl, body: bundle, json: true});
    res.status(200).json(esResBody);

  } catch (esResErr) {
    res.status(esResErr.statusCode || 502).json(esResErr.error);
  }
});
```

Inside the async function, first we build out the bundleUrl based on the provided ID. Next, we begin the try/catch block in which we'll perform all of the Elasticsearch requests and response handling.

Take a look at the first line inside the try{} block. Here, we're using await with rp() to suspend as before, but it's a parenthesized expression. Outside of the expression, we use ._source to pull out just the bundle object from the broader Elasticsearch response. This demonstrates that the results of an awaited Promise can be used in more complex expressions.

Once we have the bundle object, we overwrite its name field with the provided name parameter value. Then it's time to PUT that object back into Elasticsearch with rp.put(). The resulting Elasticsearch response body should contain information about the successful operation, which we send back through the Express response.

As usual, if anything went wrong we catch the Elasticsearch response error and report back through the Express response. One you save the file, you can try it out.

In the same terminal where you have the BUNDLE_ID still saved as an environment variable, run the following to set the bundle name to *foo*:

```
$ curl -s -X PUT localhost:60702/api/bundle/$BUNDLE_ID/name/foo | jq '.'
{
  "_index": "b4",
  "_type": "bundle",
  "_id": "AVuFkyXcpWVRyMBC8pgr",
  "_version": 2,
  "result": "updated",
  "_shards": {
    "total": 2,
    "successful": 1,
    "failed": 0
  },
  "created": false
}
```

You can confirm that it was indeed saved by retrieving the bundle using the GET bundle API.

```
$ curl -s localhost:60702/api/bundle/$BUNDLE_ID | jq '._source'
{
  "name": "foo",
  "books": []
}
```

Note that Express routes treat forward slashes as delimiters, so if you wanted to set the name of a bundle to *foo/bar*, you'd need to URI-encode the slash as *%2F*. The same goes for other special characters such as question marks and hash symbols.

Now let's move on to more complex route handlers. Next you'll learn how to manage concurrent unsettled Promises to make simultaneous asynchronous requests.

Putting a Book into a Bundle

Things are going really well for our bundle APIs. At this point, you can create a bundle, retrieve a bundle, and set the bundle's name.

However, the important feature of the bundle is its ability to store a set of books, and we don't yet have any way to manage them. In this section, you'll add an API endpoint for putting a book into a bundle.

Let's get to the code. Open your lib/bundle.js and add the following after all of the other APIs you've added, inside the module.exports() function:

web-services/b4/lib/bundle.js
```
/**
 * Put a book into a bundle by its id.
 * curl -X PUT http://<host>:<port>/api/bundle/<id>/book/<pgid>
 */
app.put('/api/bundle/:id/book/:pgid', async (req, res) => {
  const bundleUrl = `${url}/${req.params.id}`;

  const bookUrl =
      `http://${es.host}:${es.port}` +
      `/${es.books_index}/book/${req.params.pgid}`;

  try {

  } catch (esResErr) {
    res.status(esResErr.statusCode || 502).json(esResErr.error);
  }
});
```

This shell code sets up the API to PUT a book, identified by its Project Gutenberg ID, into a bundle identified by its bundle ID. The try{} block is currently empty; we'll fill that in next.

This is the first API that has to make requests to both the book's Elasticsearch index and the bundle index. So at the outset of the implementation, we compute the URL to both objects within their respective indices. We'll need to grab the book out of the books index to add it to the bundle.

The catch{} block at the bottom predictably forwards any failed request information back through the Express request like all the other APIs have done. Now let's fill in the try{} block, which introduces some new techniques. Start by adding the following:

```
web-services/b4/lib/bundle.js
// Request the bundle and book in parallel.
const [bundleRes, bookRes] = await Promise.all([
  rp({url: bundleUrl, json: true}),
  rp({url: bookUrl, json: true}),
]);
```

The Promise.all() method takes an array of Promises (technically, an iterable object containing Promises) and returns a new Promise based on all of them.[7] The all Promise will be resolved when every one of the Promises passed in has been resolved, and its returned value will be an array of the passed-in Promises' returned values in the same order.

When any of the passed-in Promises is rejected, then the all Promise is rejected immediately. This means if multiple passed-in Promises are rejected, the all Promise will only get the value of the first one.

The array of Promises we pass to Promise.all() contains the rp() invocations to retrieve the bundle and book from their respective indices. This initiates the requests in parallel.

We await the all Promise and then use destructuring assignment to pull out the respective bundle and book response objects. If either request fails, its rp() Promise will be rejected, the rejection value will be thrown, and we'll handle it in the catch{} block, passing it along to the Express response.

By contrast, consider if we'd written the code this way:

```
const bundleRes = rp({url: bundleUrl, json: true});
const bookRes = rp({url: bookUrl, json: true});
```

This would work, producing the same outcome: bundleRes and bookRes are populated. But the book request would not begin until the bundle request had already completed.

Now let's add the rest of the code in the try{} block. Add the following after the Promise.all() piece:

---

7.   https://developer.mozilla.org/en-US/docs/Web/JavaScript/Reference/Iteration_protocols

```
web-services/b4/lib/bundle.js
// Extract bundle and book information from responses.
const {_source: bundle, _version: version} = bundleRes;
const {_source: book} = bookRes;

const idx = bundle.books.findIndex(book => book.id === req.params.pgid);
if (idx === -1) {
  bundle.books.push({
    id: req.params.pgid,
    title: book.title,
  });
}

// Put the updated bundle back in the index.
const esResBody = await rp.put({
  url: bundleUrl,
  qs: { version },
  body: bundle,
  json: true,
});
res.status(200).json(esResBody);
```

First, this code uses destructuring assignment to extract and rename some variables from the bundle and book responses. This includes the book and bundle objects themselves as well as the version of the bundle. The version is needed to detect race conditions when updating the document.

After extracting the variables, we use Array.findIndex() to determine whether that book is already in the bundle. If not, we push it onto the end of the bundle.books array. Then it's time to send the updated bundle back up to Elasticsearch.

Notice that when putting the bundle document back in the bundle index, our call to rp() includes a query string (qs) field. Here we pass in the bundle version number that we previously read from the bundleRes.

When Elasticsearch receives this request, it will check that its internal version number for that document matches the query string parameter. If they don't match, then it means that the document has changed somehow and Elasticsearch will send back a 409 Conflict HTTP status code. This would cause the await clause to throw an exception, again handled by the catch{} block.

If everything went well, we send a 200 OK back through the Express response, along with the Elasticsearch response body. If you've been following along, your API code to add a book should now look like this:

web-services/b4/lib/bundle.js

```javascript
/**
 * Put a book into a bundle by its id.
 * curl -X PUT http://<host>:<port>/api/bundle/<id>/book/<pgid>
 */
app.put('/api/bundle/:id/book/:pgid', async (req, res) => {
  const bundleUrl = `${url}/${req.params.id}`;

  const bookUrl =
    `http://${es.host}:${es.port}` +
    `/${es.books_index}/book/${req.params.pgid}`;

  try {
    // Request the bundle and book in parallel.
    const [bundleRes, bookRes] = await Promise.all([
      rp({url: bundleUrl, json: true}),
      rp({url: bookUrl, json: true}),
    ]);

    // Extract bundle and book information from responses.
    const {_source: bundle, _version: version} = bundleRes;
    const {_source: book} = bookRes;

    const idx = bundle.books.findIndex(book => book.id === req.params.pgid);
    if (idx === -1) {
      bundle.books.push({
        id: req.params.pgid,
        title: book.title,
      });
    }

    // Put the updated bundle back in the index.
    const esResBody = await rp.put({
      url: bundleUrl,
      qs: { version },
      body: bundle,
      json: true,
    });
    res.status(200).json(esResBody);

  } catch (esResErr) {
    res.status(esResErr.statusCode || 502).json(esResErr.error);
  }
});
```

Save your lib/bundle.js if you haven't already. nodemon should automatically restart your service, and now we can test it.

Presuming you still have your BUNDLE_ID environment variable handy from earlier, let's add a book to it. Here we'll add *The Art of War*, which has Project Gutenberg ID 132.

```
$ curl -s -X PUT localhost:60702/api/bundle/$BUNDLE_ID/book/pg132 | jq '.'
{
  "_index": "b4",
  "_type": "bundle",
  "_id": "AVuFkyXcpWVRyMBC8pgr",
  "_version": 3,
  "result": "updated",
  "_shards": {
    "total": 2,
    "successful": 1,
    "failed": 0
  },
  "created": false
}
```

And now we can confirm that it was added by getting the bundle again using the retrieve API.

```
$ curl -s localhost:60702/api/bundle/$BUNDLE_ID | jq '._source'
{
  "name": "foo",
  "books": [
    {
      "id": "pg132",
      "title": "The Art of War"
    }
  ]
}
```

Great! We don't yet have an API to remove a book from a bundle or delete a bundle entirely. But don't worry—those will be bonus tasks described momentarily.

Wrapping Up

This was a big chapter on creating RESTful APIs using Express. Let's take a minute to reflect.

We started off with the basics—installing Express and a logging utility called Morgan. You learned how to put together the rough outline of an Express-powered web service using Node.

To manage the configuration of the service, we brought in a module called nconf. Using just three lines of code, we managed to configure the service through a config file while allowing overrides from command-line arguments and environment variables. You also learned how to use nodemon to keep your service running, automatically restarting whenever the code changes.

Next it was off to the races writing APIs that could use Elasticsearch to find books by the various fields in those documents. For this we started off using the Request module with regular callback handlers like in the previous chapter. But soon we upgraded to using Promises for managing asynchronous code flows, in particular those produced by the request-promise module.

After the search APIs, we developed APIs for working with book bundles. Building on Promises, we took advantage of async functions with the async and await keywords. This powerful combination encourages a readable, synchronous style of coding while enjoying the benefits of nonblocking, asynchronous functionality.

The followup tasks below ask you to continue filling out the suite of bundle-manipulation APIs. Take care!

Deleting a Bundle Entirely

In this chapter, you wrote a bunch of APIs for creating and manipulating book bundles, but not one to delete a bundle. Your task is to add one now.

Here's the basic shell of the API you're going to add.

```
web-services/b4/lib/bundle.js
/**
 * Delete a bundle entirely.
 * curl -X DELETE http://<host>:<port>/api/bundle/<id>
 */
app.delete('/api/bundle/:id', async (req, res) => {
});
```

Inside the Express route handler callback function, you should do the following:

- Determine the bundle's URL based on the es config object and the request parameters.

- Use await with a call to rp() to suspend until the deletion is completed.

- Wrap your await call in a try/catch block to handle any errors.

Hint: use the rp.delete() method to send an HTTP DELETE request to Elasticsearch.

Removing a Book from a Bundle

Like the previous task, this task asks you to implement a DELETE API. But this time it's to remove a book from a bundle (not delete the bundle entirely).

Here's the basic outline of your API:

```
/**
 * Remove a book from a bundle.
 * curl -X DELETE http://<host>:<port>/api/bundle/<id>/book/<pgid>
 */
app.delete('/api/bundle/:id/book/:pgid', async (req, res) => {
  const bundleUrl = `${url}/${req.params.id}`;

  try {

  } catch (esResErr) {
    res.status(esResErr.statusCode || 502).json(esResErr.error);
  }
});
```

Inside the try{} block you'll need to do a few things:

- Use await with rp() to retrieve the bundle object from Elasticsearch.
- Find the index of the book within the bundle.books list.
- Remove the book from the list. (Hint: use Array.splice().)
- PUT the updated bundle object back into the Elasticsearch index, again with await and rp().

Note that if the bundle doesn't contain the book whose removal is being requested, your handler should return a 409 Conflict HTTP status code. You can make this happen by throwing an object with a statusCode property set to 409 and an error object that contains information about what went wrong. This will be caught by the catch block and used to finish the Express response.

If you get stuck, check out the code download that accompanies this book. Good luck!

CHAPTER 8

Creating a Beautiful User Experience

APIs and command-line tools are excellent for developers to use and for systems to talk to each other. But at some point, if you're going to have nondevelopers use your software, you'll need a more friendly and beautiful user experience.

In this chapter, you'll learn how to set up a web front end for the APIs you developed across the preceding chapters. The bulk of this work is around installing and configuring webpack, a popular bundler for producing web-based UI deliverables. Doing this, we'll cover the following aspects of developing a front end for Node.js:

Node.js Core

In previous examples in the book, we've used Node.js modules that had runtime dependencies and development dependencies. In this chapter, we'll explore peer dependencies, which are often used to describe relationships between frameworks and their plugins.

Patterns

The framework-plus-plugins model is popular in front-end JavaScript development and you'll see several examples. Additionally, in modern JavaScript it's common to transpile code from one language or dialect into another. You'll learn how to use TypeScript to transpile and type-check your code.

JavaScriptisms

In the last chapter, you used async functions to write code in a synchronous style using try/catch blocks to handle the results of Promises. We'll do that again here, using the browser-native, Promise-producing fetch() method to perform asynchronous requests to the server. You'll work with other DOM APIs, too, to perform regular front-end development tasks like handling user-interaction events and navigation.

Supporting Code

Developing a web-based UI from scratch is a surprisingly large undertaking, so rather than implement everything, we'll lean heavily on supporting tools. We'll use Twitter's Bootstrap framework to provide beautiful default styles. For rendering dynamic HTML, we'll use a mature and popular library called Handlebars.

One of the things I most enjoy about Node.js development is that there's always more than one way to do anything. This is even more true of front-end JavaScript development.

There's no shortage of front-end frameworks, each with its own strengths. Both the field of frameworks and their features are in a state of constant flux.

So rather than put a stake in the sand and claim that this, that, or the other framework is the right one to use, my goal here is decidedly lower level. I'll show you how to put together a web-based UI on top of Node.js-powered APIs. Then, when it comes to writing the front-end code, we'll stick to generic techniques that transfer across frameworks. This should give you the flexibility to explore and choose from any number of frameworks and libraries you like.

With those caveats out of the way, let's start with the basics: installing and using the webpack dev server.

Getting Started with webpack

Recall that the application we've been developing is for creating and managing named reading lists called book bundles. The application, Better Book Bundle Builder, abbreviated as B4, consists only of RESTful APIs at this point.

Throughout this chapter, we'll be configuring a front-end builder tool called webpack. It takes all your front-end code and its dependencies and bundles it all up into a small number of deliverables.

For example, say you have one main JavaScript file, with two libraries that it depends on. Rather than send three individual JavaScript files to the client browser, webpack handles the job of combining these assets into a single JavaScript file. Through a variety of plugins, it can do the same for CSS, images, and other assets.

But the very first step is to create a directory to house the front-end project. Open a terminal, and create a directory called b4-app.

```
$ mkdir b4-app
$ cd b4-app
```

Next, let's make this a Node.js project by calling npm init from inside the project directory. All of the defaults are fine, but you may want to update the license property to meet your own needs.

```
$ npm init -y
Wrote to ./b4-app/package.json:

{
  "name": "b4-app",
  "version": "1.0.0",
  "description": "",
  "main": "index.js",
  "scripts": {
    "test": "echo \"Error: no test specified\" && exit 1"
  },
  "keywords": [],
  "author": "",
  "license": "ISC"
}
```

It is, of course, possible to create a web page or application without bundling your assets. But there's a host of reasons why bundling has become standard practice. Transpiling down into a common version of JavaScript and reduced latency are just two.

In a production environment, you'd perform all of this bundling activity before deployment. But during development, it's much more convenient to have the bundling occur on demand.

For this, we'll use a plugin for webpack called the webpack dev server. Installing and running the webpack dev server, conveniently, also offers an introduction to working with Node.js peer dependencies.

Typically in Node.js, when a module depends on another, it goes into a nested subdirectory deep inside the node_modules directory. Not so with peer dependencies. In Node.js, a *peer dependency* is a required sibling module. So rather than having the dependency exist in a child directory, it must be at the same level.

With a terminal opened to your b4-app project directory, install the webpack-dev-server module.

```
$ npm install --save-dev --save-exact webpack-dev-server@2.9.1
```

Toward the end of the npm install command's output, you may notice a couple of warnings about unmet peer dependencies.

```
npm WARN webpack-dev-server@2.9.1 requires a peer of webpack@^2.2.0 but none
    was installed.
npm WARN webpack-dev-middleware@1.12.0 requires a peer of webpack@1.0.0 ||
    ^2.0.0 || ^3.0.0 but none was installed.
```

To run the webpack dev server, you'll need to add a start script to your package.json file. Open that file now, and add the following start script:

```
"scripts": {
  "start": "webpack-dev-server",
  "test": "echo \"Error: no test specified\" && exit 1"
},
```

Now try to start the webpack dev server through npm.

```
$ npm start

> b4-app@1.0.0 start ./b4-app
> webpack-dev-server

module.js:472
    throw err;
    ^

Error: Cannot find module 'webpack'
    at Function.Module._resolveFilename (module.js:470:15)
    at Function.Module._load (module.js:418:25)
    at Module.require (module.js:498:17)
    at require (internal/module.js:20:19)
    at Object.<anonymous> (./b4-app/node_modules/webpack-dev-server/lib/
        Server.js:15:17)
    at Module._compile (module.js:571:32)
    at Object.Module._extensions..js (module.js:580:10)
    at Module.load (module.js:488:32)
    at tryModuleLoad (module.js:447:12)
    at Function.Module._load (module.js:439:3)
```

As you can see, webpack-dev-server's peer dependency on webpack turns our failure to install it into a runtime error.

The reason for peer dependencies is to support a plugin model. Unlike a regular dependency, where its dependent projects are meant to be smaller units of functionality, a plugin adds functionality into a larger unit or framework.

In a sense, webpack-dev-server is a plugin to the larger webpack project. It wouldn't be as correct to say that webpack-dev-server depends on webpack as it would be to say that it plugs into webpack.

Without an explicit peer-dependency mechanism in npm, you'd need to either have things like webpack-dev-server depend on the larger framework or invent your own plugin architecture.

Using plugins to augment libraries is a common pattern in front-end UI development, so we'll be working a lot with peer dependencies in this chapter.

Let's install the webpack module to resolve the peer dependency.

```
$ npm install --save-dev --save-exact webpack@3.6.0
```

To use webpack, you need to configure it in a file called webpack.config.js. We'll start with a bare-bones configuration file, then build on it.

Create a file called webpack.config.js in your project root and give it the following content:

ux/b4-app/webpack.config.js
```
'use strict';
module.exports = {
  entry: './entry.js',
};
```

This file exports a minimal configuration object, which only contains an entry property. This property points to the root file from which all other dependencies will be computed. Without an entry-point file, webpack won't do anything.

Let's create an empty entry.js now, just to get started. We'll make a more complete application entry point shortly.

```
$ touch entry.js
```

Now let's try running the dev server again. It should produce output something like the following:

```
$ npm start

> b4-app@1.0.0 start ./b4-app
> webpack-dev-server

Project is running at http://localhost:8080/
webpack output is served from /
Hash: 02f07941014e01e17c1c
Version: webpack 3.6.0
Time: 695ms
    Asset    Size  Chunks                    Chunk Names
bundle.js  314 kB       0  [emitted]  [big]  main
chunk    {0} bundle.js (main) 300 kB [entry] [rendered]
    [35] ./entry.js 0 bytes {0} [built]
    [36] (webpack)-dev-server/client?http://localhost:8080 5.68 kB {0} [built]
    [37] ./~/ansi-html/index.js 4.26 kB {0} [built]
    [38] ./~/ansi-regex/index.js 135 bytes {0} [built]
    [40] ./~/events/events.js 8.33 kB {0} [built]
    [41] ./~/html-entities/index.js 231 bytes {0} [built]
    [48] ./~/querystring-es3/index.js 127 bytes {0} [built]
    [51] ./~/sockjs-client/lib/entry.js 244 bytes {0} [built]
```

```
[77] ./~/strip-ansi/index.js 161 bytes {0} [built]
[79] ./~/url/url.js 23.3 kB {0} [built]
[80] ./~/url/util.js 314 bytes {0} [built]
[81] (webpack)-dev-server/client/overlay.js 3.73 kB {0} [built]
[82] (webpack)-dev-server/client/socket.js 897 bytes {0} [built]
[84] (webpack)/hot/emitter.js 77 bytes {0} [built]
[85] multi (webpack)-dev-server/client?http://localhost:8080 ./entry.js
     40 bytes {0} [built]
   + 71 hidden modules
webpack: Compiled successfully.
```

By default, webpack-dev-server listens on TCP port 8080. If you visit localhost:8080 in your browser, you should see a directory listing of your project directory.

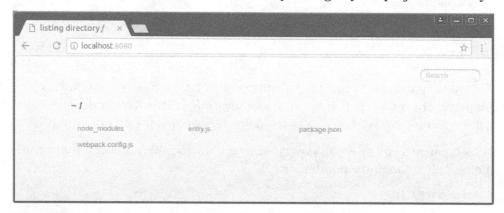

Currently, our webpack.config.js contains only an entry point, no outputs. So webpack doesn't yet pack anything. In the next section we'll use an HTML-generating plugin to construct a basic Hello World page.

Generating Your First webpack Bundle

At this point, you have the basic outline of a project that will build a front end using webpack, but currently it doesn't actually build anything. In this section, we'll get the project to the point where it generates an index.html file and produces a distributable JavaScript bundle to go along with it.

First, to generate the HTML we'll need the html-webpack-plugin module. Install it with npm.

```
$ npm install --save-dev --save-exact html-webpack-plugin@2.30.1
```

Next, open your webpack.config.js and update it to contain the following content:

ux/b4-app/webpack.config.js
```
'use strict';
const path = require('path');
const distDir = path.resolve(__dirname, 'dist');
```

```
const HtmlWebpackPlugin = require('html-webpack-plugin');

module.exports = {
  entry: './entry.js',
  output: {
    filename: 'bundle.js',
    path: distDir,
  },
  devServer: {
    contentBase: distDir,
    port: 60800,
  },
  plugins: [
    new HtmlWebpackPlugin({
      title: 'Better Book Bundle Builder',
    }),
  ],
};
```

At the top of the file, we pull in the built-in path module and use it to resolve the path to the dist directory. This is roughly equivalent to __dirname + '/dist', but uses the correct path separator for the current operating system and returns a fully resolved absolute path. We pull in the HtmlWebpackPlugin class from the included module, which we'll use in the plugins portion of the webpack config.

Next, notice that we've added an output object to the webpack config. This specifies the target output directory and the filename that the bundled JavaScript output should have. By convention, we call the bundled JavaScript file bundle.js.

Note that webpack-dev-server does not write to this output directory. Instead, it serves content like the bundle.js file directly from memory on request. Running the webpack command directly, rather than webpack-dev-server, would write content to the output directory.

The devServer object contains configuration parameters specific to the webpack-dev-server. Here we use the same dist directory to be the contentBase of the running dev server, and override the default TCP port.

Lastly, we add a plugins object to add webpack plugins to the build. In the array of plugins, we construct a new HtmlWebpackPlugin instance and configure its title. This will show up in the generated HTML file's <title> tag.

At this point the webpack config is ready, but in order to see anything other than a blank page, we should expand the currently empty entry.js file. Open that file and add the following:

```
ux/b4-app/entry.js
'use strict';
document.body.innerHTML = `
  <h1>B4 - Book Bundler</h1>
  <p>${new Date()}</p>
`;
```

All this does is insert a big header and the current date and time into the page, but it's enough to get going. Once you save the file, head to a terminal and start up the webpack dev server via npm start. If it's still running from before, use Ctrl-C to kill it first.

With the dev server running, open localhost:60800 in your browser. It should look something like the following.

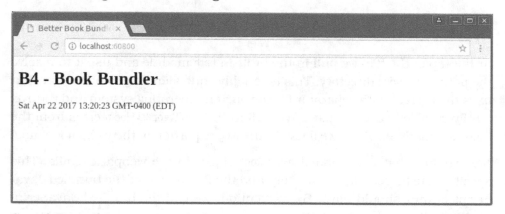

Great! Everything appears to be going smoothly so far. Next we'll bring in Bootstrap to make the page more beautiful.

Sprucing Up Your UI with Bootstrap

Bootstrap, by Twitter, is a framework for developing beautiful, mobile-first web UIs.[1] Rather than designing every aspect of the UI and then writing CSS rules by hand, we'll use Bootstrap to provide a good, basic design.

Before we pull in Bootstrap, though, we'll need some dependency plugins. For webpack to work with CSS generally, we need the style-loader and css-loader plugins. In addition, to load other static assets that CSS files might reference, like images and fonts, we'll need the url-loader plugin and its peer dependency the file-loader plugin.

Use npm to install all of those:

---

1. http://getbootstrap.com/

```
$ npm install --save-dev --save-exact \
  style-loader@0.19.0 \
  css-loader@0.28.7 \
  url-loader@0.6.2 \
  file-loader@1.1.5
```

For webpack to use those plugins, we need to add them to the config and explain which files should be handled by which plugins. Open your webpack.config.js and add the following module section to the exported webpack config object.

```
ux/b4-app/webpack.config.js
module: {
  rules: [{
    test: /\.css$/,
    use: [ 'style-loader', 'css-loader' ]
  },{
    test: /\.(png|woff|woff2|eot|ttf|svg)$/,
    loader: 'url-loader?limit=100000',
  }],
},
```

First, this tells webpack that files ending in .css should be handled using the css-loader and the style-loader. The css-loader plugin reads CSS files and resolves any @import and url() statements using webpack's require() toolchain. But after resolving the dependencies, css-loader doesn't do anything with the resulting CSS. For that, you need the style-loader plugin, which injects a <style> tag into the page containing the CSS content.

Order matters here! The plugins listed in the use list of a module rule are processed in reverse order. If you switch these around, webpack will emit an ugly error when attempting to build—try it if you're curious.

The second module rule tells webpack that a variety of files should be loaded with the url-loader. This pulls in the remote file and inlines it directly. For example, if a CSS rule uses a background image, it'll be turned into a data URI.[2]

The url-loader's limit parameter specifies the maximum file size in bytes that can be inlined. If a file is larger than this limit, then url-loader defers to file-loader, which emits the file to the output directory instead. There's no one-size-fits-all rule to determine this limit—it's a classic tradeoff between loading many small files vs. a smaller number of larger files.

Once you've saved your webpack.config.js file, it's time to bring in Bootstrap. Open your terminal and run this command:

```
$ npm install --save-dev --save-exact bootstrap@3.3.7
```

---

2. https://developer.mozilla.org/en-US/docs/Web/HTTP/Basics_of_HTTP/Data_URIs

Now the last thing to do is make use of Bootstrap in the entry.js. Open that file and replace its contents with this:

```
ux/b4-app/entry.js
'use strict';
import './node_modules/bootstrap/dist/css/bootstrap.min.css';

document.body.innerHTML = `
  <div class="container">
    <h1>B4 - Book Bundler</h1>
    <div class="b4-alerts"></div>
    <div class="b4-main"></div>
  </div>
`;
```

At the top of this file, we use the import keyword to pull in the minified Bootstrap CSS. The import keyword is part of the ECMAScript 2015 module specification, but is not yet available in Node.js. We can use it here, though, because webpack, not Node.js, is responsible for resolving these dependencies. We'll use import throughout this chapter for bringing in dependencies.

For now, consider this import line to be the same as calling require() with the same argument. When webpack encounters this dependency at build time, it matches the filename against the module.rules we added earlier in webpack.config.js. Seeing that the file ends in .css, webpack invokes the css-loader plugin to grab Bootstrap's CSS content.

After establishing the dependency on Bootstrap, we update the document.body.innerHTML to create the basic architecture of the page. The CSS class container on the outermost <div> tells Bootstrap to constrain its width if the window size is too large. Inside the container, we set up an area for alerts to notify the user, and a main content area that will dynamically change based on the application state. CSS classes that begin with the b4- prefix are specific to this application—all other CSS classes you see are part of Bootstrap.

Next, add this code to the end of the file, after setting document.body.innerHTML:

```
ux/b4-app/entry.js
const mainElement = document.body.querySelector('.b4-main');

mainElement.innerHTML = `
  <div class="jumbotron">
    <h1>Welcome!</h1>
    <p>B4 is an application for creating book bundles.</p>
  </div>
`;

const alertsElement = document.body.querySelector('.b4-alerts');

alertsElement.innerHTML = `
```

```
<div class="alert alert-success alert-dismissible fade in" role="alert">
  <button class="close" data-dismiss="alert" aria-label="Close">
    <span aria-hidden="true">&times;</span>
  </button>
  <strong>Success!</strong> Bootstrap is working.
</div>
`;
```

In this part, we grab a reference to the main content <div> by passing a CSS selector to the querySelector() method. Using this element, we insert a big welcome message styled by Bootstrap's jumbotron class.

Lastly, again using querySelector(), we get the alerts content <div> and insert an example. The CSS classes and other attributes on the various elements that compose this alert are all meaningful to Bootstrap, enabling it to layer in additional functionality post hoc. In short, this is how you create a green (success) dismissable alert box. You can read more about how to stylize alerts on Bootstrap's components page.[3]

Let's try this all out. Since you've made changes to webpack.config.js, you'll probably have to restart your webpack dev server. The webpack dev server is capable of automatically picking up changes to your content files, but not the configuration file itself.

Run npm start from your terminal. Once it starts up, navigate to localhost:60800 in your browser. It should look something like this:

If it does, great! Bootstrap is styling the page as intended.

---

3.   http://getbootstrap.com/components/#alerts

Now try to close the alert by clicking the X (close) button. It doesn't work! This is because although we brought in the Bootstrap CSS, we've yet to bring in the accompanying Bootstrap JavaScript that adds dynamic functionality. Let's do that next.

Bringing in Bootstrap JavaScript and jQuery

So far, the web application we've been building brings in Bootstrap CSS for styling, but does not include the Bootstrap JavaScript that implements the functionality of a variety of Bootstrap components. In this section we'll pull that in, as well as take care of a few other housecleaning details. After this, we'll be in a great place to begin developing the application proper.

The various webpack plugins we've been using in this chapter provide their functionality by decorating the webpack core. In like fashion, Bootstrap JavaScript works by adding its functionality to the jQuery core. Plugging in to a parent library or framework in this way has been a common pattern in the front-end JavaScript community for a long time.

What this means for us is that we need to bring in jQuery for Bootstrap behaviors to work. The first step is to install it. Run the following command from your terminal:

```
$ npm install --save-dev --save-exact jquery@3.2.1
```

Next, we need to tell webpack how to incorporate jQuery into the project. Open your webpack.config.js file and start by adding this import at the top, right after the HtmlWebpackPlugin:

ux/b4-app/webpack.config.js
```
const webpack = require('webpack');
```

This brings in the webpack module, which doubles as a namespace for built-in plugins. The one we need is the ProvidePlugin, which we can use to indicate that a particular module provides a particular JavaScript global.

In your webpack.config.js, head down to the plugins section and add a ProvidePlugin after the HtmlWebpackPlugin as follows:

ux/b4-app/webpack.config.js
```
new webpack.ProvidePlugin({
  $: 'jquery',
  jQuery: 'jquery'
}),
```

This indicates that the jquery module provides the jQuery and $ global variables.

Next, open your entry.js. At the top, right after the Bootstrap CSS import line, add the following:

```
import 'bootstrap';
```

This tells webpack that entry.js depends on the bootstrap module. Like with the CSS import, we're not setting a local variable to the returned object, because we don't need it programmatically. Bootstrap will take care of imbuing the various page elements with their functionality behind the scenes, provided it gets loaded into the browser.

Use npm start to run your webpack dev server. Once it has started, revisit the welcome page at localhost:60800 and confirm that the close button works. Now let's move on to adding our own application logic.

Transpiling with TypeScript

At this point, the basic framework of the application is in place and we're ready to start developing the application functionality. Since browsers often lag behind Node.js in terms of support for the latest JavaScript features, we need a way to convert modern JavaScript into a common dialect that browsers will understand.

The practice of compiling source code from one programming language into another (or from one language version to another version) is called *transpiling*. There is a rich tradition of transpiling in the JavaScript community—both from other languages into JavaScript and JavaScript-to-JavaScript. Today, two of the most popular JavaScript transpilers are Babel and TypeScript.

Babel transpiles code written using the latest ECMAScript techniques (like those we've been using throughout this book),[4] into a dialect of ECMAScript that's widely available in browsers. Babel can be used in conjunction with Flow, an analysis tool by Facebook, which performs type inference and type checking.[5] In many cases, Flow can infer the type of a variable and inform you of subtle code errors before they become runtime issues. If that's not enough, you can also provide specific type information about your variables that Flow will enforce.

TypeScript, by Microsoft, is a superset of JavaScript that includes typings.[6] The TypeScript toolchain performs transpiling down into common ECMAScript,

---

4.   https://babeljs.io/

5.   https://flow.org/

6.   https://www.typescriptlang.org/

as well as static type inference and checking on your source code. Like Flow, in many cases TypeScript can infer variable types, and you can also provide specific types through a rich type system.

For our immediate purpose, either Babel or TypeScript would be fine. Both are relatively easy to integrate with webpack, and both can transpile the latest ECMAScript down to a version understood by browsers. I've chosen to use TypeScript in this book for a couple of reasons.

First, since TypeScript performs type inference and checking in addition to transpiling, you get a layer of protection for free. With Babel, we'd have to add Flow to get the same benefit.

Second, TypeScript has a large and growing repository of community-contributed typings called DefinitelyTyped.[7] This repository is directly available through npm as a collection of packages that begin with the prefix @types/. For example, the Bootstrap typings are available as @types/bootstrap.

I think momentum is on TypeScript's side, but time will tell. In either case, the code that you'll be writing throughout the rest of this chapter is compatible with both TypeScript and Babel/Flow.

To use TypeScript in your project, start by installing it with npm.

```
$ npm install --save-dev --save-exact typescript@2.5.3
```

You'll also need the ts-loader plugin for webpack.

```
$ npm install --save-dev --save-exact ts-loader@2.3.7
```

To transpile TypeScript into JavaScript, you'll need a tsconfig.json to configure your project. Open your text editor and enter the following:

ux/b4-app/tsconfig.json
```json
{
  "compilerOptions": {
    "outDir": "./dist/",
    "sourceMap": true,
    "module": "CommonJS",
    "target": "ES5",
    "lib": ["DOM", "ES2015.Promise", "ES5"],
    "allowJs": true,
    "alwaysStrict": true
  }
}
```

---

7. https://github.com/DefinitelyTyped/DefinitelyTyped

Via the tsconfig.json, TypeScript allows you to fine-tune the compilation through many compiler options.[8] Here's a quick rundown of the ones we're using.

- outDir—Directory where TypeScript should emit transpiled .js files. These files won't actually appear here when using the ts-loader and webpack dev server.

- sourceMap—Whether to generate a source map along with the transpiled output. We'll explore this in more detail later.

- module—Which module system to use to represent transpiled dependencies. CommonJS is the module system used by Node.js, characterized by the require() function for pulling in dependent modules.

- target—Which version of ECMAScript to target for transpiled output. ECMAScript version 5 has wide support among modern browsers.

- lib—Collection of built-in typings that TypeScript should be aware of. In our case, we'll employ features of the DOM and presume that the user's browser has support for Promises.

- allowJs—Whether to permit TypeScript to compile .js source files as well as .ts.

- alwaysStrict—Whether to always interpret code in strict mode and emit 'use strict'; in generated files. This lets us omit the use strict clause from the tops of .ts files.

After you save this file, it's time to update your webpack.config.js. To start, open that file and update the entry to point to ./app/index.ts.

ux/b4-app/webpack.config.js
```
entry: './app/index.ts',
```

In addition to switching from a .js file to a .ts file, let's also create a subdirectory to organize the front-end code files. It is a webpack convention to call this directory app. We'll create the app directory and index.ts in a bit, but first let's finish updating the webpack config.

Down in the module.rules section of your webpack.config.js file, add a rule to the top of the list to associate the .ts with TypeScript via the ts-loader plugin. Your module.rules section should now look like this:

---

8. https://www.typescriptlang.org/docs/handbook/compiler-options.html

ux/b4-app/webpack.config.js

```
module: {
  rules: [{
    test: /\.ts$/,
    loader: 'ts-loader',
  },{
    test: /\.css$/,
    use: [ 'style-loader', 'css-loader' ]
  },{
    test: /\.(png|woff|woff2|eot|ttf|svg)$/,
    loader: 'url-loader?limit=100000',
  }],
},
```

Good—now it's time to create the app directory.

```
$ mkdir app
```

Rather than have all of the application code lumped into one file, let's split out the HTML parts into a separate file called templates.ts. Open your text editor and enter the following:

ux/b4-app/app/templates.ts

```
export const main = `
  <div class="container">
    <h1>B4 - Book Bundler</h1>
    <div class="b4-alerts"></div>
    <div class="b4-main"></div>
  </div>
`;

export const welcome = `
  <div class="jumbotron">
    <h1>Welcome!</h1>
    <p>B4 is an application for creating book bundles.</p>
  </div>
`;

export const alert = `
  <div class="alert alert-success alert-dismissible fade in" role="alert">
    <button class="close" data-dismiss="alert" aria-label="Close">
      <span aria-hidden="true">&times;</span>
    </button>
    <strong>Success!</strong> Bootstrap is working.
  </div>
`;
```

The multiline strings of HTML you see here are all copied directly from the entry.js from earlier. But rather than assigning them to the innerHTML properties of DOM elements, we're making them available through the ES6 module keyword export. This is similar to setting module.exports like you've done in previous examples in this book.

Once you save this file, start a new file in your editor for the index.ts file. Enter the following to get it started.

```
import '../node_modules/bootstrap/dist/css/bootstrap.min.css';
import 'bootstrap';
import * as templates from './templates.ts';

document.body.innerHTML = templates.main;

const mainElement = document.body.querySelector('.b4-main');
const alertsElement = document.body.querySelector('.b4-alerts');

mainElement.innerHTML = templates.welcome;
alertsElement.innerHTML = templates.alert;
```

At the outset of this file, we import the same bootstrap.css and bootstrap module as before. Note the subtle difference in the path to bootstrap.css. Now that we're down one subdirectory in app, the path to bootstrap.css starts with ../node_modules/ instead of ./node_modules/.

Next, we import all of the exported members from templates.ts into a local variable called templates. These will be used to populate the innerHTML elements in the page.

As before, in entry.js we start by populating the document.body with the main structural HTML. After that, we grab references to the mainElement and the alertsElement in which we'll render page content and notifications, respectively.

Lastly, we fill in the main content element with the HTML from templates.welcome, and the alerts element with the HTML from templates.alert. This produces the same behavior as the entry.js from earlier, and represents a good test to ensure that all of the TypeScript and webpack configuration is working.

After saving this file, restart your webpack dev server, then confirm that the page at localhost:60800 looks the same as before and the close button on the alert works as expected. If so, great!

Next, we'll add HTML templating to the project. This will afford dynamically generating HTML, rather than relying on only static strings.

Templating HTML with Handlebars

Up to this point, the B4 application only emits static HTML that is completely known in advance. For example, the alert box contains the same *Success* message every time. What we really want is the ability to render HTML for dynamic strings. For this we need templates.

Now, it's true that ECMAScript supports template strings that allow you to easily inject values into strings, and we've been taking liberal advantage of this feature throughout the book. Unfortunately, though, this technique can quickly introduce cross-site scripting (XSS) vulnerabilities when used with user-supplied data. To protect our app from XSS vulnerabilities, any content over which a user may have any control must be properly encoded.

For example, consider the case where we'll show the name of a user's bundle. You might naively implement that template like this:

```
// DO NOT USE! VULNERABLE TO XSS.
export const bundleName = name => `<h2>${name}</h2>`;
```

Here, the bundleName() takes a name parameter and returns a string including the name surrounded by a pair of <h2> tags. What could go wrong?

It turns out that this kind of templating is trivially exploitable and easy to break accidentally. Consider if the name contains an <img> tag. Your app could be inadvertently showing images where they weren't expected. Or worse, if the tag has an onload or onerror attribute, it could execute arbitrary JavaScript in the page!

Defending against these types of vulnerabilities is not easy, but fortunately you don't have to do it yourself. Modern frameworks and templating libraries handle these concerns for you.

For the purposes of this book, we'll use Handlebars, a minimal and stable templating library.[9] Handlebars can operate both as a client-side runtime library and as a build-time module on the Node.js side of things. We'll use it as a client-side library because I've found that easier to set up, but if you wanted to integrate Handlebars compilation into webpack, there is a handlebars-loader plugin for webpack that can help with this.[10]

To use Handlebars, start by installing it with npm.

```
$ npm install --save-dev --save-exact handlebars@4.0.10
```

Next, open your app/templates.ts file. Instead of exporting static HTML strings, we'll export compiled Handlebars templates. Update the file's contents to look like this:

---

9.   http://handlebarsjs.com/

10. https://www.npmjs.com/package/handlebars-loader

```
ux/b4-app/app/templates.ts
import * as Handlebars from '../node_modules/handlebars/dist/handlebars.js';

export const main = Handlebars.compile(`
  <div class="container">
    <h1>B4 - Book Bundler</h1>
    <div class="b4-alerts"></div>
    <div class="b4-main"></div>
  </div>
`);

export const welcome = Handlebars.compile(`
  <div class="jumbotron">
    <h1>Welcome!</h1>
    <p>B4 is an application for creating book bundles.</p>
  </div>
`);

export const alert = Handlebars.compile(`
  <div class="alert alert-{{type}} alert-dismissible fade in" role="alert">
    <button class="close" data-dismiss="alert" aria-label="Close">
      <span aria-hidden="true">&times;</span>
    </button>
    {{message}}
  </div>
`);
```

For each of the exported constants, now the HTML string is passed into Handlebars.compile(). This produces a function that takes in an object—a map of parameters by name—and returns a string with the appropriate replacements having been made.

The first two templates are exactly the same as before. Both main() and welcome() take no parameters and simply return a static string. Using Handlebars.compile() makes no real difference, but for consistency all of the exported members of templates.ts will be compiled template functions.

The third template, alert(), takes an object with two members: a type and a message. The type value is used to complete the alert- CSS class, which sets the color of the alert box. The four choices are *success* (green), *info* (blue), *warning* (yellow), and *danger* (red). The message value fills in the body of the alert box.

Save this file, then open app/index.ts We need to update the use of the templates members to call methods instead of using the values as strings directly. Edit that file to look like the following:

```
ux/b4-app/app/index.ts
import '../node_modules/bootstrap/dist/css/bootstrap.min.css';
import 'bootstrap';
import * as templates from './templates.ts';

// Page setup.
document.body.innerHTML = templates.main();
const mainElement = document.body.querySelector('.b4-main');
const alertsElement = document.body.querySelector('.b4-alerts');

mainElement.innerHTML = templates.welcome();
alertsElement.innerHTML = templates.alert({
  type: 'info',
  message: 'Handlebars is working!',
});
```

The only difference with respect to templates.main and templates.welcome is that now they are called as templates.main() and templates.welcome(), respectively. Note that the call to templates.alert() takes an object with both a type and a message parameter.

Once you save this file, the webpack dev server should pick up the changes and update localhost:60800 for you. It should now look like the following:

I know all of this probably seems like a lot of work to get such a simple page working, but rest assured, it's setting the groundwork for more involved functionality coming up.

Next we'll implement a simple URL hash-based routing to navigate through the app.

Implementing hashChange Navigation

The B4 application we're developing is what you might call a single-page application. The behavior of the application is driven by user interaction, and the data is supplied by RESTful JSON APIs.

Rather than request from the server new pages that live at different URLs, the user requests only the first page and its dependent content (JavaScript, CSS, images, etc.) up front. This raises the question of how to implement and track changes to the application as the user navigates through it.

For this, we'll use the URL hash: the part of the URL after the pound sign (#). We'll refer to each page the user might encounter as a *view*. The welcome view will live at #welcome, which will also be the default if the URL lacks a hash or if it has an invalid hash. Other views will live at hashes that match their purposes.

To implement hashchange navigation between views, open your app/index.ts for editing. Start by removing everything after the page-setup part that uses querySelector() to set the mainElement and alertsElement local variables. Next, add the following showView() method:

```
ux/b4-app/app/index.ts
/**
 * Use Window location hash to show the specified view.
 */
const showView = async () => {
  const [view, ...params] = window.location.hash.split('/');

  switch (view) {
    case '#welcome':
      mainElement.innerHTML = templates.welcome();
      break;
    default:
      // Unrecognized view.
      throw Error(`Unrecognized view: ${view}`);
  }
};
```

This async function starts by reading the window.location.hash string and splitting it wherever there's a forward slash (/). This will allow us to have parameterized views later, such as #view-bundle/BUNDLE_ID.

Next, we switch on the beginning portion of the hash (view) and take action appropriately. If the hash is #welcome, then we set the contents of the mainElement to contain the welcome-template HTML. If the hash is unrecognized, then we throw an exception.

Currently there's no code that would invoke showView(), but we want it to get called whenever the URL's hash changes. To get that to work, add the following:

```
ux/b4-app/app/index.ts
window.addEventListener('hashchange', showView);
```

Whenever the URL's hash changes, the window object emits a hashchange event. In answer to this, we want showView() to be invoked.

Unfortunately, the initial page load does not trigger a hashchange event, so we still need to call showView() explicitly to get things rolling. For that we need one more line of code:

```
ux/b4-app/app/index.ts
showView().catch(err => window.location.hash = '#welcome');
```

Here we call showView() directly. Since this is an async function, it returns a Promise when called. If that Promise gets rejected—which would happen if the view hash was unrecognized—then we want to explicitly set the hash to #welcome, which will trigger a hashchange event and load the welcome view.

To recap, at this point your app/index.ts should look like this:

```
ux/b4-app/app/index.ts
import '../node_modules/bootstrap/dist/css/bootstrap.min.css';
import 'bootstrap';
import * as templates from './templates.ts';

// Page setup.
document.body.innerHTML = templates.main();
const mainElement = document.body.querySelector('.b4-main');
const alertsElement = document.body.querySelector('.b4-alerts');

/**
 * Use Window location hash to show the specified view.
 */
const showView = async () => {
  const [view, ...params] = window.location.hash.split('/');

  switch (view) {
    case '#welcome':
      mainElement.innerHTML = templates.welcome();
      break;
    default:
      // Unrecognized view.
      throw Error(`Unrecognized view: ${view}`);
  }
};

window.addEventListener('hashchange', showView);

showView().catch(err => window.location.hash = '#welcome');
```

After you save this file, your webpack dev server should pick up the change. If you check out localhost:60800, it should look the same as before, with the welcome view showing, but without any alerts.

Now we have all the pieces in place to start implementing views that load data from the web services we developed in previous chapters.

Listing Objects in a View

Using the webpack dev server, it's easy to quickly see the rendered output of statically served content. But how do you access web services like those we implemented in the last chapter?

Ideally, we'd have one Node.js server that serves the front-end static content and handles the API requests. We'll achieve that in the next chapter, when we pull it all together, but for now they're two separate things.

Fortunately, the webpack dev server has a capability that can help us. By configuring proxies in the webpack.config.js file, we can have the webpack dev server reach out to API endpoints and forward the results.

Configuring a webpack-dev-server Proxy

Web browsers have strict rules about the conditions under which a page can connect to a service. A *proxy* is an endpoint that acts as a passthrough to another service. For development purposes, configuring a webpack-dev-server proxy is a convenient way to provide access to services before the whole system is ready end to end.

To configure the proxies, start by opening your webpack.config.js file for editing. In the module.exports, under the devServer configuration, add a proxy object to make it look like the following:

ux/b4-app/webpack.config.js
```
devServer: {
  contentBase: distDir,
  port: 60800,
  proxy: {
    '/api': 'http://localhost:60702',
    '/es': {
      target: 'http://localhost:9200',
      pathRewrite: {'^/es' : ''},
    }
  },
},
```

This specifies that requests to /api should be sent as is to the localhost service running on port 60702—that is, the Express server we developed in *Writing Modular Express Services*, on page 151.

It also exposes requests directly to Elasticsearch through the endpoint /es. We haven't developed APIs that work for specific users yet, so we need to bypass the API layer and go directly to Elasticsearch for some things. This is a temporary workaround that we won't need in the next chapter, when we create a consolidated server and fill in the authenticated user APIs.

Elasticsearch APIs begin at the root, so we need to strip off the leading /es, which is what the pathRewrite setting is for. You could use this same technique to proxy requests to other services as well, but you should be careful with what you proxy. Unconstrained proxy services can become vulnerabilities when they expose access to services, or levels of privilege on those services, that should not be available to the end user.

Once you save this file, you'll need to restart your webpack dev server to pick up the changes. You'll also need to make sure you're running the Express web services from the last chapter, and make sure your local Elasticsearch cluster is up and running. With those services running, now we can implement a view that uses data from them, as served through the proxy.

Implementing a View

To implement a view that lists the user's bundles, we'll need a couple of things. First we'll need a way of retrieving the bundles asynchronously from the server. Next we'll need a function that renders the list using a compiled Handlebars template to produce displayable HTML. And lastly we'll need to add the hash route to the showView() function to tie it all together.

Let's start with the bundle-retrieving task. Open your app/index.ts and insert the following getBundles() async function after the imports and page-setup part of the file.

```
ux/b4-app/app/index.ts
const getBundles = async () => {
  const esRes = await fetch('/es/b4/bundle/_search?size=1000');

  const esResBody = await esRes.json();

  return esResBody.hits.hits.map(hit => ({
    id: hit._id,
    name: hit._source.name,
  }));
};
```

This method starts off by issuing an asynchronous request to Elasticsearch through the global fetch() method.[11] This is a Promise-producing function that initiates an HTTP request with the provided settings. In this case, we're passing in an Elasticsearch query URL in which we hope to retrieve up to 1,000 bundle documents from the b4 index.

The fetch() API is relatively new, and meant to supplant the older XMLHttpRequest() API. It is widely available, with the notable exceptions being Safari and Internet Explorer. If you need to support these browsers, you can pull in a popular polyfill implementation from the npm package whatwg-fetch.[12]

As a Promise-producing request API, fetch() is quite similar to the request-promise module we used in the last chapter. One notable difference is the way that the response body content is handled. To decode the body content as JSON using the fetch() API, you need to call the response object's json() method, which is another asynchronous, Promise-producing function. So here we await the results of that operation.

Once the JSON body has been decoded, we extract the Elasticsearch results (hits.hits) as an array of objects containing the automatically generated id of the document and the name of the bundle. Since getBundles() is an async function, if anything goes wrong it will result in a rejection of the returned Promise. We're explicitly not handling those potential errors here. Instead, we'll rely on the caller to handle the error by alerting the user.

Still in app/index.ts, let's add a listBundles() function that renders the list of bundles using a Handlebars template. Insert the following after your getBundles() function.

```
ux/b4-app/app/index.ts
const listBundles = bundles => {
  mainElement.innerHIML = templates.listBundles({bundles});
};
```

Currently all this function does is render the bundles using an as-yet-unimplemented Handlebars template also called listBundles. Later we'll add more functionality to this function, but it's good enough for now.

We need to make one more change to the app/index.ts before we backfill the missing Handlebars template. Down in the showView() function, we need to add a handler for the #list-bundles hash route. Insert the following into the switch ladder.

---

11. https://developer.mozilla.org/en-US/docs/Web/API/WindowOrWorkerGlobalScope/fetch
12. https://www.npmjs.com/package/whatwg-fetch

ux/b4-app/app/index.ts

```
case '#list-bundles':
  const bundles = await getBundles();
  listBundles(bundles);
  break;
```

After you save the file, open your app/templates.ts. Add the following implementation of the listBundles() template.

ux/b4-app/app/templates.ts

```
export const listBundles = Handlebars.compile(`
  <div class="panel panel-default">
    <div class="panel-heading">Your Bundles</div>
    {{#if bundles.length}}
      <table class="table">
        <tr>
          <th>Bundle Name</th>
          <th>Actions</th>
        </tr>
        {{#each bundles}}
        <tr>
          <td>
            <a href="#view-bundle/{{id}}">{{name}}</a>
          </td>
          <td>
            <button class="btn delete" data-bundle-id="{{id}}">Delete</button>
          </td>
        </tr>
        {{/each}}
      </table>
    {{else}}
      <div class="panel-body">
        <p>None yet!</p>
      </div>
    {{/if}}
  </div>
`);
```

This template uses the array of bundle passed in to render a Bootstrap panel containing a two-column table. The left column of the table contains the name of the bundle and the right column has a Delete button. Neither the bundle-name link nor the Delete button will do anything yet—we have to add that later.

This template uses a couple of Handlebars features. First, the {{#if}}{{else}}{{/if}} block expression does what you might expect. If the condition in the {{#if}} is true, then Handlebars renders the first part; otherwise it renders the {{else}} part. So if you have no bundles, you'll see a message instead of a table.

The {{#each}} block expression iterates over an array or object. Here we create a new <tr> for each bundle, and fill it with two <td> cells. Inside the {{#each}} expression, the context is the current element, so we can use {{id}} and {{name}} to refer to the current bundle's ID and name, respectively.

Notice that the bundle name links to #view-bundle/{{id}}. Once we add #view-bundle to the showView() switch ladder, these links will take you to a view showing the particular bundle.

Finally, observe the data-bundle-id attribute on the Delete button. This is not required by Bootstrap, but exists so that we know which bundle to delete when the user clicks this button.

Once you save the app/templates.ts file, everything should be in place to see the #list-bundles view from end to end. Start up your webpack dev server, if it's not running already, then navigate to localhost:60800/#list-bundles. It should look something like this:

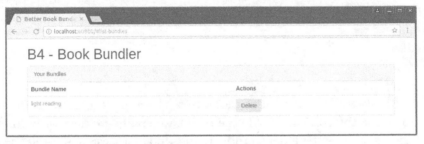

If you haven't created any bundles yet, you'll see a message stating *None yet!* instead of the table. You can create a bundle using the bundle API from *Manipulating Documents RESTfully*, on page 167, with curl and jq.

```
$ curl -s -X POST localhost:60702/api/bundle?name=light%20reading | jq '.'
{
  "_index": "b4",
  "_type": "bundle",
  "_id": "AVuFkyXcpWVRyMBC8pgr",
  "_version": 1,
  "result": "created",
  "_shards": {
    "total": 2,
    "successful": 1,
    "failed": 0
  },
  "created": true
}
```

So far so good, but what about adding a new bundle? Let's add a form to do that next.

Saving Data with a Form

It's great that our application is able to list bundles that already exist, but what about adding new ones? The right tool for this job is the venerable HTML <form> tag. Using a form, we can capture user input and process it by making a proxied call to the back-end APIs. Since the form is static HTML, we'll put it in app/templates.ts. Open that file now and add this template.

```
ux/b4-app/app/templates.ts
export const addBundleForm = Handlebars.compile(`
  <div class="panel panel-default">
    <div class="panel-heading">Create a new bundle.</div>
    <div class="panel-body">
      <form>
        <div class="input-group">
          <input class="form-control" placeholder="Bundle Name" />
          <span class="input-group-btn">
            <button class="btn btn-primary" type="submit">Create</button>
          </span>
        </div>
      </form>
    </div>
  </div>
`);
```

Like the listBundles() template, the addBundleForm() template creates a Bootstrap panel to house the content. Inside the panel, we create a <form> with an <input> where the user can enter a new bundle name, and a <button> to submit the form.

Next, open your app/index.ts for editing and head to the listBundles(). We need to add the form to this and handle form submission.

```
ux/b4-app/app/index.ts
const listBundles = bundles => {
  mainElement.innerHTML =
    templates.addBundleForm() + templates.listBundles({bundles});

  const form = mainElement.querySelector('form');
  form.addEventListener('submit', event => {
    event.preventDefault();
    const name = form.querySelector('input').value;
    addBundle(name);
  });
};
```

At the top of this function, we set the mainElement's HTML to include both the form and the bundle-listing table. After that, we grab a reference to the <form> element and capture its submit event.

The browser's default behavior when a form is submitted is to navigate away from the current page while submitting the form data to the server. Inside the submit event handler, the first thing we have to do is call event.preventDefault() to stop this from happening. After that, we extract the name from the form's <input> tag, and call the as-yet-unwritten addBundle().

To complete the functionality, we need to introduce the addBundle() async function, which takes the name of a bundle to add and asynchronously adds it, then updates the list. Whether this operation succeeds or fails, we'll need to inform the user, so add this convenience function for showing an alert to the user:

```
ux/b4-app/app/index.ts
/**
 * Show an alert to the user.
 */
const showAlert = (message, type = 'danger') => {
  const html = templates.alert({type, message});
  alertsElement.insertAdjacentHTML('beforeend', html);
};
```

This simple helper function uses the alert() Handlebars template from earlier to generate a nice-looking dismissable alert box. We inject the resulting HTML at the end of the alertsElement using the insertAdjacentHTML() method.

Finally, still inside app/index.ts, add the following addBundle() async function.

```
ux/b4-app/app/index.ts
/**
 * Create a new bundle with the given name, then list bundles.
 */
const addBundle = async (name) => {
  try {
    // Grab the list of bundles already created.
    const bundles = await getBundles();

    // Add the new bundle.
    const url = `/api/bundle?name=${encodeURIComponent(name)}`;
    const res = await fetch(url, {method: 'POST'});
    const resBody = await res.json();

    // Merge the new bundle into the original results and show them.
    bundles.push({id: resBody._id, name});
    listBundles(bundles);

    showAlert(`Bundle "${name}" created!`, 'success');
  } catch (err) {
    showAlert(err);
  }
};
```

In form, this code shouldn't appear too surprising. It's the same sort of async function you've been developing in this chapter and the previous one, with a big try/catch block to handle both synchronous exceptions and rejected Promises.

First, we await an updated list of bundles from the async function getBundles(). We have to get an updated list because it may have changed since the form was originally rendered on the page (for example, if the user took action in another tab).

Next, we issue an HTTP POST request using fetch() to create a bundle with the user-specified name. Once that returns, we extract the JSON response, which gives us access to the ID that Elasticsearch generated for the bundle.

If everything was successful to this point, we add that bundle to the bundles array and then call listBundles() to re-render the table. And lastly, we use the showAlert() function to inform the user that the operation was successful. If anything went wrong, we use showAlert() to indicate the problem in the catch block at the bottom.

You might wonder why we don't just add the bundle and then request the full bundle list and display it. The reason is something called *eventual consistency*. Elasticsearch, like many database solutions, experiences a delay between successful changes to the data and those results showing up in subsequent queries. Consider this bad implementation of addBundle():

```
// BAD IMPLEMENTATION! Subject to stale data due to eventual consistency.
const addBundle = async (name) => {
  try {
    // Add the new bundle.
    const url = `/api/bundle?name=${encodeURIComponent(name)}`;
    const res = await fetch(url, {method: 'POST'});
    const resBody = await res.json();

    // Grab the list of all bundles, expecting the new one to be in the list.
    // Due to eventual consistency, the new bundle may be missing!
    const bundles = await getBundles();
    listBundles(bundles);

    showAlert(`Bundle "${name}" created!`, 'success');
  } catch (err) {
    showAlert(err);
  }
};
```

In this bad implementation, we POST the new bundle first, then immediately invoke getBundles(), expecting it to contain all the bundles, including the brand-new one. Now, the ordering of the requests isn't itself a problem. Since we're using await at each step, the next fetch() request won't start until the previous one has finished.

However, there's very little time between the finishing of the POST and the request to get bundles. That means it's possible—and, in my experience, probable—that the result of the getBundles() request won't include the bundle that was just added.

Unfortunately, this experience is not unique to Elasticsearch. In order to handle requests at scale, many systems distribute the load across a network. Even SQL servers are not immune. One common practice is to have a central server receive write requests, then replicate data to other read-only servers to satisfy queries. Even if the delay between a central write and the replication is tiny, it's still quite possible to perform a read too soon after a write to pick up the changes.

For this reason, it's up to you to maintain the relevant data in your application and mirror the changes you're making asynchronously upstream. That's the safe way to guard against getting stale results due to eventual consistency.

Once you save these changes to app/index.ts, you should see the form above the list when you visit #list-bundles. Try adding a new bundle. It should appear in the list, with a success message up top.

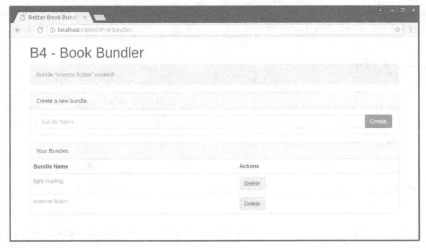

Whew! What a lot of work to get this far. There is, of course, a ton more functionality this application needs to be usable, but a lot of it is in the form of iterative features and improvements on this basic structure.

Let's quickly recap what we discussed in this chapter, then move on to wrapping it all together.

Wrapping Up

In this chapter, you learned how to set up a front-end project for Node.js using webpack. To style the application, you used Twitter's Bootstrap framework.

Rather than write front-end JavaScript code to the lowest common denominator among browsers, you installed and configured TypeScript to transpile and type-check your code. Knowing how to do this, you're now able to explore using more TypeScript features in your Node.js and front-end code.

For handling synchronous and asynchronous code flows, we doubled down on async functions paired with Promise-generating methods. You learned how to issue asynchronous HTTP requests using the fetch() method.

We explored the vulnerabilities inherent in generating HTML naively with JavaScript template strings. You learned how to sidestep these vulnerabilities by using a templating library like Handlebars.

In the next chapter we'll pull everything together. Rather than proxying Node.js APIs through the webpack dev server, we'll have an integrated application from end to end. This will require user authentication and thinking about protected APIs.

The tasks below ask you to build on the existing b4-app project you started in this chapter. If you get stuck, check out the b4-final application in the download that accompanies this book.

Extracting Text

The B4 project described in this chapter takes all the CSS from Bootstrap and puts it in a <style> at the top of the rendered index.html file. This is typically not the way you'd do things in a production-grade project. Instead you'd put the CSS in a separate file that is loaded in with a <link> tag.

A webpack plugin called ExtractTextPlugin can help with this; it's in the npm package extract-text-webpack-plugin. Your task is to incorporate it into this project (version 3.0.1).

After you install the package using npm, make the following changes to your webpack.config.js:

- Bring in the plugin with a call to require() at the top of the file.

- Replace the use field for the CSS entry under module.rules with a call to ExtractTextPlugin.extract().

- Insert a new instance of the ExtractTextPlugin class into the plugins array.

Both the ExtractTextPlugin constructor and the call to the static method Extract-TextPlugin.extract() require particular parameters. To find out exactly what they need, see the project's README.md file.[13]

You can also take a look at the b4-final project in the downloads that accompany this book.

Deleting Bundles

One feature of the B4 application we didn't discuss was how to delete bundles once they were made. In this task, you'll wire up the Delete buttons produced in the table rendered by the listBundles() in app/index.ts.

To get started, navigate to the listBundles() function and add this block of code.

ux/b4-app/app/index.ts
```
const deleteButtons = mainElement.querySelectorAll('button.delete');
for (let i = 0; i < deleteButtons.length; i++) {
  const deleteButton = deleteButtons[i];
  deleteButton.addEventListener('click', event => {
    deleteBundle(deleteButton.getAttribute('data-bundle-id'));
  });
}
```

This code selects the Delete buttons from the table and sets up a click handler for each one. The click handler extracts the data-bundle-id attribute value and passes this into a function called deleteBundle(). Your job is to implement this async function.

To get you started, here's the basic outline:

ux/b4-app/app/index.ts
```
/**
 * Delete the bundle with the specified ID, then list bundles.
 */
const deleteBundle = async (bundleId) => {
  try {
    // Delete the bundle, then render the updated list with listBundles().

    showAlert(`Bundle deleted!`, 'success');
  } catch (err) {
    showAlert(err);
  }
};
```

---

13. https://github.com/webpack-contrib/extract-text-webpack-plugin/blob/v3.0.1/README.md

Inside the try block, your task is to implement the following:

- Use getBundles() to retrieve the current list of bundles.

- Find the index of the selected bundleId in the list. (If there is no matching bundle, throw an exception explaining the problem.)

- Issue an HTTP DELETE request for the specified bundleId using fetch().

- Remove the bundle from the list by calling splice(), passing in the found index.

- Render the updated list using listBundles() and show a success message using showAlert().

If any errors occur in the above sequence, they'll show up in the catch block and show up as an alert. Good luck!

CHAPTER 9

Fortifying Your Application

Over the last couple of chapters, you've been building up the skills to create back-end APIs for a server using Express, and a front end using TypeScript and webpack. In this chapter, you'll put it all together from end to end to create a full-stack JavaScript application in Node.js.

This is the capstone course of the B4 application arc. Recall that B4, the Better Book Bundle Builder, is a Node.js application that empowers users to create named reading lists called book bundles. It relies on Elasticsearch to store information about books and book bundles. Chapters 5 and 6 were about manipulating this data, getting everything in place to build APIs on top.

In Chapters 7 and 8, you learned to create RESTful APIs and a UI that communicates with them, respectively, but they were run as separate programs. In this chapter, we'll pull them together along with authentication and session management. Users will be able to sign in with Facebook, Twitter, or Google, and then view and create book bundles.

By the end of this chapter, you'll have the foundation you need to put together Node.js-based web applications yourself, from scratch.

It's a long chapter, but even so, it doesn't cover everything there is to know about deploying your Node.js application in production. The state of the art moves too quickly for that. But you should have enough that you can ask the right questions to take you the rest of the way.

We'll cover these aspects of Node.js development in this chapter:

Node.js Core

> At this point, we're pretty far removed from the Node.js core, but we'll still touch on some important topics. You'll use the URL class from the url module to construct application-specific URLs. You'll use the NODE_ENV environment variable to control whether your application runs in development or

production mode. And you'll also use the built-in path module to perform OS-specific filesystem path manipulations.

Patterns

We'll hit on some patterns both new and old. You'll get more practice writing Express middleware, and you'll learn to encapsulate stacks of middleware and routes into Express Routers. You'll also use Passport to authenticate users and store their session state with the express-session module.

JavaScriptisms

In this chapter, you'll get a lot more practice writing async functions—the important new way of handling both synchronous and asynchronous code flows in a consistent style. You'll also make richer use of the fetch() API for performing authenticated API requests.

Supporting Code

It takes a surprising amount of supporting code to build this kind of app. You'll learn how to create and use a localhost alias for development. You'll install and use Social Bootstrap and Font Awesome, both of which provide well-designed UI components. Lastly, you'll use Redis, a fast database and caching server for storing user sessions in production mode.

Users of the B4 application that you'll be making will be able to sign in using any of three authentication services: Facebook, Twitter, or Google. I'll walk you through how to set up all of them. First we'll quickly get the initial project running locally, during which I'll explain the few bits it contains that you haven't seen yet. From there we're ready to build on top. Let's go!

Setting Up the Initial Project

Rather than write everything from scratch, you'll want to rely more on the code download that accompanies this book than in previous chapters. In the fortify directory, you'll find three subdirectories:

- b4-initial—You should copy this directory to a local directory called b4.

- b4—This represents the project as it should be at the end of the chapter. No peeking!

- b4-final—This includes everything in b4 plus more functionality—the ability to add books to bundles, book title autocomplete, etc.

The b4-initial project that you'll be building on combines the Express framework and the webpack compilation of the last two chapters. Here's a file listing of that directory:

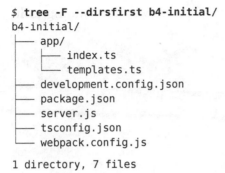

```
$ tree -F --dirsfirst b4-initial/
b4-initial/
├── app/
│   ├── index.ts
│   └── templates.ts
├── development.config.json
├── package.json
├── server.js
├── tsconfig.json
└── webpack.config.js

1 directory, 7 files
```

The app directory contains an index.ts and a templates.ts file, just like in the last chapter. These files have some minor differences from their predecessors that will make sense as you make changes during this chapter.

The tsconfig.json is identical to the last chapter's version, and the webpack.config.js is quite similar except that it uses Node.js's path module for OS-specific file-path manipulations.

development.config.json contains the configuration settings for running the project in development mode. It has Elasticsearch connection settings and a serviceURL string, which we'll discuss shortly.

The package.json file describes the project, and server.js pulls it all together. We'll dive into the server.js file in a bit.

To get started, copy the b4-initial into your own working directory called b4. Now open a terminal to your new b4 directory.

The first thing to do is run npm install to get all the dependencies.

```
$ npm install
```

And then you can start the server with npm start:

```
$ npm start
```

You can leave this running for the rest of the chapter, until we get to the part about running in production. As you make changes, nodemon will pick them up, recompile the webpack assets, and restart the server.

Next let's dive into server.js, which is core to the work you'll be doing in this chapter.

Reviewing the server.js File

The server.js file is the backbone that holds the project together. It pulls in all the modules and configures Express and related middleware.

Let's take a quick peek at this important file before we start adding to it. Here it is:

```
fortify/b4/server.js
'use strict';
const pkg = require('./package.json');
const {URL} = require('url');
const path = require('path');

// nconf configuration.
const nconf = require('nconf');
nconf
  .argv()
  .env('__')
  .defaults({'NODE_ENV': 'development'});

const NODE_ENV = nconf.get('NODE_ENV');
const isDev = NODE_ENV === 'development';
nconf
  .defaults({'conf': path.join(__dirname, `${NODE_ENV}.config.json`)})
  .file(nconf.get('conf'));

const serviceUrl = new URL(nconf.get('serviceUrl'));
const servicePort =
    serviceUrl.port || (serviceUrl.protocol === 'https:' ? 443 : 80);

// Express and middleware.
const express = require('express');
const morgan = require('morgan');

const app = express();

app.use(morgan('dev'));

app.get('/api/version', (req, res) => res.status(200).json(pkg.version));

// Serve webpack assets.
if (isDev) {
  const webpack = require('webpack');
  const webpackMiddleware = require('webpack-dev-middleware');
  const webpackConfig = require('./webpack.config.js');
  app.use(webpackMiddleware(webpack(webpackConfig), {
    publicPath: '/',
    stats: {colors: true},
  }));
} else {
  app.use(express.static('dist'));
}

app.listen(servicePort, () => console.log('Ready.'));
```

Serving Over HTTPS

At some point you'll want to launch your Express-based Node.js application externally. When you do, it's prudent to serve your content and APIs over HTTPS.

To do this, you'll need certificate files and a little extra code that makes use of Node.js's built-in https module.[a] Here's an example:

```
const fs = require('fs');
const https = require('https');
const httpsOptions = {
  key: fs.readFileSync('path/to/private.key'),
  cert: fs.readFileSync('path/to/certificate.pem'),
};
https.createServer(httpsOptions, app)
    .listen(() => console.log('Secure Server Ready.'));
```

The httpsOptions object can be configured in a few different ways, depending on whether you have .pem, .pfx, or other kinds of certificate files.

A complete discussion of how to obtain keys and certificates is outside the scope of this book, but the Node.js documentation for the tls.createSecureContext() describes, in detail, all of the available options.[b] Note that it would be better to read the file paths from nconf rather than hard-coding them as in this example.

Good luck!

_____

a.   https://nodejs.org/api/https.html
b.   https://nodejs.org/api/tls.html#tls_tls_createsecurecontext_options

Much of this should look familiar to you, so I won't go over all of it. But there are a few parts you should pay some attention to.

First, check out the part about NODE_ENV around line 13. This environment variable is widely used to indicate whether a Node.js program is running in production mode. Here we pull it from nconf, with the default set to development.

Next, on line 19, observe the serviceUrl constant. This is a URL instance implemented in the Node.js core module url and adhering to the URLInterface web standard.[1] [2] We'll use URL instances to construct URLs relative to the main service URL throughout.

Lastly, take a look at the webpack-dev-middleware part beginning on line 34. The webpack-dev-middleware module serves webpack assets directly from memory through Express.[3] When we're in dev mode, we'll serve them this way, but in

_____

1.   https://nodejs.org/api/url.html
2.   https://developer.mozilla.org/en-US/docs/Web/API/URL
3.   https://www.npmjs.com/package/webpack-dev-middleware

production mode we want to serve static files from the dist directory. This directory doesn't yet exist, but will once you invoke npm run build, which is configured in the package.json to execute webpack.

Take a minute to familiarize yourself with this file since you'll be building on top of it throughout the chapter. When you're ready, there's one more bit of setup: your localhost alias.

Configuring a localhost Alias

When developing services locally, it's typical to rely on localhost at IP address 127.0.0.1. We've been doing it all along in this book.

Unfortunately, this is a problem for authentication using OAuth, which we'll be doing later in this chapter. To be clear, nothing in OAuth specifically prohibits using localhost, but the three providers we'll be using have mutually incompatible rules around allowable domain names for development.

Facebook's app-configuration page allows you to use localhost for website URLs but prohibits 127.0.0.1. Twitter allows you to use 127.0.0.1 but disallows localhost. For its part, Google authentication is OK with both localhost and 127.0.0.1, but otherwise requires hostnames to end in a legitimate top-level domain (TLD).

We need a hostname that all three services will allow and that we can point to 127.0.0.1 for local development. For this, I've chosen b4.example.com. The .com suffix satisfies Google's TLD requirement, and the example.com second-level domain is reserved by IANA for illustrative purposes, so it can't create an accidental collision.

To point b4.example.com to 127.0.0.1, you need to add an entry to your operating system's hosts file. On Mac OS X and Linux, you can find this file at /etc/hosts. On Windows, it's at \WINDOWS\system32\drivers\etc\hosts.

Open your hosts file in a text editor (this generally requires root privileges), then add the following line:

```
127.0.0.1 b4.example.com
```

After you have saved the file, any requests you make to b4.example.com will go to your loopback interface, IP address 127.0.0.1. Try it out by opening http://b4.example.com:60900 in a browser. It should look like the figure on page 225.

If so, great! Now you're ready to start developing. Let's start by adding support for persistent sessions.

Welcome!

B4 is an application for creating book bundles.

Managing User Sessions in Express

In previous chapters, all of our APIs have placed no authentication requirements on the caller, nor made any attempt to link one request with any previous request. For users to have their own book bundles, we need some identifying token that persists between requests. This is a *session*.

Sessions are most typically implemented by giving each new user a cookie with an ID that links to some backing session data. Subsequent requests made by the user's browser (also called a user agent) will include the cookie value, allowing the server to update the user's session information.

In Express, this is all implemented with middleware. You'll need the express-session and session-file-store modules. Install those with npm.

```
$ npm install --save -E express-session@1.15.6 session-file-store@1.1.2
```

The express-session module is responsible for using cookies to associate session data with requests. By default, this will store session data in memory by using a MemoryStore. That won't work for us for two reasons—one that applies to development, and one that applies to production.

During development, nodemon will restart the server each time you save a source code file, wiping out any session data in memory. This makes it incredibly tedious to develop and test session-based code, since each time you change the code, it'll sign you out!

In production, the express-session's default MemoryStore is not recommended due to memory leaks and a single-processor limit. There's no shared memory between Node.js processes.

Instead of MemoryStore, we'll use the FileStore class from the session-file-store module during development. This session-storage implementation uses a .json file per session to store data associated with each cookie.

Open your server.js file for editing and find the line that creates the Express app instance:

```
fortify/b4/server.js
const app = express();
```

Then insert the following lines immediately below it:

```
fortify/b4/server.js
// Setup Express sessions.
const expressSession = require('express-session');
if (isDev) {
  // Use FileStore in development mode.
  const FileStore = require('session-file-store')(expressSession);
  app.use(expressSession({
    resave: false,
    saveUninitialized: true,
    secret: 'unguessable',
    store: new FileStore(),
  }));
} else {
  // Use RedisStore in production mode.
}
```

We pull in the expressSession middleware and then enter an isDev check. Using the FileStore class, the app.use() call sets up the expressSession middleware with its required options. Here's a quick rundown of each:

- resave—This option indicates whether the session should be saved on each request, even if no changes have been made. Since both the FileStore we're using now and the RedisStore that we'll be using later implement the touch() operation, we can safely set resave to false.

- saveUninitialized—This dictates whether to save new but unmodified sessions. Setting this to false protects against race conditions in which the user agent makes simultaneous cookieless requests. It's also useful if you need to get the user's permission before using cookies. During development, it helps to set this to true so you can inspect the session data even when it's empty.

- secret—This required string is used to sign cookie values, making it harder for an attacker to guess users' session IDs. In production mode, we'll pull this in from nconf.

- store—This is an instance of a class that extends the Store class of the express-session module. It is used to implement session data storage.

The FileStore can take a configuration object that allows you to specify various options.[4] The defaults are all fine in our case. This means that it will store session information in the ./sessions directory.

After you save this file, visit your running server at http://b4.example .com:60900. It should look the same, of course, but now there should be a sessions directory in your project folder that contains a JSON file. The file's name matches the session ID (the cookie value), and it contains the data associated with the session. You can take a peek by feeding the file through jq.

```
$ cat sessions/*.json | jq '.'
{
  "cookie": {
    "originalMaxAge": null,
    "expires": null,
    "httpOnly": true,
    "path": "/"
  },
  "__lastAccess": 1499592937433
}
```

The session data is pretty much empty, but at least it's there. You can use this technique at any time to inspect your session data—it's a valuable tool when debugging session-based problems. We're now in position to add the sign-in flow.

Adding Authentication UI Elements

At this point, your skeleton B4 application has session support, but no way to sign in. There are two parts to implementing the authentication flow—the front end and the back end.

On the front end, we need to add buttons so the user can choose the service with which to authenticate. The first step is to install the social buttons for Bootstrap so we can insert them into a template.[5] This module depends on Font Awesome for its icons,[6] so you'll need to install that too. Use npm for both.

```
$ npm install --save -E bootstrap-social@5.1.1 font-awesome@4.7.0
```

Next, for webpack to find and use these you'll need to import them into your index.ts file. Add these lines at the top, right after the import line for Bootstrap, then save the file:

---

4. https://www.npmjs.com/package/session-file-store#options
5. https://lipis.github.io/bootstrap-social/
6. http://fontawesome.io/

```
fortify/b4/app/index.ts
import '../node_modules/bootstrap-social/bootstrap-social.css';
import '../node_modules/font-awesome/css/font-awesome.min.css';
```

Now we can add the social sign-in buttons. Open your templates.ts file and update the welcome() template by inserting the following to the end of the .jumbotron div:

```
fortify/b4/app/templates.ts
{{#if session.auth}}
<p>View your <a href="#list-bundles">bundles</a>.</p>
{{else}}
<p>Sign in with any of these services to begin.</p>
<div class="row">
  <div class="col-sm-6">
    <a href="/auth/facebook" class="btn btn-block btn-social btn-facebook">
      Sign in with Facebook
      <span class="fa fa-facebook"></span>
    </a>
    <a href="/auth/twitter" class="btn btn-block btn-social btn-twitter">
      Sign in with Twitter
      <span class="fa fa-twitter"></span>
    </a>
    <a href="/auth/google" class="btn btn-block btn-social btn-google">
      Sign in with Google
      <span class="fa fa-google"></span>
    </a>
  </div>
</div>
{{/if}}
```

This code uses a Handlebars {{#if}} block to check if the passed-in session object has auth set to true. Recall that Handlebars is a templating language we introduced for rendering HTML in *Templating HTML with Handlebars*, on page 201. If session.auth is true, then we show users a link to where they can view and edit their book bundles. Otherwise, we show the social sign-in buttons.

Note that our code currently doesn't pass an empty session object to the welcome() Handlebars template. We'll need an API that the browser can hit to return a session object; we'll implement that shortly. But for now, Handlebars will evaluate the expression session.auth to be falsey.

Also, the links for the Facebook, Twitter, and Google social sign-in buttons go to /auth/facebook, /auth/twitter, and /auth/google. Our server.js currently implements none of these endpoints, so we'll need to do that as well.

After you save this file, head back to http://b4.example.com:60900. It should now look like the figure on page 229.

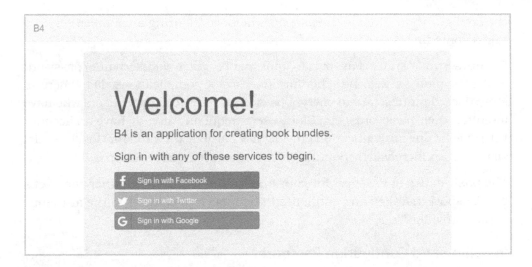

While you have templates.ts open for editing, let's make one more quick change. When a user is signed in, there are a couple of links that would be helpful to show in the nav bar up top: a link to their book bundles, and a Sign Out link.

To add those, find the main() Handlebars template and update it to look as follows by adding the {{#if}} block to the end of the .container-fluid div.

```
fortify/b4/app/templates.ts
{{#if session.auth}}
<div class="collapse navbar-collapse">
  <ul class="nav navbar-nav navbar-right">
    <li><a href="#list-bundles">My Bundles</a></li>
    <li><a href="/auth/signout">Sign Out</a></li>
  </ul>
</div><!-- /.navbar-collapse -->
{{/if}}
```

Here again, we're using {{#if}} to perform an auth check. If the user is signed in, then we'll show links to My Bundles and Sign Out.

When you save this file, there won't be any visible changes in your rendered page as yet. But once we finish the auth flow, these links will show up. Let's implement the auth flow now.

Setting Up Passport

Passport provides authentication middleware for Express-based applications. We're going to use it to implement social sign-on using three popular platforms: Facebook, Twitter, and Google. All three of these offer an OAuth flow for federated authentication, and there are Passport plugins to help simplify the configuration. Even with Passport's help, configuring all of these services takes some finesse.

Of course, you can use Passport to implement regular old username/password authentication as well, but this introduces new complications, like where to store user identities, how to encrypt passwords, how to support users who have forgotten their passwords, etc. Since users frequently already have an account with at least one authentication provider like Facebook, Twitter, or Google, social sign-in is an increasingly popular way to outsource these concerns.

The basic setup of Passport for your application is the same either way. Let's get Passport installed and configured, then use it to connect to the authentication providers.

Installing and Configuring Passport

To start, install the Passport Node.js module.

```
$ npm install --save -E passport@0.4.0
```

Next, open your server.js file for editing. After the part on configuring Express sessions that you added earlier, insert this new Passport setup section.

```
fortify/b4/server.js
// Passport Authentication.
const passport = require('passport');
passport.serializeUser((profile, done) => done(null, {
  id: profile.id,
  provider: profile.provider,
}));
passport.deserializeUser((user, done) => done(null, user));
app.use(passport.initialize());
app.use(passport.session());
```

Passport requires you to implement methods to serialize and deserialize users. That is, you have to tell Passport how to go from a user's identity token to an actual user object and vice versa. Typically, this is where you'd reach out to a database of some kind to load up an account object based on the user's ID. Both serializeUser() and deserializeUser() take a single callback function.

The callback function you pass to serializeUser() should take a Passport User Profile object,[7] and call done() with the minimum amount of data necessary to identify that user. For example, this function could query a database, then return a simple user ID string. In our case, we're not going to store per-user data in a database (aside from book bundles, which we'll get to), so all we

---

7.   http://passportjs.org/docs/profile

need is to keep track of the user's ID and which provider the user authenticated with. This is sufficient to uniquely identify a user in our system.

The deserializeUser() method takes a function that does the opposite. Given the identifier produced by your serializeUser() callback, your deserializeUser() function should retrieve the full object. In our case, the identifier is an object with the id of the user and the provider the user signed in with. Since this is all we know about the user, there's no need to perform any kind of lookup and we can just send this object to done() straight away. For more info on how to implement these callbacks, check out Passport's session documentation.[8]

After that, we call app.use() on the output of passport.initialize() and passport.session(). Order is important here! The passport.session() middleware must come after the expressSession() that you added earlier. Otherwise sessions may not be restored properly.

The next step is to set up a couple of generic session routes: /auth/session for info about the session and /auth/signout to allow users to sign off. Let's add those.

Adding Session Routes

We'll need two Express routes irrespective of which authentication provider the user signs in with. The first, /api/session, returns information about the current user session. We'll call this asynchronously from the front end in app/index.ts.

Open your server.js file for editing and navigate to the bottom. Just before the call to app.listen(), insert the following:

```
fortify/b4/server.js
app.get('/api/session', (req, res) => {
  const session = {auth: req.isAuthenticated()};
  res.status(200).json(session);
});
```

Passport adds an isAuthenticated() method to the Express request object, req. Here, the /api/session route returns an object with an auth property that'll be either true or false. After you save, you can try it out in a terminal with curl.

```
$ curl -s b4.example.com:60900/api/session
{"auth":false}
```

Now, after the /auth/session route, add the following to set up the /auth/signout route.

---

8. http://passportjs.org/docs#sessions

```
fortify/b4/server.js
app.get('/auth/signout', (req, res) => {
  req.logout();
  res.redirect('/');
});
```

Along with isAuthenticated(), Passport adds a logout() method to the req object. After calling it, we redirect the user back to the main page.

With these routes in place, we can now wire them into the front end.

Connecting the Session API to the Front End

Now that we have a /api/session route that can return a session object, let's pass this object to the templates. This is necessary so we can conditionally show session-based info to the user (like the Sign Out link).

In your app directory, open the index.ts file for editing. To simplify requests to the back end, start by adding this utility function toward the top of the file:

```
fortify/b4/app/index.ts
/**
 * Convenience method to fetch and decode JSON.
 */
const fetchJSON = async (url, method = 'GET') => {
  try {
    const response = await fetch(url, {method, credentials: 'same-origin'});
    return response.json();
  } catch (error) {
    return {error};
  }
};
```

The fetchJSON() async function takes two parameters: a required url string to fetch, and an optional method that defaults to GET. This function fetches the desired URL using the fetch API.[9]

Note the use of the credentials option. This ensures that credential information (cookies) is sent with the request. Without this option, by default fetch() will not send cookies, meaning the back end would treat the request as unauthenticated.

If the fetch() call succeeds, then we send back the Promise returned by response.json(). Callers of fetchJSON() will await the result and receive the deserialized JSON object. If anything went wrong, we return an object containing the error.

---

9. https://developer.mozilla.org/en-US/docs/Web/API/Fetch_API/Using_Fetch

Now to use fetchJSON() to get the session information. Scroll down in your index.ts file to the showView() method. In the switch block, update the #welcome case to be this:

```
fortify/b4/app/index.ts
case '#welcome':
  const session = await fetchJSON('/api/session');
  mainElement.innerHTML = templates.welcome({session});
  if (session.error) {
    showAlert(session.error);
  }
  break;
```

Now, instead of calling the welcome() template with an empty session object, we use fetchJSON() to GET /api/session, then pass the resulting object to the template. If there was an error, we use showAlert() to display it.

Scroll to the bottom of the index.ts file and find the anonymous async function that performs the page setup. Update it to read as follows:

```
fortify/b4/app/index.ts
// Page setup.
(async () => {
  const session = await fetchJSON('/api/session');
  document.body.innerHTML = templates.main({session});
  window.addEventListener('hashchange', showView);
  showView().catch(err => window.location.hash = '#welcome');
})();
```

Instead of calling main() with an empty object, here we pass it the user's session object.

It may seem odd to you that we're reaching out to /api/session twice instead of doing it just once and reusing that object throughout. The reason is that the session may change over time.

Cookies do not last forever. Eventually they expire. By default, the cookies that the Express session stack creates last about a day. This means that if users revisit the welcome page a day later, they'll be signed out.

The right thing to do in that case is show them the sign-in buttons so they can reauthenticate. Grabbing a fresh session object from /api/session inside of the showView() method ensures they're seeing session-appropriate content.

Once you save index.ts, nodemon will automatically restart your service. You won't see any visible changes in the UI yet; for that we'll need to implement at least one authentication provider and sign in with it. Let's start with Facebook, then proceed to Twitter and Google.

Authenticating with Facebook, Twitter, and Google

At this point, your full-stack JavaScript application has Passport in place for managing the authentication for user sessions. We're now ready to plug into various authentication providers, allowing users to sign in with their external accounts.

Authentication mechanisms in Passport are called *Strategies*. To support each provider, you'll need to install and configure the npm module for the provider, which includes a Strategy class that plugs into Passport.

The steps are as follows:

1. Create an app with the provider.

2. Add the app's identifier and secret information to your config.

3. Install the Passport Strategy for that provider.

4. Configure the Strategy instance in your server.js file.

First we'll go through these steps to set up authentication with Facebook, then with Twitter, and finally with Google. Since the setup for each provider involves a certain amount of boilerplate, we'll spend more time describing the Facebook authentication setup steps than the others.

Once you're done setting up Facebook, you have the option of skipping ahead to *Composing an Express Router*, on page 246. Having one authentication mechanism working is sufficient to develop the authenticated book-bundle APIs in the rest of the chapter. Let's begin!

Creating Your Facebook App

For your users to sign in with Facebook, you'll need to make a Facebook app. And to do that, you'll need a registered Facebook developer account.

If you don't yet have a Facebook developer account, you can register at the Facebook Developers page.[10]

Once you have an account, head to the Facebook Apps page and click the + Add a New App button.[11] Set the display name to *b4-dev*, then click Create App ID to continue. After you satisfy a captcha, it'll create your app and take you to it.

---

10. https://developers.facebook.com/
11. https://developers.facebook.com/apps/

When you get to your app, click the Settings link in the menu on the left sidebar. At the bottom click the + Add Platform button and select Website from the options—this will add a Website section to the page. Set the site URL to http://b4.example.com:60900. Finally, click Save Changes. When you're done, it should look like this:

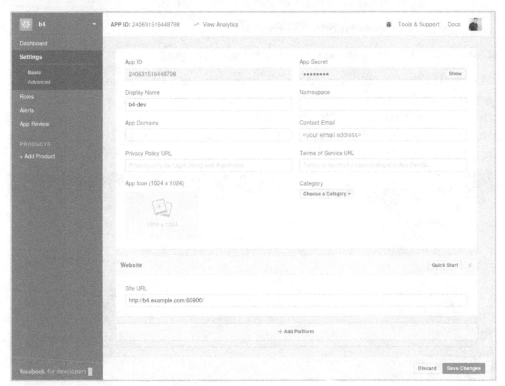

You need two pieces of information from this page in order to use the app for authentication: the app ID and the app secret. The app ID is readily visible, but you have to click the Show button to see the app secret.

Open your development.config.json for editing and add an auth section as follows:

```
"auth": {
  "facebook": {
    "appID": "<your Facebook App ID>",
    "appSecret": "<your Facebook App Secret>"
  }
}
```

Make sure to set the appId and appSecret values to those for your own project, then save the file.

Keep your app secret safe! Anyone with this string is able to perform user actions as though they were your app.

Adding the Facebook Strategy to Passport

Now that you have your Facebook app created and you've recorded the appID and appSecret in your config, it's time to install and configure the Passport Facebook npm module. This module includes a Strategy class for handling the details of connecting to Facebook for authentication.

Start by installing the module with npm:

```
$ npm install --save -E passport-facebook@2.1.1
```

To use the Facebook Strategy for authenticating with Passport, we need to set up two Express routes. The first route is /auth/facebook. When users visit this route by clicking the Sign In with Facebook button on the Welcome screen, they'll get redirected to a Facebook sign-in page. If everything goes according to plan, that'll look something like this:

The second Express route we need is /auth/facebook/callback, which is where Facebook will redirect users once they have signed in. Passport is quite flexible when it comes to exactly what these routes are, in addition to other behavior associated with the authentication process. You have a lot of choices, but that means you have to perform a lot of configuration. The code I will show you next is the minimum amount to get going—your own projects' needs may vary.

Open your server.js for editing, and find the Passport Authentication section you added earlier. Immediately below that, insert the following:

fortify/b4/server.js

```
const FacebookStrategy = require('passport-facebook').Strategy;
passport.use(new FacebookStrategy({
  clientID: nconf.get('auth:facebook:appID'),
  clientSecret: nconf.get('auth:facebook:appSecret'),
  callbackURL: new URL('/auth/facebook/callback', serviceUrl).href,
}, (accessToken, refreshToken, profile, done) => done(null, profile)));
```

This code is a little dense, but it's mostly boilerplate. First, we pull in the Strategy class as FacebookStrategy. Calling passport.use() takes two arguments. One is a configured Strategy instance and the other is a callback function to be used to resolve the user object from the Facebook profile information. Let's go over each briefly.

To configure the FacebookStrategy instance, we pass it three values. The clientID and clientSecret values are the app ID and app secret for your Facebook app. The callbackURL is a fully qualified URL that points to the /auth/facebook/callback route. Here we're using the URL class to construct such a string using the serviceUrl as a base.

Check out the user-resolving callback function—passport.use()'s second argument. Since we're not storing per-user data, the profile really is all we need, so we call done() immediately with it. Your own applications may need to do something fancier here, like reach out to a database to retrieve user information.

Note that the profile object here is exactly the input to the serializeUser() callback function that you gave to Passport. In your own applications, you may end up doing something more complex to resolve the user after Facebook sign-in. If you do, make sure you also update your Passport serialization code since these profile objects must match.

Let's look at an example. Recall the serializeUser() method from before:

fortify/b4/server.js

```
passport.serializeUser((profile, done) => done(null, {
  id: profile.id,
  provider: profile.provider,
}));
```

Notice how the callback function takes a provider object and expects it to have both an id and a provider property. Now consider the final callback function parameter to the FacebookStrategy constructor, which resolves the successful sign-in token to a user's profile object:

```
(accessToken, refreshToken, profile, done) => done(null, profile)
```

When you call done(), behind the scenes Passport and Express will take the profile object here and make sure it gets passed to your serializeUser() callback function. So while you have the flexibility to implement more complex profile objects, it's up to you to ensure that the way those objects are handled is consistent in both places. For more info on how you can configure the Facebook Strategy, including an example of how you can store richer profile information in a separate database, see Passport's documentation page.[12]

Now that Passport is configured to use the Facebook Strategy, we can finally add the Express routes. Append this code right after the passport.use() call:

fortify/b4/server.js
```
app.get('/auth/facebook', passport.authenticate('facebook'));
app.get('/auth/facebook/callback', passport.authenticate('facebook', {
  successRedirect: '/',
  failureRedirect: '/',
}));
```

When users hit the /auth/facebook route, it will redirect them to Facebook to sign in. When they've finished, Facebook will send them to /auth/facebook/callback. This may be a successful sign-in, or it could have failed for any reason. Depending on which, Passport will redirect the user to either the successRedirect or the failureRedirect.

Because B4 is a single-page application, we send the user to the web root (/) irrespective of whether the sign-in was successful. Once we add the session code to the front end, the Handlebars templates will show the correct content to the user based on whether he signed in successfully.

After you save these additions to the server.js file, nodemon should restart the service successfully. If not, stop here and troubleshoot. Remember that you can peek at the b4-final implementation in the code downloads that accompany this book.

Facebook authentication should now be all set up from end to end. To test it, navigate to your B4 application at http://b4.example.com:60900. Click the Sign In with Facebook button, then sign in. If all goes according to plan, it should redirect you back to B4, which ought to look like the figure on page 239.

If so, great, but don't get discouraged if you see the old Welcome page. I've seen this be a little flaky, so if it still shows the sign-in buttons, try clicking again.

---

12. http://passportjs.org/docs/facebook

B4

Welcome!

B4 is an application for creating book bundles.

View your bundles.

If it's not working for you, then you need to figure out whether it's a Facebook authentication problem or a code problem. The first place to investigate is the .json file for your session in your sessions directory. When Passport succeeds in authenticating with Facebook, that file should look something like this:

```
$ cat sessions/*.json | jq '.'
{
  "cookie": {
    "originalMaxAge": null,
    "expires": null,
    "httpOnly": true,
    "path": "/"
  },
  "__lastAccess": 1500116410607,
  "passport": {
    "user": {
      "id": "10155505203238200",
      "provider": "facebook"
    }
  }
}
```

If the Facebook authentication failed, then the passport section would be missing. If the passport section is there, then you may have a code problem that you need to troubleshoot. The logs in your nodemon terminal may also help.

Another benefit to having session data right in these JSON files is that you can sign users out by deleting them. When you delete a session's .json file in the sessions directory, it invalidates the session and the user must sign in again.

Once you have Facebook authentication confirmed as working, you can either skip forward to *Composing an Express Router*, on page 246, or continue to the next section to set up authentication with Twitter.

Authenticating with Twitter

In this section, you'll follow steps similar to those for setting up Facebook authentication. You'll create a Twitter app, add the identifier and secret to your config, install the Twitter Passport module, and configure the Strategy in server.js.

To create a Twitter app, start by opening a browser tab to the Twitter Apps page.[13] Then click the Create New App button. In the New App form, fill in these details of the B4 application:

- Name—b4-dev
- Description—Better Book Bundle Builder
- Website—http://b4.example.com:60900
- Callback URL—http://b4.example.com:60900/auth/twitter/callback

Click the Create Your Twitter Application button. When Twitter finishes making your app, it'll forward you to the Details page of your new app. From there, navigate to the Settings tab. It should look like this:

---

13. https://apps.twitter.com/

Make sure the check box at the bottom labeled *Allow this application to be used to sign in with Twitter* is checked.

Next, navigate to the Keys and Access Tokens tab. You'll need the consumer key and consumer secret. Open your development.config.json file for editing, then add a twitter section to auth with your consumer key and consumer secret, like this:

```
"twitter": {
  "consumerKey": "<your Consumer Key>",
  "consumerSecret": "<your Consumer Secret>"
}
```

Save this file. Next, install the Twitter Passport module with npm.

```
$ npm install --save -E passport-twitter@1.0.4
```

Now, open your server.js file for editing. Navigate to the Facebook settings you added in the previous section, then append the following code.

```
fortify/b4/server.js
const TwitterStrategy = require('passport-twitter').Strategy;
passport.use(new TwitterStrategy({
  consumerKey: nconf.get('auth:twitter:consumerKey'),
  consumerSecret: nconf.get('auth:twitter:consumerSecret'),
  callbackURL: new URL('/auth/twitter/callback', serviceUrl).href,
}, (accessToken, tokenSecret, profile, done) => done(null, profile)));

app.get('/auth/twitter', passport.authenticate('twitter'));
app.get('/auth/twitter/callback', passport.authenticate('twitter', {
  successRedirect: '/',
  failureRedirect: '/',
}));
```

This code is nearly identical to the FacebookStrategy code from earlier. We construct a TwitterStrategy and tell Passport to use it with the consumer key and consumer secret from the config file. The profile that this Strategy creates includes the id and provider that we need.

Also, just like with the Facebook setup, we need two routes. The /auth/twitter route forwards users to Twitter, where they can sign in, and the /auth/twitter/callback route is where Twitter sends users afterward.

After you save the server.js file, nodemon should pick up the change. In your browser tab with the B4 application loaded, you can now try out the Sign In with Twitter button. When you click it the first time, you should see a page like the figure on page 242.

After you click the Authorize button, Twitter will redirect you back to the B4 application, where you should now be signed in. If not, it may be because

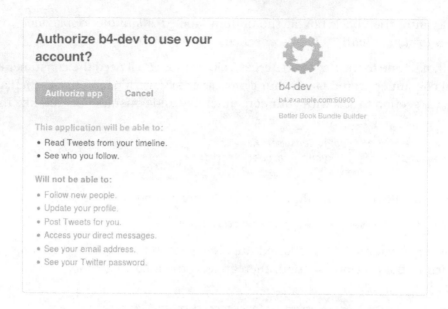

you were still signed in with Facebook. Remember that you can sign out by visiting the /auth/signout route or by deleting the .json file in the sessions directory.

If you run into trouble with Twitter, it might help to review the Passport Twitter documentation.[14]

Now let's move on to the third and final authentication provider we'll be covering, Google.

Authenticating with Google

The steps for setting up Google authentication are similar to those for Facebook and Twitter. You need to create an app, add the identifier and secret to your config, install the Passport Google module, and configure the Strategy.

To begin, go to the Google Cloud Platform page.[15] Sign in if you haven't already, then click the Console button to launch the Google Cloud Platform Console. Expand the side menu if it's not showing and choose IAM & Admin > Manage resources.

From the Manage Resources page, click the Create Project button. In the form that follows, for project name enter *b4-dev*, then click Create. When Google Cloud is finished making your project, make sure it's selected in the drop-down menu at the top of the page.

---

14. http://passportjs.org/docs/twitter
15. https://cloud.google.com

Next you'll need to enable some APIs. From the side menu, choose APIs & Services > Dashboard, then click the blue + Enable APIs and Services button at the top of the page. Scroll down and find the social APIs, then click Google+ API. This brings you to a screen describing how the Google+ API can be used for authentication, which is what we want.

Toward the top of the page, click the Enable button to turn on the Google+ API.

Next, we need to set up OAuth credentials. From the navigation bar on the left, select API Manager > Credentials. Click the Create Credentials drop-down menu and select OAuth Client ID.

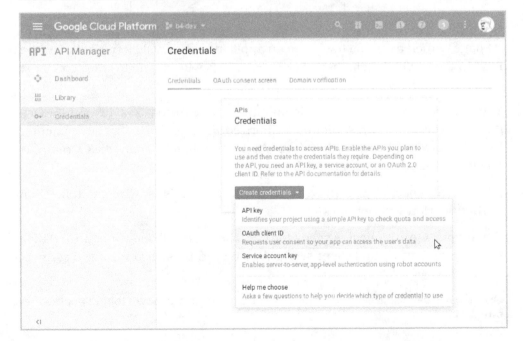

On the following screen, you may see a warning stating that you need to set up the OAuth consent screen. If so, click the link to set that up, and enter *b4-dev* for the product name shown to users.

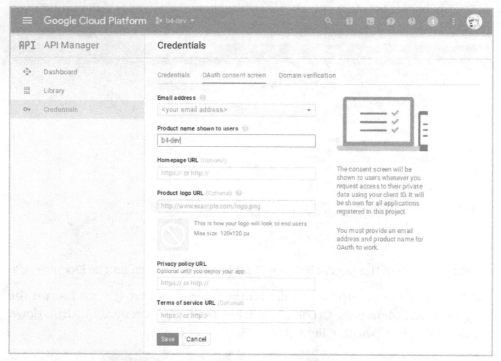

Once you save the consent-screen settings, you should be on the Create Client ID page, which asks you to choose an application type. Click the radio button next to Web Application, then click Create. This will expand to show you more options.

You can leave Name set to the default and ignore Authorized JavaScript Origins. However, you must fill out Authorized Redirect URIs. In the box, enter http://b4.example.com:60900/auth/google/callback. Then click Create as shown in the figure on page 245.

Be careful specifying your redirect URI. If there's any mismatch, then authentication will not work!

When your OAuth client is ready for use, the page will show a pop-up dialog with your client ID and client secret. You'll need these two values to connect to the service.

Open your development.config.json for editing, and add a new Google section as follows:

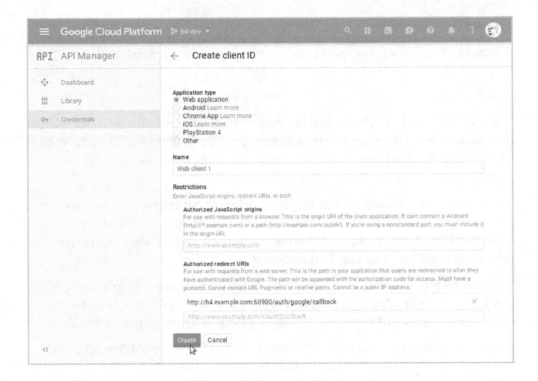

```
"google": {
  "clientID": "<your Client ID>",
  "clientSecret": "<your Client Secret>"
}
```

I've noticed that sometimes when copying the client ID and client secret, leading and trailing whitespace characters are included. Make sure to remove these when setting up your development.config.json file.

Save the file. Next, install the Passport Google module via npm.

```
$ npm install --save -E passport-google-oauth20@1.0.0
```

With that installed, all that's left is to configure the Strategy. Open your server.js, scroll down to the Twitter configuration part, and insert the following after it:

```
fortify/b4/server.js
const GoogleStrategy = require('passport-google-oauth20').Strategy;
passport.use(new GoogleStrategy({
  clientID: nconf.get('auth:google:clientID'),
  clientSecret: nconf.get('auth:google:clientSecret'),
  callbackURL: new URL('/auth/google/callback', serviceUrl).href,
  scope: 'https://www.googleapis.com/auth/plus.login',
}, (accessToken, refreshToken, profile, done) => done(null, profile)));
```

```
app.get('/auth/google',
    passport.authenticate('google', {scope: ['email', 'profile']}));
app.get('/auth/google/callback', passport.authenticate('google', {
  successRedirect: '/',
  failureRedirect: '/',
}));
```

Like Twitter and Facebook before, this code configures the provider Strategy by reading configuration settings from nconf. One difference, though, is that the Google Strategy requires a scope parameter. In this case, the scope is the Google+ API.

In addition, the configuration for the /auth/google route requires its own scope configuration. We don't need much for the user to sign in, so all we request is the email and profile scopes. When users authenticate, they'll be informed of what information your app is requesting.

For more help on how to use Google's OAuth for authentication with Node.js, see the Authenticating Users section of Google's Node.js Getting Started page.[16] You might also want to review Passport's Google Strategy documentation.[17]

Once you have your desired authentication mechanisms confirmed working, it's time to add in some more of the B4 functionality. This will combine the API and UI elements from the last two chapters while introducing an Express class called a Router for encapsulating routes. We'll start with the back-end API services, then fill in the UI.

Composing an Express Router

In this section, you'll learn how to create modular APIs using an Express Router. Organizing your APIs into Routers is a code-health technique that helps you reason about your code and facilitates refactoring and maintenance.

You can think of a Router like an Express subapplication. It has its own middleware stack and can contain routes.

With an Express Application, app, you can call app.use() to delegate to a Router. Routers themselves can use() other Routers in addition to having their own middleware and routes. This flexibility allows you to combine middleware and routes in a modular, maintainable way.

The APIs you'll develop in this section will be similar to those you worked on in Chapter 7, *Developing RESTful Web Services*, on page 147, but enhanced to

---

16. https://cloud.google.com/nodejs/getting-started/authenticate-users#authenticating_users
17. http://passportjs.org/docs/google

only allow authenticated users to access protected endpoints. Let's begin by setting up a module to house the book bundle Router.

Setting Up the Module

The first thing to do is put together the basic outline of a module that returns an Express Router. This is the cornerstone of modular Express development.

To start, create a lib directory in your B4 project. Then open your favorite text editor and enter this to start the bundle.js file:

```
fortify/b4/lib/bundle.js
/**
 * Provides API endpoints for working with book bundles.
 */
'use strict';
const express = require('express');
const rp = require('request-promise');

module.exports = es => {
  const url = `http://${es.host}:${es.port}/${es.bundles_index}/bundle`;

  const router = express.Router();

  return router;
};
```

This code sets up module.exports as a function that takes a configuration object for Elasticsearch and returns an Express Router instance.

After you save this file, open your server.js. At the bottom, right before the app.listen() line, add this:

```
fortify/b4/server.js
app.use('/api', require('./lib/bundle.js')(nconf.get('es')));
```

Here, we're calling app.use() and providing it two parameters. The first is the string /api and the second is the configured Router instance returned by the bundle.js module.

When given a path and a Router, app.use() will delegate to the Router routes under that path. For example, in a minute we'll add a /list-bundles route to the Router, which will have the application-level path /api/list-bundles.

Save your server.js file. nodemon should restart happily. Now let's add authentication middleware to the Router.

Protecting Routes with an Authentication Check

Since a Router is basically an Express mini application, it can have its own middleware that applies to all of its routes. Recall that middleware is a great way to run code on every route. For the book-bundle routes, we want all of them to be accessible only to authenticated users.

To do this, start by opening your bundle.js file. Insert this block before the return router line:

fortify/b4/lib/bundle.js

```
/**
 * All of these APIs require the user to have authenticated.
 */
router.use((req, res, next) => {
  if (!req.isAuthenticated()) {
    res.status(403).json({
      error: 'You must sign in to use this service.',
    });
    return;
  }
  next();
});
```

This block introduces a custom middleware function to the Router. Remember that Passport adds an isAuthenticated() method to the req object. We check that here, and if the user has not authenticated, we send her away with an HTTP 403 Forbidden status code. Now, any routes we add to the Router will be guarded against unauthenticated access.

Next let's add a route to list the user's bundles.

Listing a User's Book Bundles

In the last chapter, when we needed a list of bundles we proxied a direct connection to Elasticsearch through the webpack-dev-server and queried for all bundles. Instead, now our Express server will reach out to Elasticsearch and bring back only those bundles that belong to the authenticated user.

Passport adds a user object to the Express Request object req, which we can use to look up book bundles belonging to that user. Let's add a utility function to make it easy to get a user key based on the req.user object. Scroll to the top of your bundle.js file, then add the following right after the require() lines:

fortify/b4/lib/bundle.js

```
const getUserKey = ({user:{provider, id}}) => `${provider}-${id}`;
```

This terse arrow function uses nested destructuring assignment to pull out the user.provider and user.id properties from the Express Request instance passed in. The return value is a simple concatenation of these, separated by a hyphen. This will produce keys like facebook-1234512345.

Now that you have the getUserKey() utility method defined, let's add a route to list the user's bundles.

With your bundle.js still open for editing, navigate to the bottom. Just before the return router line at the bottom of the file, insert this:

```
/**
 * List bundles for the currently authenticated user.
 */
router.get('/list-bundles', async (req, res) => {
  try {
    const esReqBody = {
      size: 1000,
      query: {
        match: {
          userKey: getUserKey(req),
        }
      },
    };

    const options = {
      url: `${url}/_search`,
      json: true,
      body: esReqBody,
    };

    const esResBody = await rp(options);
    const bundles = esResBody.hits.hits.map(hit => ({
      id: hit._id,
      name: hit._source.name,
    }));
    res.status(200).json(bundles);
  } catch (err) {
    res.status(err.statusCode || 502).json(err.error || err);
  }
});
```

This code should look familiar to you based on its similarity to the API end-points you developed during previous chapters. We use router.get() to set up a handler for the /list-bundles route, which will be registered in server.js under /api.

Notice that the esReqBody performs an Elasticsearch query for documents (book bundles) whose userKey matches the user who initiated the incoming request. Next, let's add an API for creating a new book bundle.

Use router.post() to set up a handler for the route /bundle like so:

fortify/b4/lib/bundle.js

```
/**
 * Create a new bundle with the specified name.
 */
router.post('/bundle', async (req, res) => {
  try {
    const bundle = {
      name: req.query.name || '',
      userKey: getUserKey(req),
      books: [],
    };

    const esResBody = await rp.post({url, body: bundle, json: true});
    res.status(201).json(esResBody);
  } catch (err) {
    res.status(err.statusCode || 502).json(err.error || err);
  }
});
```

Make sure to include the userKey field! This is what allows /list-bundles to find it later.

Next, after that route, append this code to get a bundle by its ID:

fortify/b4/lib/bundle.js

```
/**
 * Retrieve a given bundle.
 */
router.get('/bundle/:id', async (req, res) => {
  try {
    const options = {
      url: `${url}/${req.params.id}`,
      json: true,
    };

    const {_source: bundle} = await rp(options);

    if (bundle.userKey !== getUserKey(req)) {
      throw {
        statusCode: 403,
        error: 'You are not authorized to view this bundle.',
      };
    }

    res.status(200).json({id: req.params.id, bundle});
  } catch (err) {
    res.status(err.statusCode || 502).json(err.error || err);
  }
});
```

The important part of this code is the part that checks whether the requested book bundle's userKey matches the currently authenticated user. If not, we throw an error that'll be picked up by the catch block below. The HTTP status code 403 Forbidden informs the caller she doesn't have access to the bundle.

Depending on the sensitivity of the material, another status code like 404 Not Found may make more sense in your own applications. Whether a book bundle with a particular ID exists is not a big secret, especially because the IDs are unintelligible random strings generated by Elasticsearch. But be vigilant in your own applications so you don't accidentally leak information by returning a 403 Forbidden in cases where knowledge of the existence of the document is in itself valuable.

Save your bundle.js file. With these routes in place, we have enough to build the UI on.

Bringing in the Book Bundle UI

Now that you have your Router implemented and protected by authentication checks, it's time to tack on the UI components to make it work end to end. The code for this is quite similar to the UI code you developed in Chapter 8, *Creating a Beautiful User Experience*, on page 185. And remember that you can review the b4-final application in the downloads that accompany this book, which include all of the code as well.

Open your index.ts file for editing. You'll need a couple of methods—the first of which is getBundles(). Add this code toward the top of the file, right after fetchJSON():

```
fortify/b4/app/index.ts
const getBundles = async () => {
  const bundles = await fetchJSON('/api/list-bundles');
  if (bundles.error) {
    throw bundles.error;
  }
  return bundles;
};
```

In the last chapter, the getBundles() method called out to Elasticsearch directly over the proxy provided by webkit-dev-server. This time we're using fetchJSON() to hit the /list-bundles route that you added to bundle.js.

Next, create an addBundle() async function after getBundles(). You can start with the code from *Saving Data with a Form*, on page 212, except that you should use fetchJSON() rather than calling fetch() directly.

After addBundle(), insert the following listBundles() function. This will be called to render the #list-bundles view.

fortify/b4/app/index.ts
```
const listBundles = bundles => {
  const mainElement = document.body.querySelector('.b4-main');

  mainElement.innerHTML =
    templates.addBundleForm() + templates.listBundles({bundles});

  const form = mainElement.querySelector('form');
  form.addEventListener('submit', event => {
    event.preventDefault();
    const name = form.querySelector('input').value;
    addBundle(name);
  });
};
```

And finally, you'll need to add this #list-bundles case to the switch statement inside of the showView() method.

fortify/b4/app/index.ts
```
case '#list-bundles':
  try {
    const bundles = await getBundles();
    listBundles(bundles);
  } catch (err) {
    showAlert(err);
    window.location.hash = '#welcome';
  }
  break;
```

When rendering the #list-bundles view, first we grab the user's book bundles using the getBundles() method you just added. Then we send that collection to the listBundles() method for rendering using the related templates.

If something went wrong (for example, if the session timed out), then the rejected Promise returned by getBundles() will become a thrown exception. The catch clause ensures that we notify the user of the error and send him back to the welcome screen.

Save your index.ts if you haven't already, and nodemon should acknowledge the changes. If you head back to http://b4.example.com:60900, everything should be in place to create and list book bundles associated with your account once you sign in.

Whew! That was a lot of work—but such is the nature of software development.

Filling in more of the behavior of the app will be left as an exercise for the reader. But before we close out this chapter, let's talk about serving in production.

Serving in Production

When you're actively developing your Node.js code, you want the turn-around time to be fast and its reliance on external systems to be low. So far we've been keeping things this way, using the isDev variable to occasionally make choices about whether to do things the development way.

In this section, you'll take the remaining steps to prepare the application to run in production mode. Once everything is in place, we'll clean out the project and reinstall the dependency modules to perform a clean production test run.

The first thing we need to switch out is how session data is stored. In a production environment, you're usually better off storing sessions on a service like Redis than on the filesystem.

Redis is a fast, open source, in-memory key/value store.[18] You can use it as a database, cache, or message broker, and you can control when and if it synchronizes to disk.

We're going to use Redis to store session information when NODE_ENV is set to production. To do this, you'll need to install Redis, then install the Redis session module, add a production.config.json file, and wire it up in your server.js file. Let's get started.

Installing Redis

The first step to using Redis to store session info is to install the Redis service. This varies by platform, but the Redis Download page has binaries for most popular operating systems.[19] If you're using Ubuntu, you can install the Redis server and command-line utilities from the repositories using apt:

```
$ sudo apt install redis-server redis-tools
```

On Mac OS X with homebrew, it's even easier:

```
$ brew install redis
```

Although the Redis project does not itself distribute a Windows build, you can get one from the Microsoft Open Tech group on GitHub.[20]

Once you've installed Redis, you can test if it's working with the redis-cli command-line program.

---

18. http://redis.io/
19. http://redis.io/download
20. https://github.com/MSOpenTech/redis

```
$ redis-cli
127.0.0.1:6379> ping
PONG
127.0.0.1:6379> quit
```

If you see this, great! You're ready to create a production config to point to it. Start by copying your development.config.json to production.config.json. Ideally, at this point you'd switch over all the configuration settings to more permanent production values. But for now, all we need to do is add the Redis configuration values.

Open your brand-new production.config.json file for editing, and add a section for Redis like so:

```
"redis": {
  "host": "localhost",
  "port": 6379,
  "secret": "<your Redis secret here>"
}
```

To connect to Redis, your server needs to know where to find it (the host and port). The default TCP port that Redis uses is 6379. The secret is used in the same way the FileStore used it earlier in the chapter—to sign cookies. If you ever need to simultaneously sign all users out of the system, changing the secret will do it! Once you save the production.config.json file, you're ready to wire it up to your server.

Wiring Up Redis to Express

At this point you have Redis installed and a production.config.json that contains settings for it. Now you're ready to install the connect-redis module and use it for session storage. Use npm to install it.

```
$ npm install --save -E connect-redis@3.3.2
```

Next, open your server.js file for editing and find the comment that reads, "*Use RedisStore in production mode.*" Add the following code there.

fortify/b4/server.js
```
// Use RedisStore in production mode.
const RedisStore = require('connect-redis')(expressSession);
app.use(expressSession({
  resave: false,
  saveUninitialized: false,
  secret: nconf.get('redis:secret'),
  store: new RedisStore({
    host: nconf.get('redis:host'),
    port: nconf.get('redis:port'),
  }),
}));
```

This code should look familiar to you based on its similarity to setting up the FileStore class for storage. First we pull in the RedisStore class attached to the expressSession object. From there, we call app.use(), passing in the expressSession middleware with its matching configuration.

This time, we set saveUninitialized to false. We don't want to store uninitialized sessions in production mode—we'd rather wait until the user authenticates to bother saving session information. And rather than hard-coding the secret, we pull it in through nconf.

For the store, we pass in a new instance of RedisStore, configured with settings from nconf. The connect-redis module supports additional options,[21] but these are all we need for this application.

Save your server.js file. All of the code is in place to run in production mode now except the dist directory assets. It's time to do an end-to-end test of production mode.

Running in Production Mode

At this point, all of the code is in place to run in production mode. It's time to tell webpack to build the assets.

Head to a terminal and invoke npm run build.

```
$ npm run build
```

You can confirm that it worked by taking a peek at the dist directory.

```
$ tree -F ./dist
dist
├── 674f50d287a8c48dc19ba404d20fe713.eot
├── 89889688147bd7575d6327160d64e760.svg
├── 912ec66d7572ff821749319396470bde.svg
├── b06871f2b1fee6b241d60582ae9369b9.ttf
├── bundle.js
└── index.html

0 directories, 6 files
```

Now we're ready to try a production run.

To make sure everything is working according to plan, the safest thing is to remove and reinstall all of the dependency modules in production mode. That way you don't accidentally depend on something that you forgot to save to your package.json file.

---

21. https://www.npmjs.com/package/connect-redis#options

Start by removing the contents of the node_modules. Be careful not to delete something else by accident!

```
$ rm -rf node_modules
```

Now run npm install but with NODE_ENV set to production. This will prevent npm from installing any devDependencies.

```
$ NODE_ENV=production npm install
```

And finally, start up the server in production mode.

```
$ NODE_ENV=production npm start

> b4@1.0.0 start ./code/fortify/b4
> nodemon --ignore './sessions' server.js

[nodemon] 1.12.1
[nodemon] to restart at any time, enter `rs`
[nodemon] watching: *.*
[nodemon] starting `node server.js`
Ready.
```

All that's left is to try it out! Open http://b4.exampl.com:60900/ in a browser and see if it all works. You should be able to sign in, add bundles, and sign out. Woo! Let's recap where we went in this chapter.

Wrapping Up

In this chapter, we pulled together Express-based API-serving code and webkit-built front-end code that you learned over the last two chapters to develop an end-to-end application. On top of that, we implemented authentication through Passport for three popular providers: Facebook, Twitter, and Google.

Running your Node.js project locally during development is often different than serving in production. You learned how to manage these differences with nconf configuration and the NODE_ENV environment variable.

We got deeper into Express, writing custom middleware for authentication and configuring persistent sessions. You also learned how to encapsulate stacks of middleware and routes into Express Routers—modular Express mini applications.

And as for code, you got more practice with async functions and Promises. These are crucial for writing readable, maintainable code that can handle both synchronous and asynchronous code flows in a consistent way.

At this point you're ready to set off and start developing your own full-stack JavaScript applications on Node.js. I wish you the best of luck!

In the next and final chapter of the book, we'll take a step away from the nitty-gritty of writing Node.js code by hand. Instead, you'll learn how to use Node-RED, a visual tool for composing event flow–based Node.js programs. But before you go, check out these bonus tasks. See you soon!

Upgrade Elasticsearch Configuration to URLs

As in all previous chapters, the configuration for accessing Elasticsearch in this chapter looks like this:

```
"es": {
  "host": "localhost",
  "port": 9200,
  "books_index": "books",
  "bundles_index": "b4"
},
```

And constructing Elasticsearch URLs used template strings like this:

```
const url = `http://${es.host}:${es.port}/${es.bundles_index}/bundle`;
```

But in this chapter you learned how to use the URL to construct URLs relative to other paths.

Your task is to change the configuration to look like this:

```
"es": {
  "books_index": "http://localhost:9200/books",
  "bundles_index": "http://localhost:9200/b4"
},
```

Then, with your new knowledge of the URL class, refactor the existing Elasticsearch URL building code to use it.

Extract CSS into a Separate File

Currently, webpack presses all of the CSS for the B4 app into the dist/bundle.js file. However, it typically makes sense to put the CSS in a separate distributable file from the bundled JavaScript.

Your task is to configure webpack to create a separate CSS file using the extract-text-webpack-plugin module. Start by installing it with npm.

```
$ npm install --save-dev -E extract-text-webpack-plugin@3.0.1
```

Check out the extract-text-webpack-plugin module page for instructions.[22]

---

22. https://www.npmjs.com/package/extract-text-webpack-plugin

CHAPTER 10

BONUS: Developing Flows with Node-RED

In this final chapter, I want to take you somewhere very different—to give you a peek into the future of Node.js programming. You may be surprised at what you see!

Rather than composing JavaScript in a text editor, here you'll learn how to use a visual editor called Node-RED.[1] Originally developed by IBM and now stewarded by the JS Foundation,[2] Node-RED bills itself as "a visual tool for wiring the Internet of Things." But it can do way more than that.

I like to think of Node-RED as a visual IDE, specially tuned for creating asynchronous, event-driven Node.js programs. With Node-RED, you drag and drop *nodes*—units of functionality—and connect them via their input and output ports. A node in Node-RED is a waypoint that produces, consumes, or transforms events as they flow through the system. This allows you to literally see how events will flow through your program.

You'll learn how to create an HTTP API using Node-RED without writing any JavaScript. (Well, maybe just a little.) We'll plug into Elasticsearch, like in previous chapters, but you can use the same techniques to connect to any RESTful web service.

By the end of the chapter, you should be comfortable enough with Node-RED to use it to develop your own flows from scratch. I hope you'll find it as enjoyable to use as I do!

Now let's get started with Node-RED by installing and configuring it for local development.

---

1. http://nodered.org/
2. https://js.foundation

Setting Up Node-RED

To begin, create a directory called nodered to house your Node-RED-based code. Then open a terminal to this directory and create an initial package.json.

```
$ npm init -y
```

Next, install the node-red package locally.

```
$ npm install --save --save-exact node-red@0.16.2
```

Then open your package.json in a text editor and add a start script to the scripts section like so:

```
"scripts": {
  "start": "node-red -v -u ./config -f ./config/flows.json",
  "test": "echo \"Error: no test specified\" && exit 1"
},
```

Here we're specifying a couple of command-line arguments to the node-red command. The -v flag turns on verbose mode. The -u flag is short for --userDir and specifies a path to a directory to store configuration information.

The -f flag points to a JSON file that will contain our *flows*. In Node-RED, a flow is a program that directs events as they flow through a network of nodes.

You'll be working with flows a lot in this chapter. To begin, run npm start now:

```
$ npm start

> nodered@1.0.0 start ./code/nodered
> node-red -v -u ./config -f ./config/flows.json

19 Jun 04:34:00 - [info]

Welcome to Node-RED
===================

19 Jun 04:34:00 - [info] Node-RED version: v0.16.2
19 Jun 04:34:00 - [info] Node.js  version: v8.1.0
19 Jun 04:34:00 - [info] Linux 4.4.0-79-generic x64 LE
19 Jun 04:34:00 - [info] Loading palette nodes
19 Jun 04:34:01 - [warn] ------------------------------------------------------
19 Jun 04:34:01 - [warn] [rpi-gpio] Info : Ignoring Raspberry Pi specific node
19 Jun 04:34:01 - [warn] ------------------------------------------------------
19 Jun 04:34:01 - [info] Settings file  : ./code/nodered/config/settings.js
19 Jun 04:34:01 - [info] User directory : ./code/nodered/config
19 Jun 04:34:01 - [info] Flows file     : ./code/nodered/config/flows.json
19 Jun 04:34:01 - [info] Server now running at http://127.0.0.1:1880/
19 Jun 04:34:01 - [info] Starting flows
19 Jun 04:34:01 - [info] Started flows
```

Toward the end of the output, it'll inform you that the server is listening on port 1880. If you open http://localhost:1880 in a browser you should see something like this:

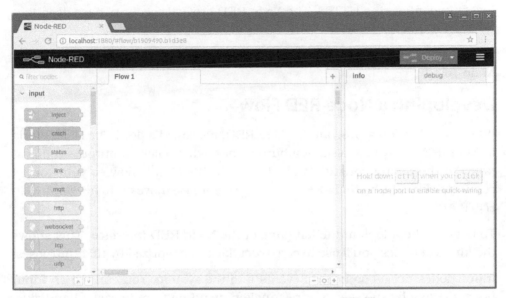

If you see this, great! Back in your terminal, use Ctrl-C to shut down the server. Next we'll set up some security around Node-RED.

Securing Node-RED

Out of the box, Node-RED has no security—anyone who can reach TCP port 1880 on your machine can deploy and run arbitrary code! This is a significant security risk, which you should mitigate in either of a couple of ways.

One solution is to use a firewall to block incoming traffic to this port from anywhere other than the loopback interface (localhost). Windows, Mac OS X, and Ubuntu all come with built-in firewalls, but they may not be enabled by default.

Another choice is to configure Node-RED itself to respond to requests only from localhost. To do this, open the settings.js file that Node-RED created in your config directory. Look for the uiHost setting in a section that reads like this:

```
// By default, the Node-RED UI accepts connections on all IPv4 interfaces.
// The following property can be used to listen on a specific interface. For
// example, the following would only allow connections from the local machine.
//uiHost: "127.0.0.1",
```

If you uncomment the uiHost line and then start up Node-RED, it will accept connections from only localhost.

Either the firewall or uiHost option works fine as long as you're working from the same machine than Node-RED is running on. If you want to access and use Node-RED remotely, you'll need to set up authentication and you should invest in configuring HTTPS. The Node-RED project's security page describes how to do this.[3]

With basic security out of the way, you're ready to develop your first flow in Node-RED!

Developing a Node-RED Flow

When you develop a program in Node-RED, it's called a flow. The Hello World of Node-RED flows consists of a button that, when clicked, outputs a timestamp to the debug console. We'll start with this simple flow so you can get comfortable with the Node-RED interface before we move on to developing an HTTP API.

To begin, take a look at the left pane of the Node-RED interface. This shows the kinds of nodes you'll use to construct flows, categorized by their purposes.

Input nodes act as sources of events into the system. You can tell an input node visually by the tiny gray rectangle protruding from its right-hand side. This gray rectangle is an *output port*.

If you hover over a node, a tooltip will pop up to give you more information about that node.

Click and drag an inject node from the left pane onto the flow pane. This will create an inject node in your flow (as shown in the figure on page 263).

Take a look at the node you just created. It will have an orange border to indicate that it's the currently selected node, and a description of the node will appear in the Info tab of the right-side pane.

The node will also have a blue dot in its upper-right corner. This signals that the node has not yet been deployed.

---

3.   https://nodered.org/docs/security

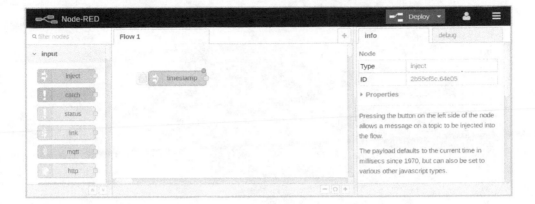

When you make changes to a flow in the editor, these changes do not take effect immediately. To get them to take effect, you have to *deploy* your flow by clicking the red Deploy button.

There are three different deployment options, ranging from a full deploy down to just the changed nodes. In this chapter, we'll always perform a full deploy.

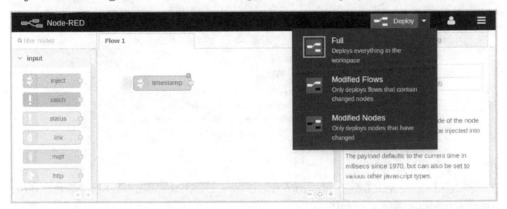

If you haven't done so already, click the Deploy button now. A *Successfully deployed* message should appear briefly at the top of the screen and the blue dot should disappear from your inject node.

When you deploy a flow, this is just like starting a server in regular Node.js code. It may not look like it's doing anything, but it's waiting for events to respond to.

Now, if you click the little square button protruding from the left side of the inject node, you should see the message *Successfully injected: timestamp* appear briefly (as shown in the figure on page 264).

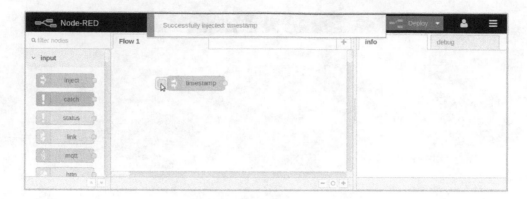

When you click the Inject button, a Node-RED event is injected into the flow. Right now nothing is set up to receive that event, so let's add a destination for it.

In the nodes pane on the left, scroll down to the output nodes. These nodes have *input ports*—little gray rectangles protruding from their left sides.

The first one in the list should be the debug node.

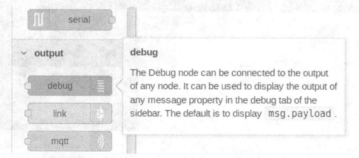

Click and drag a debug node onto the flow workspace, somewhere to the right of the inject node you added previously.

To connect the nodes, click and drag the output port of the inject node and join it to the debug node's input port (or vice versa). You should see a curvy gray line appear between the nodes.

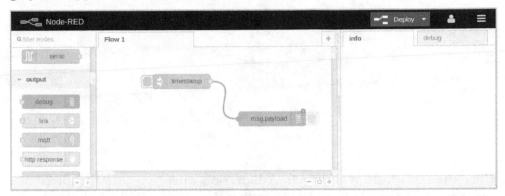

The debug node writes its output to the Debug tab of the right-side pane. Select that tab by clicking it, then deploy the flow.

Now when you click the inject node's left-side button, you should see a JavaScript timestamp logged to the Debug tab.

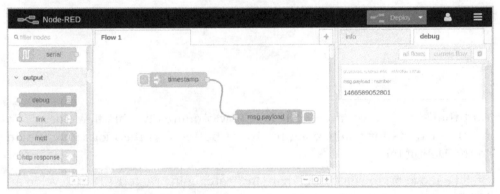

The green button hanging off of the right-hand side of the debug node toggles whether it is active. Toggling it takes effect immediately (no need to redeploy). This is convenient during development because it allows you to leave the debug nodes in your flow without having them always log to the Debug tab.

When you double-click any node, this opens the node editor, allowing you to make changes to the node's settings. Double-click the debug node now, then choose "complete msg object" from the drop-down for the Output setting (as shown in the figure on page 266).

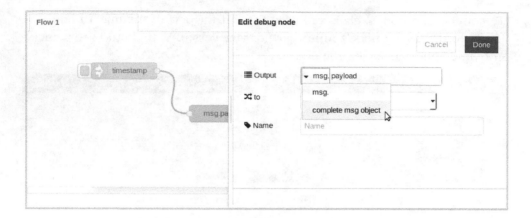

Click the Done button to close the editor. Now when you click the Inject button, you'll see the whole JSON object that it produced in the Debug tab.

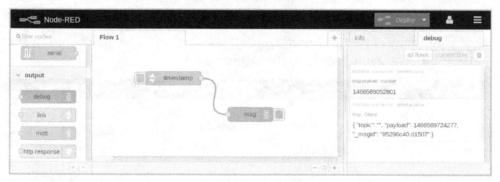

And that's it—you've made your first flow! Admittedly, this flow doesn't do much—it waits for you to click the Inject button and then logs information to the Debug tab.

So let's move on to something more intricate: using Node-RED to develop an HTTP API.

Creating HTTP APIs with Node-RED

Now that you have the basics of working with Node-RED down, let's use Node-RED to create an HTTP service. This showcases the power of Node-RED to facilitate creating server-side APIs visually.

We'll start simple, with a basic Hello World web service, then upgrade it to query Elasticsearch, much like the Express-based web services you developed in Chapter 7, *Developing RESTful Web Services*, on page 147.

Establishing an HTTP Endpoint

To start with, let's bring up a new flow. In the upper-right corner of the workspace you'll find a plus (+) button. Click this to create a new tab for your next flow.

In the top-right corner of the screen is a button to open the main menu. Under View, if you check the Show Grid option, Node-RED will draw gridlines on the flow area, making it easier to align nodes.

To begin your HTTP API flow, in the nodes panel to the left, find the HTTP input node under the inputs. Click and drag one onto your workspace.

Notice that your HTTP node has the blue circle in the upper-right corner indicating that it hasn't been deployed, and next to that there's an orange triangle. The orange triangle signifies that the node needs to be configured.

Double-click it to open the node Edit dialog.

The most important field in the dialog is URL. This is the endpoint that Node-RED will expose to callers of your API. Enter /*search* for the URL.

For any HTTP API flow to work in Node-RED, you also need an HTTP response node. Grab one now from the nodes panel.

Once both the HTTP input and HTTP response nodes are in your flow, connect the input to the output and deploy.

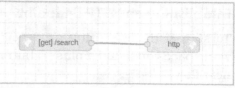

Let's give the API a try from the command line using curl. Open a terminal, then run the following:

```
$ curl -i -s localhost:1880/search
HTTP/1.1 200 OK
X-Powered-By: Express
X-Content-Type-Options: nosniff
Content-Type: application/json; charset=utf-8
Content-Length: 2
ETag: W/"2-mZFLkyvTelC5g8XnyQrpOw"
Date: Thu, 01 Jun 2017 13:45:30 GMT
Connection: keep-alive

{}
```

By using curl's -i flag, the output includes the HTTP headers. The 200 OK status at the beginning tells us that we got a positive response. The body of the output is just a pair of curly braces ({}), an empty JSON response, in the last line of the output.

By contrast, try hitting a nonsense URL to see what it produces.

```
$ curl -i -s localhost:1880/nonsense-url
HTTP/1.1 404 Not Found
X-Powered-By: Express
X-Content-Type-Options: nosniff
Content-Type: text/html; charset=utf-8
Content-Length: 25
Date: Thu, 01 Jun 2017 13:46:10 GMT
Connection: keep-alive

Cannot GET /nonsense-url
```

As you can see, if the API endpoint isn't bound, Node-RED will give you a 404 Not Found response.

Setting a Response Body

Now let's add a response body to the /search API. Back in the Node-RED editor, make some room between the HTTP input and HTTP response nodes by dragging them apart.

Next, grab a change node from the function area of the nodes panel at left. When you drag this over the connection between the HTTP input and HTTP response nodes, the line will become dashed. This means Node-RED is preparing to insert this node into the flow between the connected nodes.

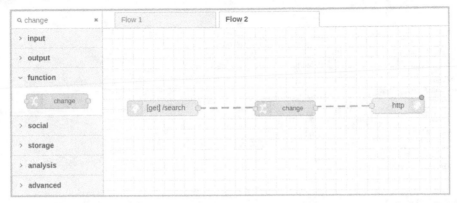

When you drop the node, the dashed lines become solid again, and the change node is ready to be configured.

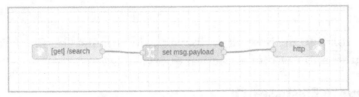

The change node allows you to modify properties of the message object (msg) as it passes through the flow. In particular, we want to set the payload property so that this value is returned to the caller in the HTTP response node.

Double-click the change node to open the Edit dialog. In the Rules section, you can add any number of modifications. For now, we only need one. In the Set rule, choose JSON from the To drop-down, then enter ["The Art of War"] in the adjacent input box. This is a placeholder value that will match our expected results once we hook the API up to Elasticsearch (as shown in the figure on page 270). Close the dialog when you're done, then deploy the flow. Now hop back over to your terminal, and let's try out the API again.

```
$ curl -i -s localhost:1880/search
HTTP/1.1 200 OK
X-Powered-By: Express
X-Content-Type-Options: nosniff
Content-Type: application/json; charset=utf-8
Content-Length: 18
ETag: W/"12-LP05bVd5cQX35db6gakpCA"
Date: Thu, 01 Jun 2017 14:16:00 GMT
Connection: keep-alive

["The Art of War"]
```

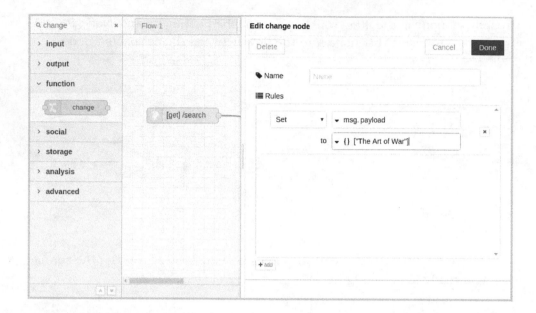

If you see this, great! Now all we have to do is make the flow reach out to Elasticsearch and perform an actual query.

Calling Out to Elasticsearch

Extending our HTTP flow to retrieve content from Elasticsearch will involve a couple of steps. First we need to craft an Elasticsearch request body using a query parameter provided by the API caller. Then we'll fire off the Elasticsearch request and format the response payload by extracting just the titles of the matching documents.

To make space, arrange the HTTP input node, change node, and HTTP response node vertically.

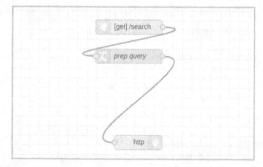

This is not strictly required, of course. Node-RED will execute the flow regardless of how the nodes are positioned graphically as long as all of the connections are in place. But this arrangement makes it easier to see what's going on and to add more nodes, as you will do shortly.

Next, double-click the change node to open the Edit dialog. The goal here is to prepare msg.payload to contain an Elasticsearch request body much like you did back in *Using Request with Express*, on page 157, when we were building out web services with Express.

Here's an example JSON request body that Elasticsearch would honor when you hit the /_search endpoint for an index:

```
{
  "query": {
    "match_phrase": {
      "title": "example string"
    }
  }
}
```

For this example, Elasticsearch would query the index for documents whose title field matches the phrase *example string*. You can read more about Elasticsearch's match_phrase feature on the Match Phrase Query documentation page.[4]

To make the change node work, we'll need to construct a payload like this, but with the user's query instead of *example string*. The change node is quite flexible, allowing you to add any number of rules to execute in sequence. There are many different ways to get this done, but here's one way:

First, set the Name property to *prep query*. This name will show for the node in the flow editor, making it easy to identify later.

Next, in the Rules section, update the Set rule's msg field from payload to payload.query. Below that, for the to field, select JSON from the drop-down and then enter {"match_phrase":{}}. Now all we need to do is set the title field.

Click the +add button at the bottom of the Edit dialog. This will add a new rule to the Rules section. In the first drop-down, change it from Set to Move—this is for relocating a property. Then set the first input to msg.payload.q and the second one to msg.payload.query.match_phrase.title. You'll have to select msg from the to drop-down to make this happen.

When you're done, the Edit dialog should look like the figure on page 272.

To finalize the configuration, click Done to close the dialog, and then deploy the flow. To test it, return to your terminal and use curl with jq like so:

---

4. https://www.elastic.co/guide/en/elasticsearch/reference/5.2/query-dsl-match-query-phrase.html

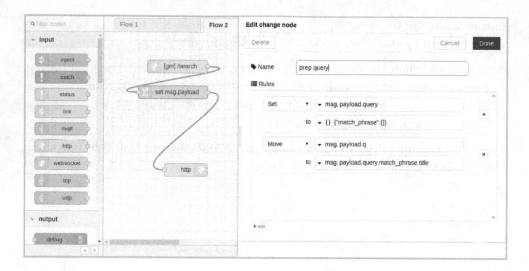

```
$ curl -s localhost:1880/search?q=example | jq '.'
{
  "query": {
    "match_phrase": {
      "title": "example"
    }
  }
}
```

So far so good! Now to feed this to Elasticsearch. In the nodes panel, find the HTTP request node under the function nodes section. Grab one, then drag and drop it onto your flow in between the prep query node and the HTTP response node.

After you drop it in place, double-click it to open the Edit dialog. Change the settings in the dialog as follows:

- Method—Set to POST.
- URL—Set to http://localhost:9200/books/_search.
- Return—Set to *a parsed JSON object*.
- Name—Set to *get /books*.

This will configure the node to POST the msg.payload to Elasticsearch and treat the response as JSON (as shown in the figure on page 273).

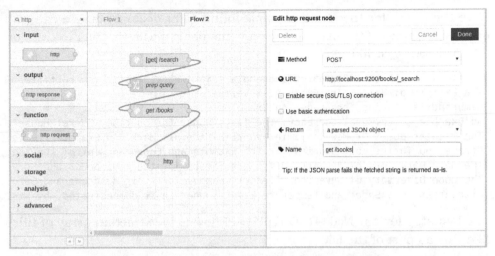

Once you click Done to save the changes and deploy the flow, it's time to try it out in the terminal. If you see something like the following, you're on track.

```
$ curl -s localhost:1880/search?q=example | jq '.' | head -n 30
{
  "took": 7,
  "timed_out": false,
  "_shards": {
    "total": 5,
    "successful": 5,
    "failed": 0
  },
  "hits": {
    "total": 8,
    "max_score": 9.897307,
    "hits": [
      {
        "_index": "books",
        "_type": "book",
        "_id": "pg22415",
        "_score": 9.897307,
        "_source": {
          "id": 22415,
          "title": "The Example of Vertu\nThe Example of Virtue",
          "authors": [
            "Hawes, Stephen"
          ],
          "subjects": [
            "Poetry"
          ]
        }
      },
      {
        "_index": "books",
```

Here the query for the string *example* found eight documents. We can pull out just the titles of the matching documents using jq with the filter expression .hits.hits[]._source.title like so:

```
$ curl -s localhost:1880/search?q=example | jq '.hits.hits[]._source.title'
"The Example of Vertu\nThe Example of Virtue"
"Rembrandt's Etching Technique: An Example"
"An Example of Communal Currency: The facts about the Guernsey Market House"
"The Printer Boy.\nOr How Benjamin Franklin Made His Mark. An Example for Yo...
"Strive and Thrive; or, Stories for the Example and Encouragement of the You...
"The Goop Directory of Juvenile Offenders Famous for their Misdeeds and Serv...
"The Goop Directory of Juvenile Offenders Famous for their Misdeeds and Serv...
"Discourses on a Sober and Temperate Life\r\nWherein is demonstrated, by his...
```

The last step for our Node-RED HTTP API flow is to extract an array of titles like this as part of the flow.

Manipulating a Message with a Function Node

At this point, your Node-RED flow should be able to receive an incoming request, reach out to Elasticsearch, and then forward its response to the original caller. The last step is to trim down the Elasticsearch response to just the content that we want to return to the caller. For this, we'll use a function node.

Grab a function node from the nodes panel and drag and drop it onto the flow before the HTTP response node.

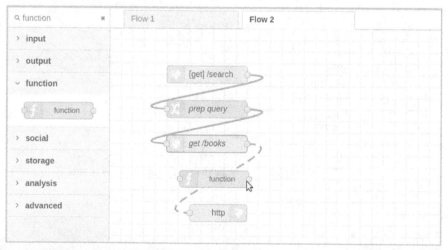

A function node gives you maximum flexibility in crafting a node's behavior because it allows you to write arbitrary JavaScript to execute. This takes us further away from the spirit of Node-RED's drag-and-drop philosophy, but it's good to know that you can drill down to this level if you need to.

Double-click the function node to open the Edit dialog. Set the name to *extract titles* to describe the behavior of this node. Then, in the Function text area, enter the following:

```
msg.payload = msg.payload.hits.hits
    .map(hit => hit._source.title);
return msg;
```

This function body iterates over the matching documents returned by Elasticsearch and, for each one, extracts the title attribute.

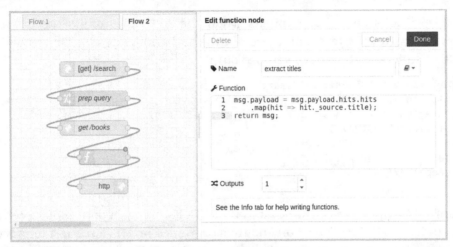

After you click Done to save changes and deploy the flow, you can test it out with curl.

```
$ curl -s localhost:1880/search?q=example | jq '.'
[
    "The Example of Vertu\nThe Example of Virtue",
    "Rembrandt's Etching Technique: An Example",
    "An Example of Communal Currency: The facts about the Guernsey Market Hous...
    "The Printer Boy.\nOr How Benjamin Franklin Made His Mark. An Example for ...
    "Strive and Thrive; or, Stories for the Example and Encouragement of the Y...
    "The Goop Directory of Juvenile Offenders Famous for their Misdeeds and Se...
    "The Goop Directory of Juvenile Offenders Famous for their Misdeeds and Se...
    "Discourses on a Sober and Temperate Life\r\nWherein is demonstrated, by h...
]
```

If you're seeing something like this, great! It means that the happy path is working as expected.

But what if the API user doesn't provide a query parameter? Or what if Elasticsearch doesn't return any results?

We'll deal with these kinds of edge cases next.

Handling Errors in Node-RED Flows

Although it's great when everything goes according to plan, sometimes it doesn't. One of the downsides of programming with Node-RED is that it can be difficult to track down problems when they occur. In this section, we'll explore a few ways the book-search API from the last section might fail and how you can investigate and mitigate these failures.

Triggering an Error

To begin, let's see what happens when the API caller omits the q query parameter. In your terminal, use curl with the -i and -v flags like so to include HTTP headers and produce verbose output:

```
$ curl -i -v localhost:1880/search
*   Trying 127.0.0.1...
* Connected to localhost (127.0.0.1) port 1880 (#0)
> GET /search HTTP/1.1
> Host: localhost:1880
> User-Agent: curl/7.47.0
> Accept: */*
>
```

From this output, we can see that Node-RED, listening on port 1880, received the underlying TCP connection and then curl issued an HTTP request for /search. But after that, we hear nothing back from Node-RED, not even HTTP headers. What's going on?

To find out, head back to your web browser and take a look in the Debug tab on the right-hand side. You should see an error reading, "TypeError: Cannot read property 'hits' of undefined". When you hover over this error, the node that produced it, the function node, will have an orange dashed outline in the flow editor.

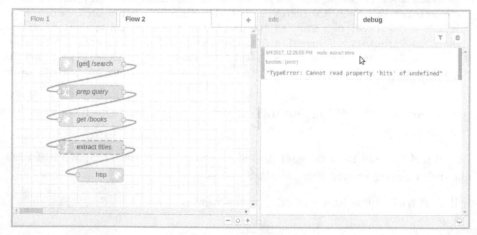

The problem seems to be with the input coming into the function node. From the error text, it seems like there's a problem in some part of the expression msg.payload.hits.hits. Let's use a debug node to investigate.

Investigating an Error

To investigate the error triggered in the last section, grab a debug node from the nodes panel and drag it onto the flow editor. Attach the debug node to the output of the Elasticsearch HTTP request node.

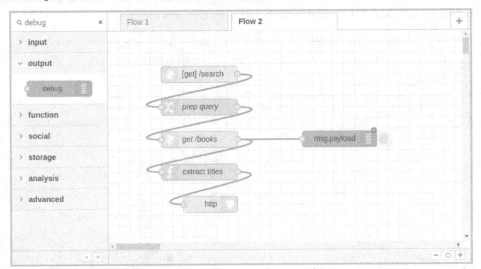

This will log to the Debug tab what's in the payload the next time Node-RED receives a request. Deploy this flow, then head back to your terminal.

Use Ctrl-C to kill the previous curl command, and then run it again. It should produce the same behavior as before, but now when you switch back to your web browser, you should see an expandable payload object in the Debug tab.

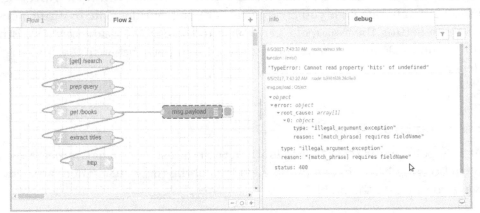

When you hover over the debug output with your mouse, the debug node will have a dashed red outline. Digging into the msg.payload object in the debug console, you'll find that there is no payload.hits field at all. Instead, the payload has an error field with a type of illegal_argument_exception and a reason of [match_phrase] requires fieldName.

That's strange because, as you'll recall, part of the prep query node's job is to set the match_phrase.title field. Let's attach the debug node to the prep query output and take a look at that next. You'll probably want to clear the debug output by clicking the trash can button in the top right.

After you deploy the change, run curl again, then flip back to the web browser. You should see more debug output this time, including an entry for the output of the prep query node.

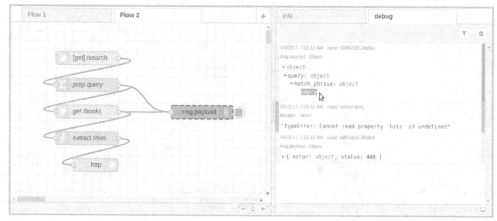

Expanding the prep query output, notice that the match_phrase field is an empty object. Its title field is missing!

And here's one of the nitty-gritty details about working with Node-RED. The prep query change node you created earlier has two rules. The first rule succeeds in setting the msg.payload.query object to the JSON {"match_query":{}}. But the second rule fails to move the msg.payload.q property because that property doesn't exist!

So let's fix it.

Handling Errors Generically

At this point, your HTTP flow fails when the request lacks a q parameter, and by debugging it you have a pretty good idea of the root cause. There are a few ways to mitigate the problem:

- Detect the absence of a q parameter early and inform the API caller with an HTTP 400 Bad Request response.

- Detect the absence of a hits field in the Elasticsearch results and skip the extract-titles step.

- Detect any error at all and return an HTTP 500 Server Error response to the API caller.

These approaches aren't mutually exclusive. Let's start with the most general approach—returning a 500 Server Error.

In the nodes panel, find the catch node under inputs. Drag one onto the flow editor. Next, drag an HTTP response node onto the editor and connect it to the catch node.

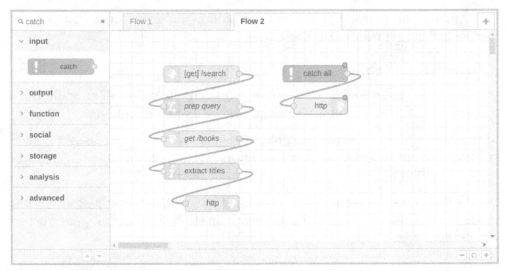

Strictly speaking, you could reuse the existing HTTP response node rather than bringing in a new one. But I find it more aesthetically pleasing to have individual HTTP response nodes for each different way the flow could terminate.

Once you deploy the flow, any unhandled error condition in the flow will trigger the catch node. If the msg object has an HTTP response object associated with it, then the attached HTTP response node will reply to the API caller.

Let's try it out in the terminal. This time, let's pipe the output of curl into jq. If you need a refresher on jq, flip back to *Shaping JSON with jq*, on page 126.

```
$ curl -s localhost:1880/search | jq '.'
{
  "error": {
    "root_cause": [
      {
        "type": "illegal_argument_exception",
        "reason": "[match_phrase] requires fieldName"
      }
    ],
    "type": "illegal_argument_exception",
    "reason": "[match_phrase] requires fieldName"
  },
  "status": 400
}
```

Great! At least the call to curl no longer hangs indefinitely.

Let's make one more improvement to the flow by detecting a bad request before handing it over to Elasticsearch.

Catching Errors Early

At this point, your flow no longer hangs indefinitely if the caller omits the q parameter. This is a big improvement, but we can do even better.

If the API caller didn't supply a q parameter, then there's no reason to reach all the way out to Elasticsearch for results. We should be able to report an HTTP 400 Bad Request response to the API caller directly.

To do this, make some room in your flow by splitting the [get] /search input node into its own column. This will leave space below for the q-parameter-checking nodes.

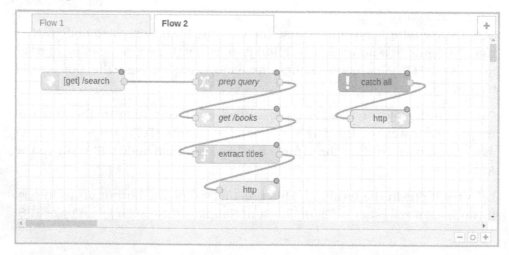

Next, in the nodes panel, find the switch node in the function section. Drag a switch node onto the flow editor under the [get] /search node. The switch node can be used to route a message along different paths, much like a switch statement in JavaScript.

To configure it, double-click the switch node to open the Edit dialog. Set the Name field to q? to indicate that we're testing for the q parameter. For the Property field, set it to msg.payload.q.

Below the Name and Property fields is an area where you can specify routing rules. In the first rule, click the drop-down and select *is not null*.

Next, click the +add button to insert a second rule. For this rule, click the drop-down and select *otherwise*.

Lastly, in the final drop-down at the bottom, choose *stopping after first match*. When you're done, the Edit dialog should look like this:

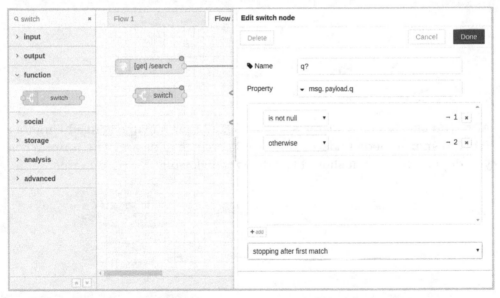

After you click Done, the switch node should now have two output ports—one for each of the two conditions, in order from top to bottom. Since the first output was for the *is not null* case, we want to wire that into the prep query node. The input to the switch node should be the output of the HTTP input node above it.

For the other switch case, we'll need a few more nodes, starting with a change node to set up the HTTP 400 Bad Request response. Drag a change node onto the flow under the switch node, connect its input to the second switch output, then double-click the change node to open the Edit dialog.

Set the change node's name to *400*. In the Rules section, first set the msg.payload to the JSON string {"error":"Query string 'q' missing."}. Then add a second rule and set the msg.statusCode to be the number 400. The HTTP response node will use this to return a 400 Bad Request status code.

When you're finished, the node editor should look like the following:

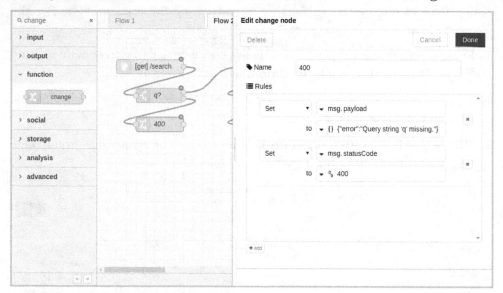

After you click Done to dismiss the dialog, all that remains is to add another HTTP response node underneath the 400 change node and wire it up. When you deploy the flow, it should look like the following:

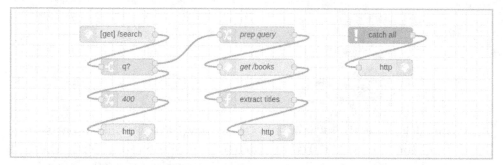

Time to try it all out. In your terminal, use curl to see how the flow deals with a missing q parameter.

```
$ curl -s localhost:1880/search | jq '.'
{
  "error": "Query string 'q' missing."
}
```

Success! Now let's reconfirm that it still returns results for expected queries.

```
$ curl -s localhost:1880/search?q=juliet | jq '.'
[
  "Romeo and Juliet",
  "The Indifference of Juliet",
  "Romeo and Juliet",
  "Romeo and Juliet",
  "Romeo and Juliet",
  "The Tragedy of Romeo and Juliet",
  "Shakespeare's Tragedy of Romeo and Juliet"
]
```

At this point you have a functioning and error-resistant HTTP API endpoint. Now let's wrap up.

Wrapping Up

Node-RED is a visual editor for developing event-based flows. In this chapter, you got Node-RED up and running and configured, and you developed a couple of flows. We explored a number of different Node-RED nodes to create, transform, and consume events.

Using HTTP input and response nodes, we stood up a simple HTTP service. By iteratively adding nodes, you learned how to manipulate the message payload. Using an HTTP request node, we issued an asynchronous request to Elasticsearch, forwarding parts of the result back to the API caller, extracted with a function node.

To handle errors, you used a catch node to guarantee that the API caller gets at least some response, even if things go wrong during any part of the flow. And finally, you learned how to conditionally direct events with a switch node to more gracefully handle error cases.

I truly hope you've enjoyed reading this book as much as I've enjoyed writing it. Good luck in all you strive to accomplish!

Setting Up Angular

In this appendix, you'll learn how to set up a basic project structure with webpack, TypeScript, and Angular, a front-end framework by Google.[1] At the end, you'll have a basis on which you can build a UI for your Node.js-powered applications.

If you're reading this appendix, you're probably already familiar with using Angular for front-end development. If not and you'd like to know more, I strongly recommend that you step through the Tour of Heroes tutorial on Angular's website.[2] It contains a step-by-step guide that'll introduce you to the relevant development concepts that are not covered here.

Setting up even a bare-bones Angular application takes a perhaps-surprising amount of boilerplate. Angular recommends using its quickstart for developing locally.[3] While this is a fast way to get started using Angular, the quickstart doesn't address how to tie Angular into a webpack project.

In the code downloads that accompany this book, you'll find a directory called extra. Inside it, there's a subdirectory named angular-webpack that contains a very simple Angular project that builds with webpack.

Like other webpack projects in this book, the angular-webpack project runs with webpack-dev-server through npm. You can start it up and take a look if you're interested in poking around.

The following is the simplest Angular project I could come up with that builds with webpack. You can use it as a reference implementation to compare against, or as a skeleton project rather than setting everything up yourself.

---

1. http://angular.io/
2. http://angular.io/tutorial
3. http://angular.io/guide/setup

```
$ cd angular-webpack
$ npm start

> angular-webpack@1.0.0 start ./extra/angular-webpack
> webpack-dev-server

Project is running at http://localhost:61100/
webpack output is served from /
Content not from webpack is served from ./extra/angular-webpack/dist
ts-loader: Using typescript@2.3.2 and ./extra/angular-webpack/tsconfig.json
Hash: 976f663472a8a9ae69c7
Version: webpack 2.4.1
```

Let's start with an overview of the directory structure of an angular-webpack project.

```
$ tree -I node_modules --dirsfirst
```

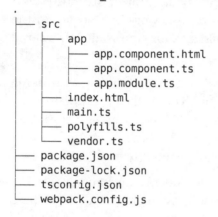

Angular recommends following the convention that source code files go under the src directory, as you see here. Top-level files are generally configuration files.

The three .ts files in the src directory are the entry points for webpack. Rather than cram all of the application's JavaScript and CSS into a single bundle.js file, Angular recommends splitting it up.[4]

Here's a brief overview of each of the top-level files in src, and how they contribute to the overall application:

- index.html—This is used as a base template for HtmlWebpackPlugin to load the main application component. It contains a <my-app> to bootstrap the rest of the application.

- main.ts—This file is the entry point for the main front-end code.

---

4.   http://angular.io/guide/webpack

- polyfills.ts—Angular takes advantage of the very latest browser features. Browsers don't always support these features, so polyfills.ts loads up the relevant polyfill implementations.

- vendor.ts—This file brings together the underlying framework and library code that your application depends on, such as Angular and Bootstrap.

The custom code for your application lives in src/app. Here's a short description of each of those files.

- app.module.ts—Defines your AppModule class using the @NgModule decorator. This class pulls all of the Angular bits together, such as your router and components.

- app.component.ts—Exports the AppComponent class using the @Component decorator. This implements your main application's <my-app> tag.

- app.component.html—Template HTML content for AppComponent.

Like webpack, Angular makes aggressive use of npm peer dependencies. As a result, it takes quite a few packages to put together an Angular project. Here are the packages you'll need for Angular:

- @angular/common @4.4.0-RC.0
- @angular/compiler @4.4.0-RC.0
- @angular/core @4.4.0-RC.0
- @angular/http @4.4.0-RC.0
- @angular/platform-browser @4.4.0-RC.0
- @angular/platform-browser-dynamic @4.4.0-RC.0
- @angular/router @4.4.0-RC.0
- @types/node @8.0.28
- core-js @2.5.1
- reflect-metadata @0.1.10
- rxjs @5.4.3
- typescript @2.3.2
- zone.js @0.8.17

The packages beginning with @angular are part of the Angular project proper. The rest are a combination of peer dependencies that Angular needs, and TypeScript typings that permit Angular to build under webpack.

Speaking of webpack, here's the stack of dependencies you'll need for it:

- angular2-template-loader @0.6.2
- css-loader @0.28.0
- file-loader @0.11.1

- html-loader @0.5.1
- html-webpack-plugin @2.28.0
- style-loader @0.16.1
- ts-loader @2.0.3
- url-loader @0.5.8
- webpack @2.4.1

The angular2-template-loader is a webpack plugin that handles tying together Angular components that have external HTML template files, like the app.component.ts and app.component.html we discussed earlier. The other packages in this list are discussed in detail in Chapter 8, *Creating a Beautiful User Experience*, on page 185.

Although much of the configuration in tsconfig.json and webpack.config.js is the same with and without Angular, there are a few differences. First, let's look at the differences in tsconfig.json.

```
{
  "compilerOptions": {
    "outDir": "./dist/",
    "sourceMap": true,
    "module": "CommonJS",
    "target": "ES5",
    "allowJs": true,
    "alwaysStrict": true,
    "lib": ["ES2016", "DOM"],
    "experimentalDecorators": true,
    "types": [ "node" ],
    "typeRoots": [ "../node_modules/@types" ]
  }
}
```

The lib options need to contain ES2016 for Angular to work, since it relies on some recent JavaScript additions such as the Map. Polyfills are added for missing features, but TypeScript needs to know that those signatures are OK.

experimentalDecorators enable the @NgModule, @Component, and other decorators that Angular depends on. Without this flag, you'll get TypeSript compilation errors.

Lastly, types and typeRoots are needed for handling the require() method. Although dependencies can usually be brought in with the import keyword, sometimes require() is needed to pull in dependencies dynamically. src/polyfills.ts contains an example of this.

Turning our attention to the webpack.config.js file, there are two changes worth noting. First is the way that .ts files are handled. Here's the rule:

```
rules: [{
  test: /\.ts$/,
  use: [ 'ts-loader', 'angular2-template-loader' ],
},{
```

The angular2-template-loader needs to be last in the list of .ts rules. This means that component templates (specified in the @Component decorator's templateUrl property) will be included properly.

The other change is the addition of a plugin to the plugins array:

```
new webpack.ContextReplacementPlugin(
  /angular(\\|\/)core(\\|\/)@angular/,
  path.resolve(__dirname, '../src')
),
```

webpack.ContextReplacementPlugin provides a means for you to tell webpack how to resolve the locations of dynamically determined source files. Without this plugin, webpack will overestimate the packages it needs to support Angular. This keeps it to the required minimum dependencies when bundling.

Feel free to poke around the angular-webpack skeleton project. If you use the tips in this appendix, you should be able to use Angular for the front end of your own Node.js projects.

Setting Up React

React is a front-end-component rendering framework by Facebook.[1] Teaching how to construct UIs with React is outside the scope of this book, but here you'll learn how to wire it into a webpack-built Node.js project. To learn to use React, I recommend stepping through the Tic-Tac-Toe tutorial.[2]

Fortunately, it doesn't take much code to get started using React, though you will need a transpiler. React typically relies on transpiling with Babel, but here we'll use TypeScript to maintain consistency with the rest of the UI code in the book. The differences between React and TypeScript are summarized in *Transpiling with TypeScript*, on page 197.

In the code downloads that accompany this book, you'll find a directory called extra/react-webpack. This directory contains a very simple React project that builds with webpack and TypeScript.

Like other webpack projects in this book, the react-webpack project runs with webpack-dev-server through npm. You can start it up and take a look if you're interested in poking around.

```
$ cd react-webpack
$ npm start

> react-webpack@1.0.0 start ./extra/react-webpack
> webpack-dev-server

Project is running at http://localhost:61200/
webpack output is served from /
Content not from webpack is served from ./extra/react-webpack/dist
ts-loader: Using typescript@2.3.2 and ./extra/react-webpack/tsconfig.json
Hash: 810e5499eb5e676ce562
Version: webpack 2.4.1
```

---

1. https://facebook.github.io/react/
2. https://facebook.github.io/react/tutorial/tutorial.html

This is the simplest React project I could come up with that builds with webpack. You can use it as a reference implementation to compare against, or as a skeleton project rather than setting everything up yourself.

Here's a listing of that project's contents.

```
$ cd react-webpack
$ tree -I node_modules --dirsfirst
.
├── src
│   ├── index.html
│   ├── index.tsx
│   └── vendor.ts
├── package.json
├── package-lock.json
├── tsconfig.json
└── webpack.config.js
```

Notice the now-familiar package.json, tsconfig.json, and webpack.config.json files. We'll discuss these in a bit, but first let's look at the src, which contains the project source code files (as per React's convention).

The src/vendor.ts file includes links to Bootstrap's CSS and JavaScript code. That way webpack will create a separate bundle file for those assets. For more on how this works, see webpack's documentation on code splitting.[3]

Next, notice the index.tsx. This is the main entry point of the application. It pulls together the React components and injects them into an element defined in the index.html file. index.html is used as a base template for HtmlWebpackPlugin to load the main application component.

The reason for .tsx instead of just .ts is that React uses JSX to allow HTML literal content inside of JavaScript files.[4] TSX is the TypeScript flavor of JSX.

To build a React-based project using TypeScript, here are the packages you'll need to add to your project:

- @types/react @16.0.5
- @types/react-dom @15.5.4
- react @15.6.1
- react-dom @15.6.1
- typescript @2.3.2

Since React is developed in regular JavaScript, the TypeScript typings are implemented separately and distributed under the @types/ prefix.

---

3. https://webpack.js.org/guides/code-splitting/#src/components/Sidebar/Sidebar.jsx
4. https://facebook.github.io/react/docs/introducing-jsx.html

For webpack, you'll need the familiar cohort of packages:

- css-loader @0.28.0
- file-loader @0.11.1
- html-webpack-plugin @2.28.0
- style-loader @0.16.1
- ts-loader @2.0.3
- url-loader @0.5.8
- webpack @2.4.1
- webpack-dev-server @2.4.3

tsconfig.json doesn't need anything special to support React above and beyond what you used in Chapter 8, *Creating a Beautiful User Experience*, on page 185. However, webpack.config.js requires one minor tweak. In the rules section, the test for .ts files needs to be extended to match .tsx files as well.

```
rules: [{
  test: /\.tsx?$/,
  loader: 'ts-loader',
},{
```

With those changes out of the way, you should be in a good spot to use React to develop the front end for your own Node.js projects. Best of luck!

Index

Secure JavaScript and Web Testing

Secure your Node applications and see how to really test on the web.

Secure Your Node.js Web Application

Cyber-criminals have your web applications in their crosshairs. They search for and exploit common security mistakes in your web application to steal user data. Learn how you can secure your Node.js applications, database and web server to avoid these security holes. Discover the primary attack vectors against web applications, and implement security best practices and effective countermeasures. Coding securely will make you a stronger web developer and analyst, and you'll protect your users.

Karl Düüna
(230 pages) ISBN: 9781680500851. $36
https://pragprog.com/book/kdnodesec

The Way of the Web Tester

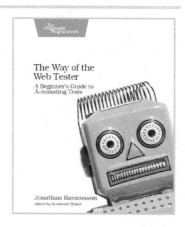

This book is for everyone who needs to test the web. As a tester, you'll automate your tests. As a developer, you'll build more robust solutions. And as a team, you'll gain a vocabulary and a means to coordinate how to write and organize automated tests for the web. Follow the testing pyramid and level up your skills in user interface testing, integration testing, and unit testing. Your new skills will free you up to do other, more important things while letting the computer do the one thing it's really good at: quickly running thousands of repetitive tasks.

Jonathan Rasmusson
(256 pages) ISBN: 9781680501834. $29
https://pragprog.com/book/jrtest

Level Up

From data structures to architecture and design, we have what you need.

A Common-Sense Guide to Data Structures and Algorithms

If you last saw algorithms in a university course or at a job interview, you're missing out on what they can do for your code. Learn different sorting and searching techniques, and when to use each. Find out how to use recursion effectively. Discover structures for specialized applications, such as trees and graphs. Use Big O notation to decide which algorithms are best for your production environment. Beginners will learn how to use these techniques from the start, and experienced developers will rediscover approaches they may have forgotten.

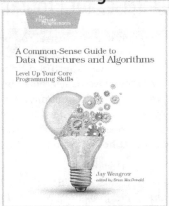

Jay Wengrow
(218 pages) ISBN: 9781680502442. $45.95
https://pragprog.com/book/jwdsal

Design It!

Don't engineer by coincidence—design it like you mean it! Grounded by fundamentals and filled with practical design methods, this is the perfect introduction to software architecture for programmers who are ready to grow their design skills. Ask the right stakeholders the right questions, explore design options, share your design decisions, and facilitate collaborative workshops that are fast, effective, and fun. Become a better programmer, leader, and designer. Use your new skills to lead your team in implementing software with the right capabilities—and develop awesome software!

Michael Keeling
(358 pages) ISBN: 9781680502091. $41.95
https://pragprog.com/book/mkdsa

Exercises and Teams

From exercises to make you a better programmer to techniques for creating better teams, we've got you covered.

Exercises for Programmers

When you write software, you need to be at the top of your game. Great programmers practice to keep their skills sharp. Get sharp and stay sharp with more than fifty practice exercises rooted in real-world scenarios. If you're a new programmer, these challenges will help you learn what you need to break into the field, and if you're a seasoned pro, you can use these exercises to learn that hot new language for your next gig.

Brian P. Hogan
(118 pages) ISBN: 9781680501223. $24
https://pragprog.com/book/bhwb

Creating Great Teams

People are happiest and most productive if they can choose what they work on and who they work with. Self-selecting teams give people that choice. Build well-designed and efficient teams to get the most out of your organization, with step-by-step instructions on how to set up teams quickly and efficiently. You'll create a process that works for you, whether you need to form teams from scratch, improve the design of existing teams, or are on the verge of a big team re-shuffle.

Sandy Mamoli and David Mole
(102 pages) ISBN: 9781680501285. $17
https://pragprog.com/book/mmteams

Put the "Fun" in Functional

Elixir puts the "fun" back into functional programming, on top of the robust, battle-tested, industrial-strength environment of Erlang. Add in the unparalleled beauty and ease of the Phoenix web framework, and enjoy the web again!

Programming Elixir 1.3

Explore functional programming without the academic overtones (tell me about monads just one more time). Create concurrent applications, but get them right without all the locking and consistency headaches. Meet Elixir, a modern, functional, concurrent language built on the rock-solid Erlang VM. Elixir's pragmatic syntax and built-in support for metaprogramming will make you productive and keep you interested for the long haul. Maybe the time is right for the Next Big Thing. Maybe it's Elixir. This book is *the* introduction to Elixir for experienced programmers, completely updated for Elixir 1.3.

Dave Thomas
(362 pages) ISBN: 9781680502008. $38
https://pragprog.com/book/elixir13

Functional Web Development with Elixir, OTP, and Phoenix

Elixir and Phoenix are generating tremendous excitement as an unbeatable platform for building modern web applications. For decades OTP has helped developers create incredibly robust, scalable applications with unparalleled uptime. Make the most of them as you build a stateful web app with Elixir, OTP, and Phoenix. Model domain entities without an ORM or a database. Manage server state and keep your code clean with OTP Behaviours. Layer on a Phoenix web interface without coupling it to the business logic. Open doors to powerful new techniques that will get you thinking about web development in fundamentally new ways.

Lance Halvorsen
(250 pages) ISBN: 9781680502435. $37.95
https://pragprog.com/book/lhelph

The Joy of Mazes and Math

Rediscover the joy and fascinating weirdness of mazes and pure mathematics.

Mazes for Programmers

A book on mazes? Seriously?

Yes!

Not because you spend your day creating mazes, or because you particularly like solving mazes.

But because it's fun. Remember when programming used to be fun? This book takes you back to those days when you were starting to program, and you wanted to make your code do things, draw things, and solve puzzles. It's fun because it lets you explore and grow your code, and reminds you how it feels to just think.

Sometimes it feels like you live your life in a maze of twisty little passages, all alike. Now you can code your way out.

Jamis Buck
(286 pages) ISBN: 9781680500554. $38
https://pragprog.com/book/jbmaze

Good Math

Mathematics is beautiful—and it can be fun and exciting as well as practical. *Good Math* is your guide to some of the most intriguing topics from two thousand years of mathematics: from Egyptian fractions to Turing machines; from the real meaning of numbers to proof trees, group symmetry, and mechanical computation. If you've ever wondered what lay beyond the proofs you struggled to complete in high school geometry, or what limits the capabilities of the computer on your desk, this is the book for you.

Mark C. Chu-Carroll
(282 pages) ISBN: 9781937785338. $34
https://pragprog.com/book/mcmath

Pragmatic Programming

We'll show you how to be more pragmatic and effective, for new code and old.

Your Code as a Crime Scene

Jack the Ripper and legacy codebases have more in common than you'd think. Inspired by forensic psychology methods, this book teaches you strategies to predict the future of your codebase, assess refactoring direction, and understand how your team influences the design. With its unique blend of forensic psychology and code analysis, this book arms you with the strategies you need, no matter what programming language you use.

Adam Tornhill
(218 pages) ISBN: 9781680500387. $36
https://pragprog.com/book/atcrime

The Nature of Software Development

You need to get value from your software project. You need it "free, now, and perfect." We can't get you there, but we can help you get to "cheaper, sooner, and better." This book leads you from the desire for value down to the specific activities that help good Agile projects deliver better software sooner, and at a lower cost. Using simple sketches and a few words, the author invites you to follow his path of learning and understanding from a half century of software development and from his engagement with Agile methods from their very beginning.

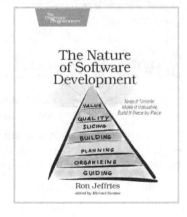

Ron Jeffries
(176 pages) ISBN: 9781941222379. $24
https://pragprog.com/book/rjnsd

The Pragmatic Bookshelf

The Pragmatic Bookshelf features books written by developers for developers. The titles continue the well-known Pragmatic Programmer style and continue to garner awards and rave reviews. As development gets more and more difficult, the Pragmatic Programmers will be there with more titles and products to help you stay on top of your game.

Visit Us Online

This Book's Home Page
https://pragprog.com/book/jwnode2
Source code from this book, errata, and other resources. Come give us feedback, too!

Register for Updates
https://pragprog.com/updates
Be notified when updates and new books become available.

Join the Community
https://pragprog.com/community
Read our weblogs, join our online discussions, participate in our mailing list, interact with our wiki, and benefit from the experience of other Pragmatic Programmers.

New and Noteworthy
https://pragprog.com/news
Check out the latest pragmatic developments, new titles and other offerings.

Save on the eBook

Save on the eBook versions of this title. Owning the paper version of this book entitles you to purchase the electronic versions at a terrific discount.

PDFs are great for carrying around on your laptop—they are hyperlinked, have color, and are fully searchable. Most titles are also available for the iPhone and iPod touch, Amazon Kindle, and other popular e-book readers.

Buy now at *https://pragprog.com/coupon*

Contact Us

Online Orders:	*https://pragprog.com/catalog*
Customer Service:	*support@pragprog.com*
International Rights:	*translations@pragprog.com*
Academic Use:	*academic@pragprog.com*
Write for Us:	*http://write-for-us.pragprog.com*
Or Call:	+1 800-699-7764